TRACES OF WAR

Parallax: Re-visions of Culture and Society

Stephen G. Nichols, Gerald Price, and Wendy Steiner,
Series Editors

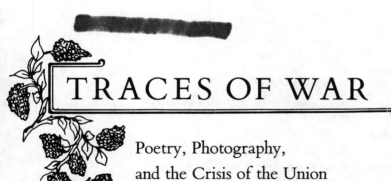

TRACES OF WAR

Poetry, Photography,
and the Crisis of the Union

Timothy Sweet

THE JOHNS HOPKINS UNIVERSITY PRESS

BALTIMORE AND LONDON

©1990 The Johns Hopkins University Press
All rights reserved
Printed in the United States of America

The Johns Hopkins University Press, 701 West 40th Street,
Baltimore, Maryland 21211
The Johns Hopkins Press Ltd., London

The paper used in this book meets the minimum requirements
of American National Standard for Information Sciences—
Permanence of Paper for Printed Library Materials,
ANSI Z39.48-1984.

Library of Congress Cataloging-in-Publication Data
Sweet, Timothy, 1960–
   Traces of war : poetry, photography, and the crisis of the Union/
Timothy Sweet,
   p. cm.—(Parallax: re-visions of culture and society)
   Includes bibliographical references.
   ISBN 0-8018-3959-9 (alk. paper)
   1. American poetry—19th century—History and criticism. 2. United
States—History—Civil War, 1861–1865—Literature and the war.
3. United States—History—Civil War, 1861–1865—Photography.
4. Literature and photography—United States—History—19th century.
5. War poetry, American—History and criticism. 6. War photography—
United States—History—19th century. 7. Whitman, Walt, 1819–1892.
Drum-taps. 8. Melville, Herman, 1819–1891. Battle-pieces. I. Title.
II. Series: Parallax (Baltimore, Md.)
PS310.H57S94   1990
811'.409358—dc20   89-38436 CIP

To my parents

Contents

List of Illustrations   *ix*

Acknowledgments   *xi*

Introduction   *1*

1. Whitman's *Drum-Taps* and the Rhetoric of War   *11*

2. "The Real War Will Never Get in the Books"   *46*

3. Photography and the Scene of History   *78*

4. Some Versions of Pastoral: Brady and Gardner   *107*

5. Barnard and the American Picturesque   *138*

6. Melville's *Battle-Pieces* as a Trace of War   *165*

Epilogue: "For the Union Dead"   *201*

Notes   *207*

Bibliography   *227*

Index   *235*

Illustrations

1. Thomas Nast, "Our Arms Victorious," *Harper's Weekly*, 24 June 1865.   *19*

2. George Barnard, "The Woodsawyer's Nooning" (1853).   *83*

3. Thomas Cole, *Consummation of Empire*, from *The Course of Empire* (1833–36).   *96*

4. Thomas Cole, *The Pastoral State*, from *The Course of Empire* (1833–36).   *98*

5. Eastman Johnson, *Old Kentucky Home* (1859).   *100*

6. Alexander Gardner, "War, effect of a shell on a Confederate soldier at Battle of Gettysburg" (1863).   *108*

7. "Stone Church, Centreville, Va., March, 1862," *Gardner's Photographic Sketch Book of the Civil War*.   *112*

8. "Scenes on the Battlefield of Antietam," *Harper's Weekly*, 18 October 1862.   *114–15*

9. "Ruins of Stone Bridge, Bull Run, Va., March, 1862," *Gardner's Photographic Sketch Book of the Civil War*.   *121*

10. "Fortifications on the Heights of Centreville, Va., March, 1862," *Gardner's Photographic Sketch Book of the Civil War*.   *123*

11. "A Harvest of Death, Gettysburg, July, 1863," *Gardner's Photographic Sketch Book of the Civil War*.   *126*

12. "Field Where General Reynolds Fell, Gettysburg, July, 1863," *Gardner's Photographic Sketch Book of the Civil War*.   *127*

13. "A Sharpshooter's Last Sleep, Gettysburg, July, 1863," *Gardner's Photographic Sketch Book of the Civil War*.   *129*

14. "Home of a Rebel Sharpshooter, Gettysburg, 1863," *Gardner's Photographic Sketch Book of the Civil War*.   *131*

15. "What Do I Want, John Henry? Warrenton, Va., November, 1862," *Gardner's Photographic Sketch Book of the Civil War*.   *134*

16. "A Burial Party, Cold Harbor, Va., April, 1865," *Gardner's Photographic Sketch Book of the Civil War*.   *134*

17. "Collecting the Remains of Union Soldiers for Re-Interment in National Cemeteries," *Harper's Weekly*, 24 November 1866.   *136*

18. "'The Halt'—A Scene in the Georgia Campaign,"
    Harper's Weekly, 30 June 1866.   *146*
19. "View from Kenesaw Mountain, Ga.,"
    Photographic Views of Sherman's Campaign.   *147*
20. "City of Atlanta, Ga., No. 1,"
    Photographic Views of Sherman's Campaign.   *150*
21. "City of Atlanta, Ga., No. 2,"
    Photographic Views of Sherman's Campaign.   *151*
22. "Savannah River, near Savannah, Ga.,"
    Photographic Views of Sherman's Campaign.   *152*
23. "Buen-Ventura, Savannah, Ga.,"
    Photographic Views of Sherman's Campaign.   *153*
24. "Chattanooga Valley from Lookout Mountain, No. 2,"
    Photographic Views of Sherman's Campaign.   *154*
25. Thomas Cole, *Oxbow*
    (*The Connecticut River Near Northampton*) (1836).   *155*
26. "Mississippi," *Harper's Weekly*, 6 January 1866.   *158*
27. "Georgia," *Harper's Weekly*, 12 May 1866.   *160*
28. "Ruins in Charleston, S.C.,"
    Photographic Views of Sherman's Campaign.   *162*

Acknowledgments

I am especially grateful to Eric Sundquist for his helpful reading of the manuscript, to Michael Hancher for his invaluable advice on all phases of the project, and to John Mowitt and Donald Ross, Jr., for their critical attention to early drafts. The New-York Historical Society, the Metropolitan Museum of Art, the International Museum of Photography, the Library of Congress, and the University of Virginia Library granted permission to reproduce materials from their collections. A fellowship from the University of Minnesota Graduate School supported my initial research. Finally, I thank Laura Brady for the loving and patient support that made it possible for me to complete this book.

TRACES OF WAR

Introduction

*The real value of the Iliad or [Raphael's] Transfiguration
is as signs of power.* —Emerson, *"Art"*

THE American Civil War arose from a crisis in political representation. Emerson, in his "Speech on Affairs in Kansas" (1856), describes the breakdown of all structures of representation, including language itself, during the decade before the war: "Language has lost its meaning in the universal cant. *Representative Government* is misrepresentative; *Union* is a conspiracy against the Northern States which the Northern States are to have the privilege of paying for; the *adding of Cuba and Central America* to the slave marts is *enlarging the area of Freedom. Manifest Destiny, Democracy, Freedom,* fine names for an ugly thing" (*W*, 11:259).[1] The Kansas-Nebraska Act had declared the Missouri Compromise inapplicable to the named territories; it prescribed that the question of slavery be determined not by the existing prohibition of slavery north of 36 degrees 30 minutes (in Louisiana Purchase territories) but rather by the constitutions of the created state or states. The subsequent violence between slaveholding and small-farming partisans in the territories indicated that the normal structures of representation were in crisis.[2]

With the outbreak of war, the critical question—whether physical violence could produce a legitimate ideological consensus where language had failed—became relevant not merely to certain sparsely populated territories but to the American nation(s) at large. The apparatus of political representation, subject to the crisis Emerson had predicted in his speech on the violence in Kansas, was reconfigured with the outbreak of the war such that a large number of supposedly free individuals became the property of the military state (soldiers). The governmental apparatus that in peacetime represented the autonomous subject to the state demanded in wartime that this representational relationship be altered.

A soldier in wartime represents the state, but he cannot be said to represent himself in any usual sense (and certainly not in Emerson's antebellum sense of "self-reliance").[3] Elaine Scarry provides an analysis of the peculiar representational status of the body of the soldier in wartime in the second chapter of *The Body in Pain*. Violence to the body of the soldier, "the main purpose and outcome of war," is made to substantiate the ideology of the victor by means of a complex semiotic process. In

1

the first step in this process, "injuring disappears from view as the central act of war" along any of three rhetorical paths: omission, redescription, or marginalization (63–64). Although it "disappears,"

> wounding is able to open up a source of reality that can give the issue [i.e., the political relation or ideological structure at stake] force and holding power. That is, the outcome of war has substantiation not in an absolute inability of the defeated to contest the outcome but in a *process of perception* that allows extreme attributes of the body to be translated into another language, to be broken away from the body and relocated elsewhere at the very moment that the body itself is disowned [and] made to disappear. (124, emphasis added)

The "extreme attributes of the body" to which Scarry refers are wounds. Her point is that wounds come to be perceived in separation from bodies, as objects in themselves. As material facts, wounds are so palpable that they make the ideological outcome of a war "*seem real* until there is time for the issues to be universally acted on and in this way *made real*" (121). The displacement of the body by ideology is possible because wounds are referentially unstable and thus can be appropriated rhetorically as signs of the legitimacy of an ideological position.

Thus, ideologies and political structures are overturned or conserved as a result of war, while the violation of human bodies never bears any direct referential relation to the issues that wars are said to be about. Our Civil War, for example, is often said to have been fought entirely by "Americans," entirely on the soil of the "United States." But this conventional description of the war was itself one of the representational questions at issue—for it is only possible to say in retrospect that the Confederates were rebellious "Americans" because the Northern states won the war. (Conversely, we do not continue to refer to our polity as a confederation of British colonies.) Poetic and photographic representations of the war aided political discourse in the project of legitimating the violent conservation of the Union by reflecting on and participating in the transformation of wounds into ideology during and after the Civil War.

Scarry can argue that the process she describes is, in general, morally acceptable because she assumes that the "belief" that is to be substantiated by means of injury "*belongs* to the person whose body is used in its confirmation" (149, emphasis added). There are serious gaps in this moral argument, especially in the assumption that a soldier's motivations for fighting are identical to those of the nation–state whose uniform he wears.[4]

In the absence of the utopian state of internal political relations that Scarry must assume in order to find a morally acceptable, genuinely informed consent for war, the cultural work of the semiotic processes that mediate between human bodies and ideology is: first, to manufacture and maintain the consent of believing subjects who will submit their bodies to violence; second, to manufacture and maintain the consent of the others who are not involved in the war as combatants but who will be affected by its outcome. This is not to deny that physical coercion is a significant factor in the mobilization of troops. Conscription, which is *prima facie* evidence of a lack of consent, was first instituted on a national level during the Civil War in both the North and the South; the antidraft riots of 1863 indicated some resistance among the working classes in cities such as New York and Detroit (Cook; McPherson, 609–10; Zinn, 187). But the militia volunteers who answered Abraham Lincoln's (or Jefferson Davis's) first call for troops did not need to be physically coerced.

The ideology that prompted the volunteer soldier of the Civil War to subject himself to the state and to "consent" to the violent use of his body, was constructed not only politically, but also aesthetically. Scarry argues that "the idiom of 'heroism,' 'sacrifice,' 'dedication,' 'devotion,' and 'bravery' conventionally invoked to describe the soldier's individual act of consent over his own body is neither inappropriate nor false" (112). Nevertheless, these descriptions of soldiers' beliefs are aesthetic legitimations for wounding and killing, suffering and dying. Products of romantic representations of war, they provide a soldier with motivations for fighting but do not bear any relation to the political issues over which the war is being fought. As in any war, the idioms of heroism, sacrifice, and so on were spoken alike by Union and Confederate soldiers and civilians, to justify killing and dying "for" their respective causes.

For a great many soldiers in the Civil War, political "belief" was less important than a naive desire for the romance and adventure that war was often supposed to supply. Consider, for example, the critiques of the textually coded bases of adventure, heroism, and patriotism in Twain's "Private History of a Campaign that Failed" and the sections of *Life on the Mississippi* that attribute the cause of the Civil War to a literal reading of Walter Scott's romances. Of course, Northerners were equally susceptible to the romantic view of war. One recruit from Maine reports that "although [he] had *no* inclination for the business," he enlisted in 1862 "in a momentary spasm of enthusiasm," and thus found himself "face to face with the alternative of going or showing a white liver by backing out." His actions are prescribed by the idioms of bravery and

3

manliness, of the sort Scarry identifies. Additionally, the possibilities of romance and adventure offered by war seem to excite this recruit: "I should, if I lived, have a chance to see some of the country and *might* witness a battle, which I greatly desired, only I wished to be a safe distance from it" (Haley, 23–24). He desires the experience of battle, but only as mediated by the sort of aesthetic distance provided by literary and pictorial representations of war. Caught up in the enthusiasm of a farewell celebration, he asks (with a touch of irony), "Why shrink from that which is so desirable as the glory of war? I am just perverse enough to want to share it" (27). The protagonist of Stephen Crane's *The Red Badge of Courage* is even less critical of the glorifying representations of war that consume him: "He had burned several times to enlist. Tales of great movements shook the land. They might not be distinctly Homeric, but there seemed to be much glory in them. He had read of marches, sieges, conflicts, and he had longed to see it all. His busy mind had drawn for him large pictures extravagant in color, lurid with breathless deeds" (46). Crane thus suggests that visual representations of war, such as historical paintings and engravings, refer to a framing ideological text. Ambrose Bierce's "Chickamauga" (which, like many of his stories, reflects critically on his own Civil War experiences) describes a similarly seductive aesthetic derived from "military books and pictures" (27).

Patriotism is an aesthetic product like romance and adventure; the patriotic response is stimulated by icons or emblems that serve as loci of the state's supposed values.[5] Whitman, for example, uses popular images such as the American flag and the allegorical figure of Liberty to evoke the contemporary aesthetics of patriotism. A recruit reports that such patriotic responses "prompted most of [the men of the 17th Maine Regiment] to enter the service" (although he himself claims to have possessed "very little of what goes by that name") (Haley, 24). Propagandistic magazine illustrations by the likes of Thomas Nast and songs such as Julia Ward Howe's "The Battle Hymn of the Republic" (which appeared in the *Atlantic Monthly* in 1862) helped to mobilize the patriotic responses of civilians and soldiers.[6] Such aesthetic structures aided political structures in producing consent for the war and in negotiating the meaning of the war even before it had ended.

Although the literature of the Civil War is vast, Daniel Aaron argues that very few American writers have said anything "revealing about the meaning [or] the causes of the War" (xxii). His thesis is that the war was, and continues to be, "unwritten" in an important (if not literal) sense. Edmund Wilson remarks that too much of the contemporary lit-

4

erature on both sides was merely partisan and propagandistic: "Automatically, on both sides of the contest, as soon as it had come to war . . . a divided and arguing public opinion [was] converted overnight into a national near-unanimity" (xxxii). He argues that poetry, especially, suffered during the war; in the vast outpouring of "versified journalism," any "authentic kind of poetry scarcely leaks through at all"; some of Whitman's poems, those in which he "does not write editorials on current events but describes his actual feelings" are nearly the only exceptions (479, 487, 483).[7]

In his assessment that very little good poetry was produced during the war, Wilson assumes that for poetry to be "authentic" (fresh, lyric, spontaneous) it must be apolitical. But this assumption dissociates literature from its cultural function in nineteenth-century America. Aaron reports in contrast that, far from desiring an apolitical literature, "almost immediately after Appomattox Northern commentators began to complain about the failure of American writers to do justice to the recent strife" (xix). The public (or at least the critics) wanted a literature that made ideological reference to the war, in order to explain and justify its horrors. Melville's *Battle-Pieces*, in response, "rais[ed] subversive doubts about the war's announced objectives and about the men who fomented it, fought it, survived it, indeed about the God who ostensibly orchestrated it" (Aaron, xv). That this was not the kind of political literature the public wanted is evident from sales figures—only 525 copies in the ten years following the war (Melville, *CP*, 446n.2).[8] Whitman's poetry had not been widely popular before the war (he was no Longfellow) but *Drum-Taps* was "more calculating and concessive" than his earlier work. Yet Aaron argues that Whitman needed to affirm the war primarily for personal reasons: "His psychic safety depended upon the Union's preservation. Given his personal expectations and his prophecies of American promise, he had to insist on the providentiality of the War and to wring optimistic conclusions from its horrors" (Aaron, 59, 67, 68). Our usual sense of Whitman's egoistic persona may invite us to read *Drum-Taps* primarily for personal significances. Yet war poetry—especially that written by noncombatants—is finally significant in only its engagement with other cultural mediations of war. Whitman's (and especially Melville's) relative lack of contemporary popularity suggests that this engagement was not always simply affirmative. If Whitman ultimately does provide an affirmative representation of the war, it is only after a revelation that the transformation of wounds into words is, for the ideologically aware individual, an extraordinarily problematic endeavor.

Whitman, as if to anticipate Aaron's conclusion about all Civil War literature, claimed that "the real war will never get in the books" (*PW*, 1:115).[9] What did get in the books were attempts to envision the meaning of the war in terms of existing ideological schemata. One important ideological issue, as George M. Fredrickson argues, concerned the value of institutions. Prior to the war "the dominant American belief" of Northern intellectuals such as Emerson had been "that the individual could find fulfillment outside of institutions"; the war displaced this "anti-institutionalist" ideology and substituted a belief in the necessity and value of political and cultural structures (22). It has lately been recognized that photographs and photographic albums played a central role in this ideological negotiation. Alan Trachtenberg's insightful analysis of Civil War photography draws some conclusions similar to Fredrickson's study of Northern intellectuals' responses to the war. The "subliminal lessons" of the war, argues Trachtenberg, include the promotion of institutionalism; many photographs emphasize "the importance of hierarchy, of subordination and obedience [to economic and political institutions]," legitimating these lessons by means of the photograph's apparently natural claims to truthfulness (25). Northern intellectuals' responses to the war involved a perceptual problem: they hoped that the violence of the war would strengthen the American aristocracy while "purging the nation once and for all of self-seeking, materialism, and corruption," but the aftermath of the war revealed the "illusory" nature of these hopes (Fredrickson, 183). Photographic scenes of destruction portended a similar "potential fissure" in the ideology of the Northern intellectual, which had to be covered in a similar, "self-blinding" perceptual dynamic (Trachtenberg, 10, 12). The fact that the "real war" did not get in the pictures or texts that purport to represent it, while so many were willing to believe that it did, aided the construction of an affirmative, nationalist ideological meaning for the war.

In Chapter 1 of this study, I analyze Whitman's treatment of the rhetorical operations by means of which the body of the soldier disappears into the ideological discourse of the state. I argue that Whitman, saturated in the ideology of his milieu, mobilized several culturally prevalent rhetorical topoi (of the sort outlined by Scarry) in order to negotiate the meaning of the Civil War in *Drum-Taps*. These topoi often invite Whitman to evade critical questions, such as the legitimacy of the use of violence in substantiating or conserving any ideology, in his production of affirmative meaning. In subsequent chapters, I focus primarily on two specific mechanisms of the evasive production generally exemplified in *Drum-*

Taps. Arguing that the pastoral and picturesque aesthetics were important in the constitution of a nationalist ideology in the antebellum period, I analyze the ways in which Whitman and the photographers mobilize the idealized representation of the Union encoded in these aesthetics to heal the wounds of war and to envision the restoration of the nation. Melville, as we might suspect, is a good deal more skeptical of the terms of this restoration. Where Whitman and the photographers draw a pastoral or picturesque frame around the war, and thereby enlist nature in the service of legitimating its violence, Melville's *Battle-Pieces* reflect critically on any such attempt to naturalize the war or its ideological implications.

Since the term *pastoralism* bears a good deal of weight in this study, some explication is in order. Annabel Patterson remarks that the "attempt to define the nature of the pastoral" is "a cause lost as early as the sixteenth century" and has become even more hopeless since Empson and his followers have found "'versions of pastoral' in the most unlikely places" (7). Nevertheless, in regarding the pastoral not as a narrowly defined genre but as a "trick of thought"—an attitude of "putting the complex into the simple"—Empson provides some direction for the present study (23). At first a war may seem to be an unlikely place to find the pastoral; but war has figured in its margins since Virgil's first *Eclogue*. One speaker in this poem, Meliboeus, has had his land expropriated by Octavian to reward the veterans of the Roman civil war; the other, Tityrus (who is sometimes assumed to speak for Virgil himself), has retained his land through Octavian's generosity (as Virgil in fact did). The two farmers share a world view, but Meliboeus has been displaced from his world and must try, tomorrow, to reestablish it elsewhere, using the memory he shares with Tityrus as a guide (Alpers, 68–95). In this eclogue are all the attitudes generally thought to characterize the pastoral. The aesthetic "harmony" of the poem—a balanced doubleness of point of view and a symmetry of stasis and displacement—"holds potential conflicts in suspension" (Alpers, 65). The pastoral poet often "creates an illusory world through gestures in the direction of the conventional one." Especially in more realistic versions of pastoral, this world is "not a separate world but a microcosm: it is not set apart from some other way of life for purposes of comparison," but reconciles us to our lives (Ettin, 14, 31). Yet it is the illusory nature of this world that provides the reconciliation, by temporarily satisfying a "longing after innocence and happiness, to be recovered not through conversion or regeneration but merely through a retreat" (Poggioli, 1). Historically, literary pastoralism has often flourished in periods following great wars: after Alexander's conquests,

7

there was the escapist charm of Theocritus; after Caesar and Octavian, Virgil; and after the French Revolution of 1789, a renewed interest in classical pastoralism. Beginning with the Romantics, however, "the connection between an idealized pastoral and violent political experience would usually remain unspoken" (Patterson, 251–52).

Nineteenth-century America was, of course, a vast distance from Virgil's Rome, but the pastoral attitude survived, especially in the discourse of the agrarian ideal which provided a cultural paradigm for the settlement of the Mississippi basin (Smith, 138–200; Gridley). Leo Marx argues that by 1785 the "pastoral ideal of America . . . had developed into something like an all-embracing ideology" (*Machine*, 88). The most important aspect of pastoralism for nineteenth-century America was the vision of a microcosm—a sociopolitical configuration that could typify American life. The American pastoral ideology entailed the representation of small-farm, free-labor agriculture as a paradigm of identity, as in Crèvecoeur's third letter, "What is an American?" (Marx, *Machine*, 107–17).[10] Virgil's two characters were fused, and in the fusion all political tensions were displaced to the outer edge of white society. Indians played out Meliboeus's forced exile, their lands expropriated in order to clear the ground for the American pastoral. With this government support, the nineteenth-century Tityrus was free to enjoy the fruits of his labor (as in Virgil's pastoral) or to replay Meliboeus's role, but in a pleasant way, by leaving his pastoral home freely to create another one farther to the west.

The Civil War, however, disrupted any such reproduction of the pastoral scene—to a much greater extent than the War of 1812 (which had a minimal effect on the farmers of the interior) or the Mexican War (the political effects of which would be strongly felt only in their eventual eruption in the Civil War). In late 1861 Bryant, perhaps America's foremost literary pastoralist in the antebellum period, declaimed:

> Lay down the axe; fling by the spade;
>   Leave in its track the toiling plow;
> The rifle and the bayonet-blade
>   For arms like yours were fitter now;
>
> . . . .
> Our country calls; away! away!
>   To where the blood-stream blots the green.   (2:96)

This announcement of disruption also predicted the drawing of a recuperative pastoral frame around the violence with the end of the war. The pastoral, as a literary mode and an American ideology, contained the means to restore itself. While death has always lurked in the margins of the pastoral ("et in Arcadia ego"), the modally prescribed response to the thought of death, even one's own death, is to take consolation from nature. Bryant had counseled in "Thanatopsis," "Go forth, under the open sky, and list / To Nature's teachings." Here one learns that one will return in death to the earth,

> To mix forever with the elements,
> To be a brother to the insensible rock
> And to the sluggish clod, which the rude swain
> Turns with his share, and treads upon.   (1:18)

In this vision the American will always be a part of the pastoral landscape, cultivating it in life and fertilizing it in death.

The consolation offered in "Thanatopsis" is that death is part of the natural process and, simultaneously, part of the nationalist process of transforming all America into a pastoral landscape. Drawing such a pastoral frame around death *in war*, however, usually implies that death resulting from war is somehow as natural as any other death. If death in war is natural, then war itself, and the politics of war, may be regarded as natural; in such a case the ideology or politics that demand death in war cannot be effectively criticized as cultural structures which it is possible to modify or dismantle. Even Wilson, who withholds any suggestion that the Civil War was noble, glorious, or liberating, appeals to the reassurance of nature when he explains that "the wars fought by human beings are stimulated as a rule primarily by the same instincts as the voracity of the sea slug. . . . The unanimity of men at war is like that of a school of fish, which will swerve, simultaneously and apparently without leadership, when the shadow of an enemy appears" (xi, xxxii). During the Civil War the appeal to nature takes on a more benign aspect than is evident in Wilson's representation of the moral neutrality of nature; yet here as well, naturalization is the ideological trope of last resort.

The contemporary naturalization of the Civil War (by Northerners) involved a twofold strategy. First, the characteristic nostalgia of the pastoral mode assured its own preservation as an idealized image of America; thus Lincoln could claim that the pastoral topos, "our national homestead," was the essence of America—which was disrupted but not demolished during the war—and actually guaranteed the eventual restoration of the Union (5:529). Second, by appealing to the solid ground of a typified, pastoral image of America and to the ideology of Union as inscribed on the landscape by the aesthetic of the picturesque, Whitman and the photographers found verbal and visual rhetorics that enabled them to naturalize the war's central events (violence) and its central outcome (the conservation of the Union). Melville was perhaps no less a Unionist than Whitman, Brady, Gardner, and Barnard, and he often used the same recuperative topoi to explore the meaning of the war. But his poetic representations criticized such strategies, even while mobilizing them. He found no means to affirm that the crisis of representation that erupted in the war had been resolved.

1. Whitman's *Drum-Taps* and
the Rhetoric of War

EVER since the first edition of *Leaves of Grass* appeared in 1855, critics have attempted to describe its structures of representation.[1] Typification, an idealizing form of synecdoche, is one of the most distinctive of these structures.[2] Allen Grossman finds typification central to Whitman's poetics, arguing that his "originality consisted in the discovery of a regulative principle that permitted an art *based in the representative function itself*, and organized in its ideal-typical moments . . . as a taxonomy of which the sorting index is mere being-at-all" (188, emphasis added). Typification organizes the representation of the Civil War in *Drum-Taps* by substituting paradigmatic instances for the myriad events and experiences of the war. The resulting interplay of interdiction and representation produces a unified, nationalistic meaning for the war.

Whitman had argued for the political significance of his poetry since the first edition of *Leaves of Grass*. But the war posed a peculiar threat to the possibilities of both poetic and political representation. In response to this threat, typification—the master trope of Whitman's poetics— emerges in four characteristic rhetorical systems. Whereas in the antebellum editions of *Leaves of Grass* "representation (the class of all classes) was itself an implicit unification" (Grossman, 187–88), the war tested such a representation of unity in Whitman's poetics and in national politics as well. *Drum-Taps* is important not for the poetic originality or uniqueness of expression for which the early editions of *Leaves of Grass* are renowned, but rather for its revealing treatment of some of the common rhetorical structures that explained and justified the war.[3] By means of a complex set of ideological operations, the poems both reflect and reflect on the contemporary construction of the "reality" of the war.

The first section of this chapter locates *Drum-Taps* with respect to Whitman's antebellum poetics as grounded in the proclamation that "the United States themselves are essentially the greatest poem" (*LG 1855*, 5). The Civil War threatened to deconstruct this poem along with the political Union, and thus to fragment the ideological ground of Whitman's poetics. *Drum-Taps* presents itself as a recuperative political-poetic response. Whitman mobilizes four topoi of the Unionist rhetoric which legitimated the prosecution of the Civil War. These topoi are: the body politic (discussed in section II), ritual sacrifice (section III), the cost of war in terms of the purchase of ideology (section IV), and the unifying, democratic love of comrades-at-arms (section V). Each topos is organized around a governing trope that makes possible the representation of the war by *typifying* some aspect of it; these tropes are, respectively: embodiment, substitution, exchange, and adhesion.

There are rare moments in *Drum-Taps*, however, in which Whitman seems to find the war unrepresentable—that is, in which representations of war are *interdicted* in some way. In such moments Whitman appeals to "adhesiveness" (*PW*, 2:271) in order to recuperate the thematized absence. The final section of this chapter expands the discussion of adhesion initiated in section V. Here I argue that reflections on problems of representation as such are in fact written into the typifying poetic-political tropes that organize the representations of war. The tropes of embodiment, substitution, exchange, and adhesion are figures for aspects of the process of semiosis in general. That is, embodiment, substitution, and exchange can be said to represent representational operations in such a way as to foreground the instability of structures of typification. In contrast, the trope of adhesion operates in the unrepresentable moments, attempting to recuperate ideological instability and to heal injuries to the structure of political and poetic representation produced by the war.

I   *"The United States themselves are essentially the greatest poem."*

In the preface to the Centennial Edition of *Leaves of Grass* (1876), Whitman returns to his perennial theme, that his poetry reflects on and clarifies "the vital political mission of the United States" (*PW*, 2:465). He goes on to claim that *Drum-Taps* is "pivotal to the rest entire" (469) of *Leaves of Grass* because the Civil War is the most significant event in American history: "Within my time the United States have emerged from nebulous vagueness and suspense, to full orbic (though varied,) decision— . . . and are henceforth to enter upon their real history—the way being now (*i.e.*, since the result of the Secession War,) clear'd of death-threatening impedimenta" (473). When Whitman locates the Civil War in American history—and, implicitly, *Drum-Taps* within *Leaves of Grass*—he represents the war as an action that ensured the safety of America conceived as a single figure, a body politic which after its "adolescence" is now ready "to enter on its full democratic career" (468). The substitution involved in the metaphor of a body politic requires an abstraction, in which millions of actual bodies are transformed into a single, powerful figure. This embodiment of a single, national intention indicates Whitman's desire to make the war meaningful in terms of the Unionist ideology.

The occasion of the American centennial required that the preface to the 1876 edition of *Leaves of Grass* present an affirmative view of the Civil War, of *Drum-Taps*, and of American history and culture in general. A safe and healthy body politic is one of several affirmative images produced by representational systems that function, in the "Drum-Taps" cluster of this edition, to shape the war and its results into a meaningful segment of the narrative of American history. In other texts, however, Whitman criticizes the framework within which he conceived the recuperative project of *Drum-Taps*. Even before the war, he had written some poems that questioned the efficacy of the symbolic systems that ground *Leaves of Grass*, and that in fact suggest a crisis of representation *as such*—for example, "As I Ebb'd with the Ocean of Life." These early, sporadic representations of the disruption of semiosis prefigure a critique of representation elaborated in Whitman's prose essay *Memoranda during the War*. The latter text, a meditation on the (im)possibility of representing "the real war," must locate ideological value not in the representation of war but in the interdiction of representation.

The Civil War was "pivotal" for Whitman in that it problematized representation in both the political and the poetic-mimetic senses. In the preface to the first edition of *Leaves of Grass* Whitman aligns these two kinds of representation: "The Americans of all nations at anytime upon the earth have probably the fullest poetical nature. The United States themselves are essentially the greatest poem" (*LG 1855*, 5). In this he is responding to Emerson, who had written in 1844 that "America is a poem in our eyes; its ample geography dazzles the imagination, and it will not wait long for metres" (*W*, 3:38). The Civil War threatened to devalue the "greatest poem" by deconstructing the political and poetic phrase "*United* States" and fragmenting its ideological geography. As Emerson proclaimed in 1856, in response to the fighting between proslavery and free-soil partisans in Kansas, "Language has lost its meaning in the universal cant. *Representative Government* is misrepresentative" (*W*, 11:259). He found that politically motivated violence—a harbinger of the coming Civil War—was destroying the capacity of the American political lexicon to represent its world. In *Drum-Taps* Whitman attempted to repair the representational function of the words whose wreckage Emerson had lamented. But during the war Whitman could not help but see a frag-

13

mentation of meaning—the violent destruction of individuals who were supposedly represented by the "poem" of the "United States" and who also represented it, even as they died for it. In order to affirm the restoration of the Union, Whitman needed to transform such violence into ideologically productive signs.

While war in general was regarded contemporarily as "a continuation of political commerce, a carrying out of the same by other means" (Clausewitz, 1:23), the conduct of politics by means *other* than "political" ones posed special problems in American political representation, because the government of the United States was not a system in which a sovereign "represented" his or her subjects. Instead, "individuals" theoretically exercised a measure of power by means of their representation in government. Republican structures of representation were (perhaps still are) thought to produce the political "meaning" of America; for example, espousal of the spread of the American system of political representation throughout North America ("manifest destiny") was considered by many to be an important component of national meaning during the first half of the nineteenth century. In a republican system of representation the consent of the governed is theorized as active rather than passive (as in the case of a sovereign system). But "representation" was explicitly the set of issues over which the Civil War was fought. Issues such as who counted as a "person" with rights of representation and what were the respective powers of state and federal governments within the system of representation were considered to be the primary causes of the war. The war put the antebellum structure of representation into question, not only as regards emancipation and states' rights but also as regards the *consent* of represented subjects. To go to war in support of an ideology would seem to be to exercise an active consent—except in the important case of conscription (first instituted in this country during the Civil War). And yet in giving his "consent" (whether coerced or not) the individual partly dissociates himself from the continuance of genuine consent, for once enlisted he has no choice in his mode of political representation. In fighting "for" freedom in the abstract he surrenders his own individual freedom—that is, his body disappears into an ideological text. (The very terms "en*list*ment" and "con*scription*" mark the first step in the textual appropriation of his body.) Whether it will reappear unscathed and once again autonomous, after his period of enlistment, is something over which he has minimal control (unless he deserts). The Civil War is not unique with respect to this dynamic, of course. But in a war in which the continuance of slavery was an important issue, the idea of surrendering one's freedom to die "for" freedom has special irony.

14

In *Drum-Taps* Whitman attempts to make sense out of the violence of war, in terms of political representation, by mobilizing rhetorical topoi which detach wounds and deaths from the body (often, without explicitly acknowledging them) and attach them to the discourse of the state. The topoi deny that violence is meaninglessness; this denial requires that the individual body disappear into ideology. Whitman's description of *Drum-Taps* in 1865 alludes to four such topoi:

> But I am perhaps mainly satisfied with Drum-Taps because it delivers my ambition of the task that has haunted me, namely, to express in a poem (& in the way I like, which is not at all by directly stating it) the pending action of this *Time & Land we swim in*, with all their large conflicting fluctuations of despair & hope, the shiftings, masses, & the whirl & deafening din, (yet over all, as by invisible hand, a definite purport & idea)—with the unprecedented anguish of wounded & suffering, the beautiful young men, in wholesale death and agony, everything sometimes as if in blood color, & dripping blood. (*C*, 1:246-47)

As in Adam Smith's *The Wealth of Nations*, the "invisible hand" signifies that, regardless of the intentions motivating individual actions, those actions will produce transcendent and beneficent effects (1:421). Economic self-interest produces a nation's wealth; similarly, self-preservation in war (killing the enemy in order to stay alive) paradoxically produces social and political union.

In Whitman's letter, the invisible hand is a synecdoche for a guarantor of national meaning. The topos of the *body politic* of the Union displaces individual bodies with an allegorical figure such as "Libertad," which represents an abstract, ideological construct. This abstract body, unlike the individual bodies it comes to represent, is inviolable; the system of the body politic recuperates wounding and death in war by omitting any description of them and focusing on ideology. Whitman does not, however, always ignore the "unprecedented anguish of wounded & suffering" that is the result of the central activity of all wars. *Drum-Taps* thus appeals also to a second topos, that of the *ritual sacrifice*. Here violence is seldom described in any detail, but at least it is acknowledged. Death is recuperated by its figuration as divinely sanctioned—the common paradigm in nineteenth-century America being the sacrifice of Christ. An innocent body is selected to become a symbolic victim; the ritual structure surrounding the death is proposed as a means of unifying the community ("America") that conducts the sacrifice. Whitman's metaphor of "wholesale" death alludes to a third topos which recuperates death and unifies the community without requiring an appeal to God or Christ. The idea of sacrifice is redescribed in secular terms as an *exchange of life for ideology* (rather than for theology). The governing trope for this topos derives from the economic configuration of mercantile capitalism, as Whitman found it circa 1860.

In each of these systems the body disappears into an ideological construct. Attempting to find a place within ideology for individual bodies as such, Whitman often describes them as "beautiful young men." To take account of the materiality of the body and recuperate the horror of its violation, he develops a fourth topos, that of a *unifying love of comrades*. Here the individual exists *in* himself, in the configuration of his body, as well as *for* the political Union that the war was being fought to conserve. The governing trope of this topos is "adhesiveness," Whitman's figure not only for homoerotic love but more broadly for the source and essence of democracy. Yet adhesive love is also a figure of typification; despite Whitman's implications to the contrary, it has no privileged claim to represent the myriad individual experiences of the war. Like the other figures, it interdicts difference in order to promote an ideology of union. More than the other figures, however, it is grounded in the American landscape. Whitman found the naturalizing potency of this figure, the roots of which are sunk deep in the pastoral scene, especially effective for the recuperation of violence and the restoration of the Union.

II. *"Yet over all, as by invisible hand,*
     a definite purport & idea."

In *Drum-Taps* the interrelation of the destruction of bodies and the reconstruction of ideology is often represented in terms of a body politic. This body of America becomes the agent of an action which represents the summation of myriad actions conducted by hundreds of thousands of individual bodies. Because of its implications of a single national destiny and mission, this figure clearly represents Whitman's ongoing project of the construction of national meaning.[4] Moreover, the general issue of the representation of bodies is important in *Drum-Taps* because an "insistence on the body as text and text as body" is often considered to be the motivating force of Whitman's poetics (Kronick, 75).[5] The violation of bodies in war poses a threat to such a project. Whitman's perception of suffering during his time as a volunteer nurse in army hospitals "undermined the poet's health and his easy confidence as the spokesman of physical perfection" (Aspiz, 94). An analogy might be drawn between

16

his roles as nurse and poet, suggesting that his attempt to heal wounded men was also an attempt to heal a violated poetics. With the coming of the war the singer who in 1855 had proclaimed, "Who degrades or defiles the living human body is cursed," was forced to come to terms with degradation of bodies on a hitherto unimagined scale (*LG 1855*, 123). The texts of American culture supplied dressings for the wounds, but too often they were only cosmetic fabrications that merely hid the wound from sight.

The politics of a civil war always reveals a fundamental instability within the representational figure of the body politic, because it is never clear how many bodies ought to be represented at any given time. In the case of the American Civil War, the Unionist position was that there was only one body. The rebellious element was either an internal threat to the health of the body, such as "tumors and abscesses of the land" (*PW*, 2:428–29), or an external danger, for example a venomous snake such as a "Copperhead."[6] Secessionists, however, had to appeal to the idea that there were at least two bodies politic living on American soil. That there were even more was implied by a strong version of a states' rights or "popular sovereignty" reading of the Constitution.

The topos of the body politic in *Drum-Taps* transforms Northern cities into armed bodies. Whitman also uses the more conventional device of a personified abstraction such as "Libertad," girded for war.[7] These figures embody the Unionist values that Whitman, like many Northerners, claimed the war was "about"—and yet they also force the realization that any representation of a body politic is both internally and externally unstable. Populations and ideologies are fluid in this poetry and can be split, regrouped, and reconfigured in any number of ways. "American" (which is to say Northern) values are embodied either singly (in the figure of "Libertad") or multiply. "First, O songs for a prelude" tells the story of "Manhattan," a female colossus,

> How she led the rest to arms—how she gave the cue,
> How at once with lithe limbs, unwaiting a moment, she sprang;
> (O superb! O Manhattan, my own, my peerless!
> O strongest you in the hour of danger, in crisis! O truer than steel!)
> How you sprang, how you threw off the costume of peace
> with indifferent hand.   (*DT*, 5)

But in a significant portion of the middle of the poem, this colossus is displaced by a catalogue of some types of the individuals—mechanics, lawyers, drivers, and salesmen—who comprise the body of "Manhattan."

The constructed image becomes a grotesque, like the "million-footed Manhattan" of "A Broadway Pageant" (61). The reabsorption of these individuals into "Manhatta a-march," smiling with exultation (7), by the end of the poem indicates the fluidity with which the structure operates to represent—in this case, by means of displacement—myriad individuals by attributing to them a unified intention. Later in the volume, the structure returns, with even greater fluidity. Individual bodies are completely absent, but embodied cities are absorbed into an embodied idea, in an image typical of nineteenth-century political allegory:

> Manhattan, rising, advancing with menacing
> front—Cincinnati, Chicago unchain'd;
> . . . .
> How DEMOCRACY, with desperate vengeful port strides on,
> shown through the dark by those flashes of lightning! (36)

One line of the poem recognizes that "Democracy" is a figure for "torrents of men," again emphasizing not the reality of individual bodies, but the fluidity of the representational structure ("Rise O Days from your fathomless Deeps," 36).

The allegorical figures of Liberty, Democracy, and the like (including cities and states) are conventionally female. "Years of the unperform'd" provides clear examples:

> I see Freedom, completely arm'd, and victorious, and very
> haughty, with Law by her side, both issuing forth
> against the idea of caste. (53)

The conventions of gender here reproduce the ideology of Union. In her analysis of the allegory of the female form, Maria Warner argues that while male figures such as Uncle Sam and John Bull "appear to be in command of their own characters and their own identity," female figures such as Liberty are "one-dimensional" (12). The female figure of Liberty could effectively be used to embody a single, unified "national" action precisely because of the cultural restrictions on the actions of women. Paradoxically, Liberty represents the subordination of individual liberties to the goal of the state—in this case, "issuing forth" to battle the South. Thomas Nast, whose illustrations for *Harper's Weekly* include some of the best-known allegorical representations of the Civil War, observed prevalent conventions in using a single image for Liberty, Victory, and Justice, varying only the props that the figure carried (flag,

Fig. 1. Thomas Nast, "Our Arms Victorious," *Harper's Weekly,*
24 June 1865, pp. 392–93.

sword, shield, scales) to specify the concept being allegorized. Similarly,
Whitman does not individualize the figures he names, but varies only
the props and poses. (It is interesting that Whitman inscribed a copy
of the 1867 edition of *Leaves of Grass*, which contains *Drum-Taps*, to Nast.)[8]

Colossi in *Drum-Taps* are never represented in the act of fighting.
They symbolize either the strong will of the nation prior to battle, or,
as in some of Nast's illustrations, a national attitude of thanksgiving for
victory.[9] Nast also produced several images of the dominance of the victor
over the vanquished; for example, a two-page illustration for *Harper's*
shows Victory, being crowned with laurels, kneeling with one foot on
the prostrate figure of the "C.S.A."—the now vanquished Confederate
States of America (fig. 1). In keeping with the conventions of the female
allegory, Whitman's poems of the body politic marginalize the reality

19

of actual men, wounded and dying in battle, in favor of a "healthy" assertion of ideals. (One figure does represent an actual individual, but only in an allegorically prescribed role: the bust of Lincoln asserts the president's quasi-monarchical status as the head of the victor state.) The black man and the broken manacle refer to the emancipation; yet the brutish, crouching, subservient figure is not a very hopeful allegory of the prospects of free blacks. They are not yet part of the American body politic—since they are embodied in a *separate* figure—and they seem not to participate in the ideals of liberty and justice allegorized in the engraving. Perhaps unintentionally, Nast's representation of the American body politic at the close of the war ironically displays the marginalization of an important constituent of the political character of America. Whitman's poems also marginalize the interests of blacks, if less dramatically, by simply excluding them from poetic representation. Whitman is primarily interested instead in the representational status of the white, Northern soldier, yet in mobilizing the allegory of the body politic he also marginalizes the reality of their experience of war.

Actual bodies of soldiers are marginalized because the representation of a single, powerful figure (with a single will) is appropriate to the assertion of the priority of order over chaos, whereas an individual man can seldom be represented with this sort of power. It is a tenet of the structure of allegory that an idealized concept-figure like "Democracy" cannot be killed or even injured; "Libertad," for example, emerges from the war "unharm'd, in immortal soundness and bloom" (*SDT*, 23). When a sign of pain threatens to manifest itself, the tone of the poem simply becomes more assertive:

> (Yet a mournful wail and low sob I fancied I heard through
> the dark,
> In a lull of the deafening confusion.)

> 3
> Thunder on! stride on Democracy! strike with vengeful
> stroke!   (*DT*, 36)

Whitman's "Years of the unperform'd" admits that a body politic is comprised of individuals. But because of the fluidity of the poetic structure (as opposed to the stasis of visual allegory) an "average man" can replace the initially thematized colossus without a simultaneous representation of individuality. As in "First O songs," Whitman's treatment of the body politic in "Years" is fluid:

Never was average man, his soul, more energetic, more like a God;
. . . .
His daring foot is on land and sea everywhere—he colonizes the
    Pacific, the archipelagoes:
. . . .
Are all nations communing? is there going to be but one
    heart to the globe?
Is humanity forming en-masse?—for lo! tyrants tremble, crowns
    grow dim.   (*DT*, 53-54)

Abstract man's single "daring foot" is a synecdoche for the bodies of the many men who fought battles of empire. By means of the synecdoche the histories of those men are interdicted; yet even such a partial representation of a supposedly average man is enough to legitimate the imperialist project in which he participates. The embodiment of ideology requires the deformed representation of individual subjects, whose bodies no longer have their own hearts (in either the literal sense, or the figurative sense of the source of will and emotion), but whose blood is commingled in one great heart. The proposed unification is as yet, according to the title of the poem, "unperform'd." But this implies that the Civil War is the prologue to a drama of empire in which America will eventually absorb all other players.

The representational structure of an *American* body politic competed with an equally prevalent representation of America as a nation of autonomous individuals. A problem for an ideology of "autonomy" is the manufacture of consent for a war in which (like many American wars) those who are called on to fight have nothing to gain and their lives or limbs to lose. The fluidity of the representational structure of the body politic in *Drum-Taps* is symptomatic of this contradiction between national consensus and autonomy. Yet we have seen that if that fluidity threatens to burst through the confines of the structure, Whitman does not hesitate to provide reinforcement, in the form of a particularly strong assertion of totalizing embodiment which marginalizes the question of autonomy.

It is not until well after the war, and then only in his prose, that Whitman comes close to admitting that the war dramatized the instability of this topos. In "Origins of Attempted Secession," he argues that the war was "a conflict . . . between the passions and paradoxes of one and the same identity—perhaps the only terms on which that identity could really become fused, homogeneous and lasting" (*PW*, 2:427). But the rhetoric of embodiment cannot quite manage the resolution, because a

Union which is not totalitarian must, when represented as a single body, seem at least schizophrenic if not physically fragmented. Although Whitman claims that after the war the states are "no more divided in their spinal requisites, but [are] a great homogeneous Nation" (433), the text also contains assertions to the contrary. The body of the Union is said still to be unhealthy, in that the "putrid conditions" which caused the war continue to exist and "still result in diseases, fevers, wounds—not of war and army hospitals—but wounds and diseases of peace" (430). At the close of the essay, the aftermath of the war is not represented in the conventional image of a single, healed nation. Instead there are two bodies:

> More than any of the rest, and, in my opinion, more than the north itself, the *vital heart and breath of the south* have escaped as from the pressure of a general nightmare, and are henceforth to enter on a life, development, and active freedom, whose realities are certain in the future . . . . And I predict that the south is yet to outstrip the north. (433, emphasis added)

Thus the potential for a recurrence of conflict, unavailable in the case of a singular body, is implicit in the prediction of two, competing bodies.

But in *Drum-Taps* Whitman does not publish this sort of critique of the representational structure of the body politic, because in 1865 the image of the Union as a single colossus had so much ideological value. Instead, the structure of embodiment is reinforced, in several poems, by attributing to the body politic a theological significance.[10] In such poems the combatants of the war are represented as sons of the "mother of all," a quasigoddess who guides her family's destiny. (In such a case the war would have to be regarded as an outbreak of sibling rivalry.) Whitman's treatment of the theological allegory is not always systematic. The divine figure is sometimes masculine (as in "Chanting the Square Deific") and sometimes feminine. The stereotyped attributes of either gender are used to establish different tones. The feminine figure appears in "Over the carnage rose prophetic a voice" and "Pensive on her dead gazing, I heard the mother of all." The representation of the divine being as specifically feminine alters the conventional naming of God the Father. This alteration is not an expression of anti-Christian sentiment (on the contrary, as Thomas Crawley has demonstrated, Whitman's poetry often depends on a Christian sense of prophecy). Rather, the feminine attributes of the "mother of all" indicate a relation to the system of allegorized female bodies, such as "Libertad." The feminine figure is devoid of character and individuality, as Warner's analysis would predict, and thus conducive to the assertion of Union over autonomy. In Whitman's transformation of allegory to theodicy, the masculine Christian God is often represented as stern and vengeful, whereas a mother is conventionally a nurturing figure who would not *willingly* let harm come to her sons. (For example, Whitman never suggests, as Lincoln sometimes does in his public discourse, that the war was God's punishment for the nation's sin of slavery.)[11] Violence to the body, then, becomes merely a sad and unavoidable consequence of a struggle for the legitimation of ideology, rather than the central fact of that struggle.

"Chanting the Square Deific," in contrast, employs a conventional representation of the stern, masculine God the father: "Relentless, I forgive no man—whoever sins, dies; I will have that man's life" (*SDT*, 15). But responsibility for the war is incorporated into the godhead in the figure of Satan, who is the third face of a divine tetrarchy. This poem has been read as Whitman's "final word on the Civil War," according to which all suffering and hate was to be "understood as part of a spiritual dialectic" (Fredrickson, 96). But the poem does not quite achieve synthesis; instead it reflects the popular Northern attitude that the South was the locus of evil. Consider Satan's description of himself:

> Aloof, dissatisfied, plotting revolt,
> Comrade of criminals, brother of slaves,
> Crafty, despised, a drudge, ignorant,
> With sudra face and worn brow—black, but in the depths of my
>   heart, proud as any;
>
> . . . .
>
> Defiant, I, SATAN, still live—still utter words—in new lands duly
>   appearing, (and old ones also;)
> Permanent here, from my side, warlike, equal with any,
>   real as any.   (*SDT*, 16)

Although Satan is traditionally "black" (as, for example, in Puritan representations), the poem demonstrates that during the war the most culturally powerful locus of "blackness" was the South: the third line, especially, is a caricature of a black slave. Victims of slavery were often blamed as the cause of the war and its suffering, by common soldiers (Glatthaar, 54–55) as well as by politicians; Lincoln, for example, seemed to share this sentiment when in 1862 he proposed a scheme for ridding the country of blacks entirely by colonizing them in Central America (Lincoln, 6:370–73; McPherson, 508–09). Many of the attributes of Satan in these lines would also have been applied, by Northerners, to the secessionists. Many white Southerners were literally the "brother[s] of slaves," because female slaves often were forced to supply the sexual demands of their masters.[12] Furthermore, the "revolt" of secession was generally said to be "criminal." Southern whites, especially of the planter class, were popularly represented in the North as "proud," "defiant," and "warlike."[13] Satan thus appears to be a figure for a sort of sinister body politic—a composite of rebellion and blackness—never to be placated, his "brow"

> Lifted, now and always, against whoever, scorning, assumes
>   to rule me;
> Morose, full of guile, full of reminiscences, brooding, with
>   many wiles,
> (Though it was thought I was baffled and dispell'd, and my wiles
>   done—but that will never be;)   (16)

The South, as they say, will rise again.

III. *Sacrificial Violence*

When history is narrated as theodicy, rather than as the triumph of an abstract political entity, evil becomes not a contingent problem which an increase in liberty or democracy can solve, but an existential fact which can only be rationalized. In a discussion of the Civil War as a "theodicean problem," Wolosky argues that in "Chanting the Square Deific" "Christ's passion emerges as the war's figure, bestowing upon it the force of purgation" so that the violence becomes "sanctified" (71). In the structure of the poem, however, Satan speaks after Christ, as if to answer his claims. Although the poem addresses the theodicean problem, it leaves open the question of whether the violence of the war fulfilled the sanctifying function required by the structure.

The representation of violence as somehow sacred is an important mechanism for the theodicean rationalization of evil. In "Lo! Victress on the Peaks," Whitman represents himself in the act of offering poetic representations of violence to the figure of "Libertad" (who occupies the position of divinity on a mountain-top):

> No poem proud I, chanting, bring to thee—nor mastery's
>   rapturous verse;

> But a little book, containing night's darkness, and blood-dripping
>   wounds,
> And psalms of the dead.   (*SDT*, 23)

Whitman's representations of sacrifice continue a long-standing tradition of mobilizing religious discourse in the service of politics. Other Civil War poetry such as Brownell's *War Lyrics* and Howe's "Battle Hymn of the Republic" also represented the prosecution of the war in militantly Christian terms. But the idea of a civil war, of internal political violence, problematizes any simple recuperation in terms of a Christian narrative. Whitman's poems, unlike those of Howe, Brownell, and others, demonstrate an awareness of this problem even as they write a sacrificial narrative of the war.

René Girard, in an analysis of sacrificial violence in "primitive" and Christian religions, argues that the sacrifice of a surrogate victim transforms the universal human impulse toward violence from a potentially divisive and reciprocal internal force into a unifying principle of society. Civil war in general is thus often represented in terms of sacrificial violence as a "foreign war" in which the enemy is a guilty victim (*Violence*, 249). Girard's analysis is relevant here because Christian narratives of sacrificial violence were often mobilized to produce the meaning of the Civil War. For example, Northern representations of the Civil War as a "Holy Crusade" guaranteed the guilt of the victim: slavery and secession were plagues, the bringers of which had to be violently expelled (Moorhead, 35–41). The allegorization of the South in the figure of Satan in "Chanting the Square Deific," as we have seen, exemplifies this identification of the victim as outside of the community to be unified.

The operation Girard describes—in which a human body is figured, prior to sacrifice, as a scapegoat or lamb of God—is, he claims, archetypal or universal. But the legitimation of a *civil* war by means of the structure of sacrifice is paradoxical. The object of violence is supposed to come from outside the community because violence toward a member of the community, "far from reiterating the effects of a generative violence, . . . would inaugurate a new crisis" of unity (*Violence*, 269). But Lincoln's official position on secession—that the Confederacy did not exist, and that those who aligned themselves with this nonexistent government were merely rebellious Americans—conflicted with this structural requirement of ritual sacrifice. According to Lincoln's policy, all potential victims belonged to the single community of the United States. After secession the Confederacy, on the contrary, regarded the North as a foreign power bent on imperial conquest. Thus, the violence of the Civil War could not fulfill its supposed unifying function, because of disagreement over what constituted unity and over how many societies could have been unified. As the third section of "Chanting the Square Deific" suggests, the conception of the Civil War as a case of ritual violence provided, at best, only a temporary sign of union; for Satan says, "it was thought I was baffled and dispell'd, and my wiles done—but that will never be" (*SDT*, 16).

In addition to the Old Testament narrative of a holy war, Whitman also appeals to the recuperative paradigm of Christ's passion, which was a highly accessible narrative of sacrificial violence in nineteenth-century America. The distinction between the two structures is important. As Girard argues, the Gospels, unlike earlier mythological texts (including the Old Testament), demystify the representation of the sacrificial victim as necessarily "guilty." The Gospels "tell us explicitly that the victim is a scapegoat" who is killed even though everyone knows that he is innocent—unlike, say, Oedipus, who is persecuted because he is guilty of incest and parricide and thus supposedly responsible for the evils that plague Thebes (Girard, *Scapegoat*, 117). The Gospels are thus Whitman's paradigm for the death of the Northern soldier who is represented as an innocent victim whose noble death ought to bring about ritual reunification.

But although Christ's death made possible the *communal* celebration of his resurrection by the church, in *Drum-Taps* the hope of union provided by Christ's passion is not always fulfilled. "Come up from the fields, father"—in which a family receives a letter describing how "the only son" died in a hospital after being shot in battle—suggests that death in war produces only grief and consequent isolation in those who are supposed to participate, by means of sacrifice (according to Girard's analysis), in a renewed and unified society. This letter intrudes a representation of the war into the pastoral scene of a small Ohio farm; the family realize that their son had offered himself as an innocent scapegoat. But rather than feeling any sense of communal renewal, the mother of the son withdraws from earthly social intercourse:

> By day her meals untouch'd—then at night fitfully sleeping,
> often waking,
> In the midnight waking, weeping, longing with one deep longing,

O that she might withdraw unnoticed—silent from life, escape
    and withdraw,
To follow, to seek, to be with her dear dead son.   (*DT*, 40)

The war thus becomes an inversion of ritual unification. The soldier, the actual victim, is inside the community represented by his family; but his sacrifice produces only the mother's longing for a unity which the son's death has made impossible on earth. Since the soldier comes from Ohio, he is also "inside" the community of the Union from the beginning of the war. Whitman thus demonstrates that the representation of death in war as a Christlike sacrifice of "the only son" no longer has the potency to renew and reunify a society, because death produces only disunity at even the most local level.

In "Reconciliation," the penultimate poem in the *Sequel to Drum-Taps*, the "enemy" is the only represented object of violence. Yet unlike the culturally pervasive representations of the war as a victorious crusade (such as Howe's "Battle Hymn of the Republic"), Whitman's poem casts a Southerner in the divine role: "For my enemy is dead—a man as divine as myself is dead" (*SDT*, 23). The second half of this line suggests that the victim also belonged to the newly unified community and was an innocent scapegoat. But, after all, "reconciliation" was only possible because the war effected the dominance of the ideology of the Union. For Whitman's ideal democratic state, as for the constitutional Union (in the terms of which Southerners were rebellious citizens of the United States), there was in theory no "outside" of the community which could provide a "guilty" sacrificial victim. In terms of the theodicean model, the war entailed the sacrifice of hundreds of thousands of "innocent" victims. In order to make such violence culturally acceptable, the narrative of ritual sacrifice had to be reinforced with parallel secular narratives. Thus death in war came to be represented additionally as a political and economic sacrifice.

IV. *"The priceless value of our institutions"*

Because it involves a *substitution* (of specific violence for the threat of general violence, of actual victim for surrogate victim), sacrifice is a species of exchange. In the case of the Civil War, substitution was not only, or even primarily, figured as the displacement of violence upon slaves by violence upon their masters. Lincoln uses the figure of exchange only

27

late in the war, proclaiming that the war will continue "until every drop of blood drawn with the lash, shall be repaid with another drawn by the sword" (8:333).[14] Such a representation of violence disguises the fact that as many Northerners as Southerners were objects of military violence. But the violence of the war was often admitted to be more or less equally distributed. To account for the deaths of Northern soldiers, Unionists could represent their deaths as necessary sacrifices not to God but to the legal institutions: "The great battle between anarchy and law, between rebellion and government, is now to be fought. The fair fabric, whose stones were cemented with the blood of our fathers, is now to be defended. Can any offering be too great in such a cause? Can a life be more worthily or sacredly given up than upon the altar of our country?" (Perkins, 1067). The implication is that the victim is both inside society, as a citizen/ subject, and outside the government which is to be revitalized through sacrifice, as a property owned by the state. In other words, both the Christian and pre-Christian paradigms of sacrifice described by Girard are present, on different levels, and yet American institutions are the only source of authority. Another editorial represents this reciprocating substitution in a slightly different way, and more overtly assumes an equivalence between the sacrifice of lives and more conventional forms of economic exchange: "We shall come out of the present struggle impoverished in many ways. . . . We shall expend hundreds of millions of treasures and sacrifice thousands of lives" (Perkins, 1089). Thus the trope of sacrifice enlists economic metaphors—that human life is "priceless," human blood "precious"—in support of war (*DT*, 32, 71). It is clear that lives are expended to maintain the political economy of America.

The central "hermeneutic principle" of Abraham Lincoln's explanation of the war was, as Grossman maintains, "an exchange of life for meaning" (191). This principle governed a great many contemporary responses to the Civil War. "Exchange" is, in fact, one of the most common topoi in the rhetoric of war in general. We have been told, for example, that "Freedom" and "Democracy" were worth the cost of lives lost in the Revolution, or in Vietnam. But this is merely a recent version of Horace's dictum that it is beautiful and fitting for a young man to die "pro patria" (exposed by Wilfred Owen during the Great War as "the old lie"). The "pro" indicates the dual representational status of the death of the soldier in the rhetoric of war: he can be thought of as dying "in exchange for" the ideology of his country or "on behalf of" that ideology as its representative. While the life of the soldier is represented as a commodity, Whitman recognizes that the body of the soldier is also a figure for representation itself, inasmuch as the body, intact or violated, stands at once for the "patria" and for the quasi-political process— dependent on the possibility of death in war—by means of which the "patria" maintains its power to continue to exist.

Grossman argues that in "When Lilacs Last in the Dooryard Bloom'd" Whitman "translates Lincoln's death without exchanging it for any term whatsoever, and 'the slain soldiers of the war' without the commutation of any rational value" (201).[15] But in *Drum-Taps*, "rational," calculable economic values are sometimes placed into a system of exchange along with human life and the abstract "values" of ideology. The war threatens to disrupt this stable system of exchange. But because commodities appear to have a natural value in an exchange economy, representations of the general process of exchange function as naturalizing guarantees of meaning—even when the values exchanged are not commodities in the strict sense.

Some poems in *Drum-Taps* use a structure of exchange to support another metaphoric system such as a body politic. For example, in "Pensive on her dead gazing I heard the mother of all," the earth of America is itself a body, in which the blood of all its brave soldiers is commingled and circulated; but circulation takes on an economic sense as well, which becomes naturalized:

> Absorb them well, O my earth, she cried—I charge you, lose not
> my sons! lose not an atom;
> And you streams, absorb them well, taking their dear blood;
> . . . .
> My dead absorb—my young men's beautiful bodies absorb—and
> their precious, precious, precious blood;
> Which holding in trust for me, faithfully back again give many a
> year hence,
> . . . .
> O years and graves! O air and soil! O my dead, an aroma sweet!
> Exhale them perennial, sweet death, years, centuries hence.
>
> (*DT*, 71)

Although the poem does not name overtly an exchange of lives for an ideology of Union, the "mother of all" (a benevolent if vaguely defined divine figure) is said to place the lives of soldiers "in trust." The return on this investment is payable "years hence"; thus the "trust" is an optimistic speculation in the future of the Union. The authority of the central metaphor of absorption and exhalation is grounded (in two senses) in the guarantee of equal exchange value implicit in the economic structure. The poem, like any investment, posits a confidence in the market.

Of all the *Drum-Taps* poems, "Song of the Banner at Day-Break" best exemplifies the prevalence of the topos of economic exchange in the cultural rhetoric that legitimated the war. Here the flag, rather than the earth, becomes the site of the transaction; but like "Pensive on her dead gazing," this poem is also governed by the representational structure of commodity exchange.[16] "Song of the Banner" is the longest poem in *Drum-Taps*. It purports more than most to dramatize the problem of representing the war in the face of conflicting ideologies. There are three voices, plus the song of the poet who, in searching for his own voice, finds that he can only "weave the chord and twine in" (9) the other voices. The voice of the "pennant and banner" is at first merely aesthetically seductive: "Come up here dear little child / To fly in the winds with us and play with the measureless light" (10). Later it proclaims more overtly the pro-war position. Necessarily this voice of ideology is ignorant of legitimating arguments; it knows that there are economic and moral arguments against the war, and yet it must have war. Thus the voice of the flags appeals for its legitimation to the aesthetic discourse of poetry:

> Where our factory-engines hum, where our miners delve the
> ground,
> Where our hoarse Niagara rumbles, where our prairie-plows are
> plowing;
> Speak, O bard! point this day, leaving all the rest, to us over all—
> and yet we know not why;
> For what are we, mere strips of cloth, profiting nothing,
> Only flapping in the wind? (11)

Thus the flags pronounce the role of poets and other rhetoricians during wartime—which is to represent aesthetic resolutions to the material contradictions surfaced by the war in the ideology of a capitalist society.

A child, naively in awe of the symbolic power of the banner, debates with a father who argues that to go to war is "to gain nothing, but risk and defy everything" (14). The father's lines make it clear that the peace position is a materialist position, as they counsel the child to resist the sway of ideology: "behold not the banners and pennants aloft, / But the well-prepared pavements behold—and mark the solid-wall'd houses" (11). The child's response indicates that to go to war is to embody the ideology proclaimed by the flags, which is to surrender values established in peacetime:

30

> O my father, I like not the houses;
> They will never to me be anything—nor do I like money;
> But to mount up there I would like, O father dear—that banner
>   I like;
> That pennant I would be, and must be.   (13)

But the contradictions in an economic legitimation of the war are not easily resolved. One pro-Lincoln paper claimed that the cause of the war was "excessive prosperity"; another exulted that the war had "broken up the nightmare of commerce" that was weakening American values (Perkins, 1065, 1071). In contrast, another pro-Lincoln paper affirmed the mercantile system by arguing that the war was "worth all its costs" and by suggesting that the nation would in fact net "a thousand fold" return on its investment: "Every drop of blood that has been shed—every dollar that has been expended—every purpose that has been baulked and hope that has been crushed—will fructify into future blessings" (Perkins, 1089–90).

The voices of child, father, and banner, having established the sense that the debate over the war is to be conducted in economic terms, give way to the poet, who finds his voice in the debate:

> —my theme is clear at last:
> —Banner so broad, advancing out of the night, I sing you haughty
>   and resolute;
> I burst through where I waited long, too long, deafen'd and
>   blinded;
> My sight, my hearing and tongue, are come to me (a little child
>   taught me;)   (15)

The opening of the poem had prepared us for a synthesis of positions—"Man's desire and babe's desire—I'll twine them in" (9). Yet in the ensuing dialectic, the naive thesis of the child subsumes the antithesis of the father's economic position. If the war will be, in the father's words, filled with "passions of demons, slaughter, premature death," then the poet is willing to affirm this: "Demons and death then I sing" (14). The father's "desire" is not synthesized but merely excluded; it no longer signifies a legitimate ideological position.

Although the father had argued that the ideology represented by the banner bears no relation to the material significance of labor, of goods "valued and toil'd for" (10), the poet suggests in his final apostrophe to the banner that value derives only from the existing network of political relations:

> Not houses of peace are you, nor any nor all of their prosperity,
>   (if need be you shall have every one of those houses to
>   destroy them;
> You thought not to destroy those valuable houses, standing fast,
>   full of comfort, built with money;
> May they stand fast then? Not an hour, unless you, above them
>   and all, stand fast;)
> —O banner! not money so precious are you, nor farm produce
>   you, nor the material good nutriment.   (15)

Since the flag itself has been exchanged metonymically for the state which it represents, and thus for the ideology of an exchange society, this sign of the dominant ideology becomes the sign which guarantees all value. There follows a catalogue of economic goods, after which the poet continues:

> O you up there! O pennant! where you undulate like a snake,
>   hissing so curious,
> Out of reach—an idea only—yet furiously fought for, risking
>   bloody death—loved by me!
> So loved! O you banner leading the day, with stars brought from
>   the night!
> Valueless, object of eyes, over all and demanding all—O banner
>   and pennant!   (15–16)

Here the flag is shown to be the ultimate commodity—the very source of exchange which consumes all use-value. Thus it is "valueless," a word which cuts two ways. On the one hand a "valueless" commodity is worthless; like the fiat money first printed by the United States government during the war to pay the war debt, it possesses no intrinsic use-value (except as mere paper).[17] On the other hand it is priceless, consuming ("demanding all") the exchange-value of all the ordinary commodities listed in the poem's catalogue; thus it can only be exchanged for something of equal (valueless) value such as the "priceless blood" of soldiers (*DT*, 32). Both of these significations argue that, although poems may revalue the commodity of the soldier's life, nothing is outside the general system of exchange. Two revisions for the 1871 edition of *Leaves of Grass* (which stood through the subsequent editions) are significant in this context. One deletes the phrase "a snake, hissing," creating a more positive image of the flag. The other clarifies somewhat the economic relations in the poem: the flag is represented as the "absolute owner of all," which confirms the sense of the 1865 version that the flag has the power of life and death over those who are its property (*LGV*, 2:465). The implicit claim of the banner, naively accepted by the child who is himself willing to go to war, is that ideology is beyond the economic concept of "value" and yet must be understood in those terms.

In spite of the poem's representation of internal contradictions in the ideological structure that justifies war in economic terms, the poet remains blind. The ideology signified by the flag maintains its status as the master of its representatives, the child-soldiers of the Civil War. The "call and demand" of the flag is recognized to be "ironical," and yet the poet surrenders to it:

> I too leave the rest—great as it is, it is nothing—houses, machines
>   are nothing—I see them not:
> I see but you, O warlike pennant. O banner so broad, with stripes,
>   I sing you only,
> Flapping up there in the wind.   (*DT*, 16)

The blindness of the poet seems to be the only available source of insight. His exclusive focus on the appearance of the flag calls attention to the aesthetic value of the sign of ideology. Walter Benjamin would argue, albeit in a different political climate, that the aestheticization of politics is a sufficient sign of fascism (241–42). In Whitman's poem it is clear that ideology has the power of an aesthetic object to minimize all peripheral claims on the subject's attention. This "object of eyes" (*DT*, 16) is a source of blindness—which can be read, but only against the grain, as a source of insight. Whitman seems to recognize that to consent to war is to renounce the materialist position that holds productive labor to be the source of value. But at the same time he remains mystified, arguing the case that ideology has a supreme value of its own—turning, as F. O. Matthiessen argues he often does, toward idealism when materialism proves inconvenient (521). In this tendency as much as in anything else, Whitman is thoroughly representative of the ideology that legitimated the war. The economic structure of representation used here to produce the meaning of the war is grounded in the assumption that the source of value is *exchange*. The labor of the soldier does not produce material value; rather, his body is expropriated and exchanged by the state for the maintenance of its ideology. The poet claims to have no choice but to exchange a peacetime, materialist economics for the idealist, exchange-based system, symbolized by the aesthetically seductive flag, which the legitimation of war required. Or, as one pro-Lincoln editor phrased it, the war was "teaching the people the priceless value of our institutions" (Perkins, 1093).

V. *"Affection shall solve the problems of freedom."*

Whitman attempted to ground an effective political ideology in a poetics of "adhesiveness," the mutual, democratic love of "comrades." Whether or not this poetics originated in Whitman's own homoerotic experiences or desires, in his texts the love of male comrades is always represented as the originating impulse of democracy.[18] In the preface to the 1876 edition of *Leaves of Grass*, Whitman asserts that "this universal democratic comradeship—this old, eternal, yet ever-new interchange of *adhesiveness*" is the real ground of the American political system, which is identical with the Union:

> The special meaning of the "Calamus" cluster of "Leaves of Grass" (and more or less running through the book, and cropping out in "Drum-Taps,") mainly resides in its political significance. In my opinion, it is by a fervid, accepted development of comradeship, the beautiful and sane affection of man for man, latent in all the young fellows . . . that the United States of the future, (I cannot too often repeat,) are to be most effectually welded together, intercalated, anneal'd into a living union. (*PW*, 2:471)

In "States," one of the poems in the "Calamus" cluster of the 1860 edition, Whitman identifies the crisis of political representation that would soon erupt in the war:

> States!
> Were you looking to be held together by the lawyers?
> Or by an agreement on paper? or by arms?   (*LGV*, 2:371–72)

His response to this threat of fragmentation is the cultivation of the adhesive sentiment, for which his poetic persona provides a model:

> There shall from me be a new friendship—It shall be called after
>   my name,
> It shall circulate through The States, indifferent of place,
> It shall twist and intertwist them through and around each other—
>   Compact shall they be, showing new signs,
> Affection shall solve every one of the problems of freedom,

34

Those who love each other shall be invincible,
They shall finally make America completely victorious,
    in my name.

. . . .

No danger shall balk Columbia's lovers;
If need be, a thousand shall sternly immolate themselves
    for one.   (372)

The rhetoric of adhesiveness, however, is contiguous in these lines with the rhetoric of war. The assertion of the political virtue of "affection" is followed closely by assertions of invincibility and victory and of the potential of sacrificial immolation, as if it is impossible for Whitman to develop his American nationalist poetics without a concomitant valor-ization of military conquest. Thus the trope of adhesion seems to encode not an ideology of autonomy, but a democracy motivated by the absorption of all it contacts.

Like "Come up from the fields, father," "States!" includes a rep-resentation of ritual sacrifice. Etymologically, *immolate* indicates a spe-cifically sacrificial death (derived from the Latin "*mola*," a millstone, it refers to a custom of sprinkling sacrificial victims with meal). In "Come up from the fields," the lonely grief of the mother permits a critical perspective on the idea of sacrificial violence, since there it produced only alienation. "States," however, gives an affirmative perspective on sacrifice. The difference between the two poems lies not only in the fact that in one case death is actual and in the other it is only hypothetical, "if need be." In "States!" the unity that Girard claims is produced through ritual sacrifice is shown to be prior to the sacrificial act; there is no need for sacrifice if "affection" can be mobilized in another way.

Whitman dropped "States!" from subsequent editions of *Leaves of Grass*, but he recycled many of its lines in the *Drum-Taps* poem "Over the carnage rose prophetic a voice." However, the lines that derive from the prewar poems bore a new significance after the outbreak of the war had shown that affection had not been mobilized in the way Whitman had proposed in the "Calamus" cluster of the 1860 edition:

Be not dishearten'd—Affection shall solve the problems of
    freedom *yet*;
Those who love each other shall become invincible—they shall
    yet make Columbia victorious.

. . . .

No danger shall balk Columbia's lovers;

> If need be, a thousand shall sternly immolate themselves
> for one.   (DT, 49, emphasis added)

The hypothetical sacrifice of "thousands" may be an attempt to effect the sort of ritual unification described by Girard. Christ's passion is repeatedly represented in the liturgy of the church; thus Christians experience vicariously their own death and resurrection and the communal staging of this experience effects the unification of the community. In the antebellum context of "States!" the poetic representation of sacrifice may be read as an analogously vicarious experience. But in war, the enactment of death is more than symbolic—it is actual—and it is not followed by the resurrection of the body that is killed. There is now a conflict between the symbolic level, on which the body politic is reborn, and the material level, on which the soldier remains dead. His body has been consumed by the ideology that demands his death.

Whitman attempts the reconciliation of these levels by means of the power of adhesiveness; in "Over the carnage rose prophetic a voice," the lines that immediately follow the reference to immolation contain synecdoches of Unionism:

> One from Massachusetts shall be a Missourian's comrade;
> From Maine and from hot Carolina, and another an Oregonese,
> shall be friends triune,
> More precious to each other than all the riches of the earth.
>
>   (DT, 49)

These lines displace the deaths of the Civil War and substitute the adhesive figuration of Unionism, whereas prior to the war in "States!" the hypothesis of sacrifice had been explored with greater specificity: "The Kanuck shall be willing to lay down his life for the Kansian, and the Kansian for the Kanuck, in due need" (LGV, 2:372). "States!" is hopeful, as if the love of comrades might yet avert the war. However, although it seems to identify the hope of union, "affection" also names a cause of the war since it represents the ideology of the Union from which the Southern states attempted to dissociate themselves.

In "Over the carnage" the contiguity of the tropes of sacrifice and adhesion indicate their political interconnection. The query that had opened "States!" becomes in Drum-Taps a description of history:

> Were you looking to be held together by the lawyers?
> Or by an agreement on paper? or by arms?
> Nay, nor the world, nor any living thing, will so cohere.   (50)

The poem has identified "manly affection" as the paradigm of political cohesion (49). This figure interdicts the representation of death in war—for although the title refers to "carnage," the poem never actually describes the aftermath of a battle. Such traces of war are instead displaced by figures of the coherence of the Union, as Whitman attempts to reaffirm the political potency of adhesiveness in the face of evidence of its impotence provided by the war.

VI. *"Many a soldier's kiss dwells on these bearded lips"*

Each of the topoi that function in *Drum-Taps* to produce the meaning of the war contains a trace of the war as a rupture of representation. This is not so much because the metaphor of the body politic, the narratives of divine sacrifice or the economic exchange of life for ideology, and the rhetoric of adhesiveness represent the war (for in important respects they do not), but because they are products of the ideology of Union which required the war in the first place. They were already in place before the war. But these structures also—in their internal contradictions—were symptomatic of the war as a crisis of representation.

While the topoi of the embodiment of abstract ideas, ritual sacrifice, the exchange of life for ideology, and the democratic, adhesive love of comrades organize the production of meaning in *Drum-Taps*, the governing tropes of these topoi are in themselves figures for aspects of the process of semiosis in general. A reflection on the problem of representation *as such* is written into all four rhetorical systems—and this is not, for Whitman, merely an artistic concern, because since his proclamation that the "United States are the Greatest Poem" he had treated representation as simultaneously a poetic and a political problem (*LG 1855*, 5). The *Drum-Taps* poems show that different figurations of representation contain different political implications. More than just structures of representation mobilized by poems, the tropes of embodiment, substitution, exchange, and adhesion denote alternate ways of thinking about the relations between the parts of any semiotic system. As such the first three figures (embodiment, substitution, exchange) reflect on the ways in which a system threatens to come apart, thematizing the dissipation of the "typifying" sign in an oscillation between the signified (for example, a single experience of a representative soldier) and the referent (the myriad experiences of other, equally representative soldiers). Adhesion is in contrast a figure which proposes the coherence and cohesion of the sign. Long

37

recognized as Whitman's special concern, the "interchange of adhesiveness" or the "love of comrades" is the figure that Whitman found most appropriate to represent the ideology of Union in a positive light. He found this particular specification of the typical most conducive to the unified treatment of poetics, politics, and metaphysics; that is, he regarded adhesiveness as a representational system that is "about" what holds representational systems together. But rare moments in *Drum-Taps*—those that most clearly thematize the question of the representation of horrors of war—put the adhesive function of the sign to the test.

In the following discussion of the ways in which the figures of embodiment, substitution, exchange, and adhesion can be said to represent representation, I draw on Hanna Pitkin's study of the ways in which political representation has been conceptualized. Substitution, according to Pitkin, is a case of "standing for" in which the representation bears a descriptive or mimetic relation to the referent (60–91).[19] Girard, whose work has already helped to orient my reading, also speaks of substitution as a case of resemblance when he identifies the mimetic function of ritual violence, which resembles and displaces (and thus dissipates) the originary violence that constitutes the root of social organization (*Violence*, 101–3). However, perfect resemblance is logically impossible as well as impossible in practice (Plato, *Cratylus*, 432b); thus a consideration of representation as a substitution based on resemblance reveals the absences which any sign-system necessarily contains and covers.

Exchange and substitution, as the preceding sections have suggested, are closely related figures. The most important theory that conceives representation as *exchange* is an overtly critical one: in his analysis of the logic of exchange in capitalist economies, Marx treats the commodity as a complex signifier—a "social hieroglyphic"—attached by convention to a fictional signified (exchange value) and by material fact to a real, but obscured referent (labor) (167). We have seen how Whitman's "Song of the Banner," in its blindness, also achieves Marx's insight. While Pitkin does not treat Marx, it is clear that she would regard the sign-function that authorizes commodity exchange as a case of "standing for" in which the representative symbolizes the referent on a symbolic (that is, a conventional) rather than descriptive (mimetic) basis (92–111). Here, as in the case of substitution, there is room to focus on the lack encoded into the representational system. (Pitkin argues that the symbolic theory of representation is essentially "nonrational" and potentially "fascist" [107].)

The origins of the theory of representation as embodiment can be located in the medieval juridical theory according to which the king's "body politic" is said to represent the bodies of his subjects (Rogin, "King's Two Bodies"). In the nineteenth century, the most important theories conceptualizing the state as a person or other organism were imported from Germany by the likes of historian George Bancroft (Coker; Callcott, 6–10). This nonmimetic conception of political representation grounds the relation between sign and referent in a theory of agency—that is, of "acting for" (Pitkin, 112–43). If a text is to be representative in this sense, it must be conceptualized as an agent. A well-known example of Whitman's insistence that the text is an acting body occurs in "So Long!" (1860):

> Camerado, this is no book,
> Who touches this touches a man.   (*LGV*, 2:452)

The trope of embodiment can be unstable in the case of a civil war, in which the configuration of the body politic is necessarily uncertain. In "So Long!" stability is finally achieved only in the absence of the body; the death of the body in some sense produces the essence of the poet: "decease calls me forth" (452). As with substitution and exchange, embodiment represents the possibility of a fragmentary force acting within the representational structure. The trope of adhesion, signaled by a declaration of love addressed directly to the reader-"Camerado," provides a centripetal force that counterbalances the centrifugal force represented by embodiment.

"As I Ebb'd with the Ocean of Life," another poem from the 1860 edition, describes a crisis of representation that Whitman inherited from Emerson; as in "So Long!" adhesion provides the only hope of resolving the crisis. In one sense this poem reveals Whitman's growing mistrust of the body from about 1860 on, a mistrust which was to have profound effects on his poetics, possibly causing a "decline in the quality and adventurousness of his poetry" (Rosenblatt, 105-6). We would expect to find in this mistrust a suspicion of the efficacy of the trope of embodiment. Jon Rosenblatt argues that the poem "shows that Whitman's entire method of reading the world as a series of shifting signifiers that are unified in the poet's self is on the verge of collapse" (106). In another sense, however, "As I Ebb'd" is a poem of broader political significance, reaching beyond Whitman's own "self." The representational crisis in "As I Ebb'd" is first announced with reference to the Swedenborgian structure of types and correspondences. As the poet examines the implications of Emerson's critique of the static character of Swedenborgian semiotics in *Representative*

Men, he sees a dissipation of the power of his own master-trope of typification:

> Chaff, straw, splinters of wood, weeds, and the sea-gluten,
> Scum, scales from shining rocks, leaves of salt-lettuce, left by
>   the tide,
> Miles walking, the sound of breaking waves the other side of me,
> Paumanok there and then I thought the old thought of likenesses,
> These you presented to me, you fish-shaped island,
> As I wended the shores I know,
> As I walked with that eternal self of me, seeking types.
>
> 2
> As I wend to the shores I know not,
> As I listen to the dirge, the voices of men and women wrecked,
> . . . .
> At once I find, the least thing that belongs to me, or that I see or
>   touch, I know not;
> I, too, but signify, at the utmost, a little washed-up drift,
> A few sands and dead leaves to gather,
> Gather, and merge myself as part of the sands and drift.
>
> (LGV, 2:319–20)

Having identified himself with nature in the form of the junk on Paumanok's shore, Whitman "can only follow the 'drift' of this signifier into dissolution and inexpressibility" (Rosenblatt, 107). "As I Ebb'd" describes a crisis of representation in general, figured not only as the dissolution of embodiment, but also as the absence inherent in the figuration of representation as embodiment, exchange, or substitution. The representational relation of "standing for" produces only a lack: "These little shreds, indeed, shall stand for all" (*LGV*, 2:320); the relation of "acting for" is available only in aimless, intentionless drift.

Fragmentation remains in the final image of the poem; the body, the object of the poet's discourse and of his desire, is represented in parts: "You up there walking or sitting, / Whoever you are, we too lie in drifts at your feet" (322). In keeping with the sense of instability which pervades the poem, the antecedent of "You" is unclear. Within the poem, it is primarily the ebbing "ocean of life" itself. As a speech-act of direct address, it involves the reader in the crisis. But "You" at the same time addresses the "father" of the third section of the poem—for here, if anywhere, is the source of hope for a coherent poetics, in the only indication of a voice:

I throw myself on your breast, my father,
I cling to you so that you cannot unloose me,
I hold you firm, till you answer me something.

Kiss me, my father,
Touch me with your lips, as I touch those I love,
Breathe to me, while I hold you close, the secret of the wondrous
    murmuring I envy,
For I fear I shall become crazed, if I cannot emulate it, and utter
    myself as well as it. (321)

Fragmentation is Whitman's figure for the crisis within the system of representation; in the case of the war, fragmentation takes on the political sense of dis-Union. The only hope of preserving the system—and the desperate tone indicates that it is fleeting—is adhesiveness. The object of desire is fragmented, in images of the poet clinging to the breast, kissing the lips of the father. Before the war Whitman had written that "a true composition in words, returns to the human body, male or female—that is the most perfect composition, and shall be best-beloved by men and women, and shall last the longest, which slights no part of the body, and repeats no part of the body" (*AP*, 27–28). The adhesive tendency, that is, dictates the "perfect" representation of a unified, inviolate body (poetic or politic). The adhesion figured in the line "I cling to you so that you cannot unloose me" represents the object of desire in such a way that the "emulative"—the mimetic (substitution) or symbolic (exchange)—function of the system will continue to be productive rather than fragmentary and destructive.

Whitman does not value adhesiveness above embodiment, substitution, or exchange because it is a "better" description of representation. Rather, it is a question of different functional levels of a system. Adhesiveness allows the other representative operations to take place, but it does not displace them. For Whitman, the ground of representation and the "Base of all Metaphysics" was the "dear love of man for his comrade, the attraction of friend to friend" (*LGV*, 3:629). Whitman suggested that the origin of language—itself a "sort of universal absorber"—was its adhesive tendencies and that slang was the "germinal element" because it was closest to the originary, adhesive function of language: "something arising out of the work, needs, ties, joys, affections, tastes of long generations of humanity" (*PW*, 2:572–73).

The Civil War and the events that led up to it—debates over the nature of the Union and, finally, secession—produced a fragmentation of political experience and thus put the adhesive function into question. In *Drum-Taps*, dead or wounded soldiers are the most significant images of fragmentation. As these images appear they threaten the collapse of the representational structure (poetic and political) of the poem of America; for—to return to a consideration of Scarry's thesis—the wound is an unstable signifier. Whitman in turn invokes adhesiveness, in the form of the love of comrades, as the only healing power that might hold together not only the wounded body of the soldier (even though in the literal sense the body could never be made whole again) but also his poetics and ultimately the Union.

"A March in the ranks hard-prest, and the road unknown," a vignette from the life of an anonymous soldier-poet, thematizes the potential unrepresentability of the war, bringing the trope of adhesion to bear on the problem of representation. The presence of a temporary hospital, containing wounded from a battle in which the army was "foil'd with loss severe," appears as a diversion on the march:

> Till after midnight glimmer upon us, the lights of a dim-lighted
>   building;
> We come to an open space in the woods, and halt by the
>   dim-lighted building;
> 'Tis a large old church, at the crossing roads—'tis now an
>   impromptu hospital;
> —Entering but for a minute, I see a sight beyond all the pictures
>   and poems ever made:
> Shadows of deepest, deepest black, just lit by moving candles
>   and lamps,
> . . . .
> At my feet more distinctly, a soldier, a mere lad, in danger of
>   bleeding to death, (he is shot in the abdomen;)
> I staunch the blood temporarily, (the youngster's face is white as
>   a lily;)
> Then before I depart I sweep my eyes o'er the scene, fain to absorb
>   it all;
> Faces, varieties, postures beyond description, most in obscurity,
>   some of them dead. (*DT*, 44)

The narrator's experience of seeing the violated bodies of his comrades is unrepresentable and yet somehow partly represented. The poet appeals twice to the inexpressibility of the scene, which justifies the interdicted representation. A wound is named, but not described in any detail.

In this poem Whitman comes much closer to a representation of violated bodies of soldiers than in the poems of the body politic, theodicy, and exchange, in which the representational structure functions to obscure the reality of violence through a redescriptive transference. Here the sense of fragmentation which prohibits full visual or textual representation— "beyond all the pictures and poems"—is self-reflexively acknowledged, and thus never quite recuperated. But the march and the narrative can continue after a significant moment shared by the narrator and a wounded soldier, which provides a closure to the scene of "postures beyond description" that threatens the possibility of representation. In this moment Whitman appeals to the adhesive topos to restore the narrative structure:

> But first I bend to the dying lad—his eyes open—a half-smile he
> gives me;
> Then the eyes close, calmly close, and I speed forth to the
> darkness. (45)

The image of the closing eyes prefigures the interdiction of any further representation of the scene of horror. The poet's own eyes are closed— by the "darkness," but also by his bond with the soldier produced in the adhesive moment. The love of comrades, if it cannot actually reunify the fragmented body of the dying soldier, at least allows the completion of the poetic structure: the narrative is restored and the narrator, himself both a poet and a military representative of his country, can continue to execute his two representational activities. That his efficacy as a political representative depends on the possibility of his own death (prefigured in the scene itself, which interrupts the narrative) is an irony on which he does not comment. The adhesive structures of representation will function, it seems, with or without the presence of this soldier-poet.

Another poem involving the interplay among representation, fragmentation and the healing power of adhesiveness is "The Dresser"—the prelude to which, a short poem entitled "Quicksand years that whirl me I know not whither," refers to the dissipating drift of sands and signs in "As I Ebb'd." In "The Dresser," entry into an army hospital is represented as, potentially, reentry into the representational crisis of that poem from 1860. But "The Dresser" also includes a reference to the "father" invoked in "As I Ebb'd" as a possible resolution of that crisis (just as "Vigil strange I kept on the field one night" represents the grieving soldier as the father of the dead soldier):

> But in silence, in dream's projections,
> While the world of gain and appearance and mirth goes on,

> Soon what is over forgotten, and waves wash the imprints off
> the sand,
> In nature's reverie sad, with hinged knees returning, I enter the
> doors—(while you up there,
> Whoever you are, follow me without noise, and be of strong
> heart.)   (DT, 32)

In "Quicksand years," as in "The Dresser," Whitman returns to his already established poetics to recuperate the presence of the dead and wounded; and yet this move is inflected by uncertainty. In the former poem, the confident assertions of selfhood from "Song of Myself" (1855) are transformed into a searching question:

> Out of politics, triumphs, battles, death—what at last finally
> remains?
> When shows break up, what but One's-Self is sure?   (DT, 30)

Despite this attempt at confidence in "One's-Self," in the context of the war Whitman found his own "self" to be unstable. During his years as volunteer nurse in army hospitals he suffered physical and emotional breakdowns, in 1863 and again in 1865 (Aspiz, 25–27). The grounding of poetics in "myself" or in the "body electric" as constructed in the first edition of *Leaves of Grass* was brought into question by the violence of the war.

The poem, the self, the concept (if not the reality) of the body are all tenuously cemented by the homoerotic moment—an element of the earlier poetics which Whitman cannot bring himself to question, even rhetorically, as the ground of meaning:

> The hurt and wounded I pacify with soothing hand,
> I sit by the restless all the dark night—some are so young;
> Some suffer so much—I recall the experience sweet and sad;
> (Many a soldier's loving arms about this neck have cross'd
> and rested,
> Many a soldier's kiss dwells on these bearded lips.)   (34)

The verb "dwells" (in the present tense, rather than the past-perfect of "have cross'd") attempts to preserve the healing, adhesive moments by asserting their continual presence. There is no doubt that the love of comrades is an article of Whitman's faith in representation. In the context of the army hospital Christ becomes both the subject and object of desire: "I think I could not refuse this moment to die for you, if that would

save you" (32). In "A Sight in camp in the day-break" he finds a reflection
of this Christlike self in the face of a wounded soldier:

> Then to the third—a face nor child, nor old, very calm, as of
>   beautiful yellow-white ivory;
> Young man, I think I know you—I think this face of yours is the
>   face of the Christ himself;
> Dead and divine, and brother of all, and here again he lies.
>
> (*DT*, 46)

Adhesiveness—the poetic representation of homoerotic desire—functions
as a guarantee that all the subjects of the war are one. Whitman is not
a millennialist in any conventional sense of the term; and yet the desired
unity in Christ invokes a teleology that proposes a way out of, or an
end to, politics and history.

Adhesiveness is always recuperative in Whitman's texts, since it forms
the political, representative ground for re-Union. However, in the context
of the aftermath of the war, there is a suggestion that a lack of representation has in itself a restorative power, as for example in "Reconciliation," the penultimate poem in the *Sequel to Drum-Taps*, in which the
absence produced by death is juxtaposed to the homoerotic moment:

> Word over all, beautiful as the sky!
> Beautiful that war, and all its deeds of carnage, must in time
>   be utterly lost;
> That the hands of the sisters Death and Night, incessantly softly
>   wash again, and ever again, this soil'd world:
> . . . For my enemy is dead—a man divine as myself is dead;
> I look where he lies, white-faced and still, in the coffin—
>   I draw near;
> I bend down and touch lightly with my lips the white face
>   in the coffin.   (23, Whitman's ellipses)

The second line may be expressing the hope that internal strife in the
body politic of America would henceforth disappear. But the proposed
disappearance is as much textual as material, for the "Word over all"
is what is "beautiful." Discourse itself is represented as possessing the
aesthetic power to make war disappear. Whitman explores such interdictive operations in greater detail in the *Memoranda during the War*. There
he returns to the antebellum locus of the moment of "adhesiveness"—
the pastoral scene—to find that with the war it has become a site not
of unification but of fragmentation.

2. "The Real War Will Never Get in the Books"

IN 1875 Whitman published a prose account of his Civil War years entitled *Memoranda during the War*. The primary sources for this text were notebook and diary entries that Whitman recorded during the war.[1] As it was for *Drum-Taps*, the impetus for the *Memoranda* was Whitman's immediate response to the war. But the mediation of the war takes a different form in the prose text. The *Memoranda* are more reflective than *Drum-Taps*, sometimes critical and even skeptical about the possibilities of representation. They appear to be working through those rare moments in *Drum-Taps* in which the war is said to pose representational problems, in an attempt to find aesthetic and ideological solutions.

Whitman identifies these problems in passages such as the following:

> Of scenes like these, I say, who writes—who e'er can write, the story? Of many a score—aye, thousands, North and South, of unwrit heroes, unknown heroisms, incredible, impromptu, first-class desperations—who tells? No history, ever—No poem sings, no music sounds, those bravest men of all—those deeds. No formal General's report, nor print, nor book in the library, nor column in the paper, embalms the bravest, North or South, East or West. Unnamed, unknown, remain, and still remain, the bravest soldiers. Our manliest—our boys—our hardy darlings. Indeed no picture gives them. Likely their very names are lost. (*M*, 16)

This reflection on representation reveals a double absence. Whitman deplores the lack of adequate accounts of the war—textual or otherwise—but provides no causal explanation for this absence. Additionally, the metaphor of embalming specifically criticizes the textual mode of representation in general by suggesting that texts preserve only the empty form of experience. (There is no reason to believe that he excepts his own *Drum-Taps* poems from this critique.) Such absences—of and within representation—might have critical consequences for the ideology of Unionism, because representational plenitude was the theoretical foundation, not only of Whitman's poetics, but of American politics as well.

Poetry stands in the same relation as all other representational apparatuses to the unnamed, unknown referents. In 1865 Whitman had claimed that *Drum-Taps* expressed the "pending action of this *Time & Land we swim in*," even if "not at all by directly stating it" (*C*, 1:246). The *Memoranda* interrogate this claim. Exploring the limits of representation, Whitman in one respect comes to reaffirm his antebellum poetics by returning to his master trope of typification, which subsumes the specific figures for representation (embodiment, substitution, exchange, adhesiveness) that organize the meanings of the war in *Drum-Taps*. The *Memoranda* legitimate typification by appealing to the ancient topos of inexpressibility, but in such a way as to reveal the ideological operations of a poetics organized around "ideal-typical moments" (Grossman, 188). At crucial moments of the *Memoranda*, the rhetorics of inexpressibility and typification intersect in the pastoral scene. In *Drum-Taps* Whitman marginalizes the pastoral topos in an attempt to shield its figures of wholeness and integrity from wartime violence and violation. In the *Memoranda*, however, he returns to the pastoral scene to find that it *has* been a site of violence during the war. This acknowledgment is the first step in Whitman's recovery of pastoralism and with it a nationalist ideology appropriate to reconciliation. In "When Lilacs Last in the Dooryard Bloom'd" he interdicts the critique of history posed in the *Memoranda* by retrieving the culturally powerful but historically evasive pastoral mode, in an effort to restore his poetics (especially in their implications for a nationalist ideology) to representational plenitude. The possibility of an affirmative American history depends, for Whitman, on the fact that "the real war will never get in the books" (*PW*, 1:115).[2]

I.   *"Associations never to be possibly
      said or sung"*

The title of the 1875 volume implies that it exteriorizes and textualizes memory; this implicit claim to represent and thereby preserve the contents of memory seems to conflict with Whitman's explicit assertion that "the real war will never get in the books." But etymologically a memorandum is something that *ought* to be remembered (in the future); it is not so much a description as a prescriptive agenda for memory. Memory is enabled, but also distorted, by schemata. Textual structures—rhyme, parallelism, organic rhythm, rhetorical tropes—are analogous to these mnemonic structures, as Whitman recognized.[3] While memory and text represent or re-create, they also interdict certain aspects of "reality," "experience," and the like. That is, even though in *Drum-Taps* Whitman

47

seemed to have found a guarantee of poetic representation in tropes of adhesiveness, the very notion of a memorandum implies that a text is not thoroughly adhesive. And yet untextualized memory cannot in itself preserve history for the future.

Whitman opposes textual representation to the unrepresentable traces of war in a prefatory note to *Specimen Days*, in which he describes the process of composing the *Memoranda*. The mediating term is memory, which here assumes the form of inarticulate "associations":

> I have dozens of . . . little note-books left, forming a special history of those years, for myself alone, full of associations never to be possibly said or sung. I wish I could convey to the reader the associations that attach to these soil'd and creas'd livraisons, each composed of a sheet or two of paper, folded small to carry in the pocket, and fasten'd with a pin. I leave them just as I threw them by after the war, blotch'd here and there with more than one blood-stain . . . . Most of the pages from 26 to 81 are verbatim copies of these lurid and blood-smutch'd little note-books. (*PW*, 1:2)

These papers affect Whitman not so much because of their words, but because they bear traces of the violated human body which cannot be represented and thus must fail to become part of the public record of the war. The very presence of the "blood-stain[s]" prevents Whitman from representing them; their reality thwarts textualization.

In the face of the acknowledged impossibility of full representation, the *Memoranda* propose a system of the typical as the form for the historical representation of war. The basic trope of this system is synecdoche, in which a single event or experience replaces the whole of the war. (The very title of *Specimen Days*, in which the *Memoranda* were later reprinted, foregrounds synecdoche). The rhetorical structures of *Drum-Taps*—for example, the allegory of "Libertad" or the exchange of life for ideology (as discussed in the previous chapter)—might be supposed to typify various experiences of the war, but at the expense of individual subjectivity. The *Memoranda* qualify the device of typification by developing arguments for a proposition only occasionally hinted at in *Drum-Taps*—namely, that the lived experience of war will always exceed the representational capacity of any medium. Such representational absences are ideologically productive, however: by despairing of the possibility of a comprehensive history of violence, the *Memoranda* affirm the prosecution of the war.

48

Whitman does not flinch from a direct account that includes many "realistic" details, as in this description of a scene from the battle of Chancellorsville:

> [There were] many good fellows lying helpless, with new accessions to them, and every minute amid the rattle of muskets and the crash of cannon, (for there was an artillery contest too,) the red life-blood oozing out from heads or trunks or limbs upon that green and dew-cool grass. The woods take fire, and many of the wounded, unable to move, (especially some of the divisions in the Sixth Corps,) are consumed—quite large spaces are swept over, burning the dead also. (*M*, 14)

Yet the "realistic" description is always fragmentary, and framed by claims, such as the one quoted above, which question the possibility of representation and suggest that "the real war will never get in the books." The vivid details function, paradoxically, to indicate a lack of adequate detail.

Whitman introduces this passage about Chancellorsville with the Romantic device of the incomplete view ("just a glimpse"), which excludes—how much, we will never know:

> We already talk of Histories of the War, (presently to accumulate)— yes—technical histories of some things, statistics, official reports, and so on—but shall we ever get histories of the *real* things? . . . . [Whitman's ellipses] There was part of the late battle at Chancellorsville [that] . . . I would like to give just a glimpse of—(a moment's look in a terrible storm at sea—of which a few suggestions are enough, and full details impossible). (13)[4]

Having set up the passage by foregrounding the problem of representation, Whitman closes it in a similar way—this time, however, at greater length, and with specific reference to the historiographical nature of the problem:

> What history, I say, can ever give—for who can know—the mad, determin'd tussle of the armies, in all their separate large and little squads—as this—each steep'd from crown to toe in desperate, mortal purports? . . . Who paint the scene, the sudden partial panic of the afternoon, at dusk? (15)

The cultural memory of the war, in the form of historical representation, is addressed (especially in the last sentence of the passage) as an aesthetic problem. But the aesthetic problem derives from a prior epistemological one: "who can know?"

Typification is presented as the only adequate resolution of the conflicting impulses of representation and interdiction that motivate the *Memoranda*. Whitman's use of the trope is explicit in the following passage on death in war:

> Our manliest—our boys—our hardy darlings. Indeed no picture gives them. Likely their very names are lost. Likely, the *typic* one of them, (standing, no doubt, for hundreds, thousands,) crawls aside to some bush-clump, or ferny tuft, on receiving his death-shot—there, sheltering a little while, soaking roots, grass and soil with red blood . . . and there, haply with pain and suffering, (yet less, far less than is supposed,) the last lethargy winds like a serpent around him— the eyes glaze in death—none recks—Perhaps the burial squads, in truce, a week afterwards, search not the secluded spot—And there, at last, the Bravest Soldier crumbles in the soil of mother earth, unburied and unknown. (16, emphasis added)[5]

If Scarry's thesis is correct—that pain is inexpressible because "the most crucial fact about pain is *its presentness*" (9)—then a schema of typification may seem to be the most adequate semiotic possible. But in fact Whitman is claiming here that suffering *is* representable, since he ventures to correct a shared norm of what is "supposed." Yet at the same time, he refuses any representation of either the suffering or its measure, the norm. The qualifier "haply" even suggests disturbingly that the suffering of the soldier is only incidental to the representation of the event. The text dwells instead on the natural scene that encompasses the body of the soldier, ignoring his consciousness (which would, at that moment, be proving the norm). The pastoral frame interdicts traces of the soldier's (or is it soldiers'?) political experience. By naturalizing his (their) presence in this garden, it also naturalizes the historical-ideological forces responsible for such deaths.

A *type*, as Whitman seems to be using the term, is decontextualized to the extent that individual circumstance, difference and variation regarding the referent(s) are erased. The representation of a single soldier displaces the universal experience of (hundreds of) "thousands." Those men who entered the war self-aware and willing to die (there must have been a few), those who were innocent or ignorant of the horrors of war, those who were ideologically coerced or mystified by the demands of patriotism, those who were conscripted and could not afford the $300 necessary to buy substitute bodies, "regular army" soldiers who had enlisted before the war expecting to kill Indians and not Southern whites— all these different types (imagine the project of describing all the in- dividuals in all of these categories) are represented as having a single, universal experience.

At certain moments in the text, the formal (epistemological-semiotic) problem of representation is considered also as a moral or volitional problem. It is as if, after the war, any consideration of morality would be counterproductive to the goal of the war: "Future years will never know the seething hell and the black infernal background of countless minor scenes and interiors (not the few great battles) of the Secession War; and *it is best they should not*" (5, emphasis added). Perhaps if we knew the "interiors" of the war we would criticize its prosecution, weighing the ends against the means. As it is, Whitman's repeated in- terrogations of the possibility of historical representation shield the means from a too scrupulous examination.

This moral configuration of the problem is evident, for example, in a passage describing a raid on a troop train by some of Mosby's guerrillas, who were subsequently taken prisoner and then massacred by Federal troops.[6] The description ends with a summary of the attitudes of those troops: "There was no exultation, little said; almost nothing; yet every man contributed his shot" (36). By thus naming a particularly cruel and repulsive historical event—and one that reflects badly on the morality of soldiers who represented the Union interest—Whitman implies a jus- tification for interdicting historical representation; even the soldiers en- gage in their own form of interdiction by speaking "almost nothing."

There are occasional passages in which Whitman more actively demonstrates the mnemonic suppression of certain possible narratives; for example, the dramatized parenthesis: "(We hear of some poor fighting, episodes, skedadling on our part. I think not of it. I think of the fierce bravery, the general rule)" (14). Such passages, while rare, suggest Whit- man's awareness that the willful operation of memory is a determining factor in the epistemology of written history. Writing the typical—"the general rule"—is a means of disguising the process of selection which is common to all histories. One can "think not of" any given experience by assigning it to the unauthorized category of the atypical.

There was no doubt something repugnant, even to Whitman's om- nivorous sensibility, in an extensive catalogue of the evils of war. Typ- ification could thus ease the moral burden of representing repulsive events. The "scene, or a sample of it" of the massacre of Mosby's men closes

as follows: "Multiply the above by scores, aye hundreds—verify it in all the forms that different circumstances, individuals, places &c., could afford— . . . and you have an inkling of this war" (36). The only way to "verify" a scene, however, is to return to a memory (of an experience), and relatively few readers (none, today) have the capacity to do this. Whitman himself did not work from any experience of combat, but got his narratives from the recollections of soldiers. The reader is made responsible for *inventing* his or her own memories of the war by particularizing the represented types supplied in this indirect way.

The device of typification is legitimated in the *Memoranda* by the ancient topos of "inexpressibility," in light of which the volitional (moral) aspect of the problem of representation figures as an alibi for the processes of selection and interdiction that are inevitable in the composition of any text.[7] The argument that poetry is not produced through an exertion of the will is an old one. Whitman knew it as formulated by Shelley, who held that poetic representation cannot restore the plenitude of experience, but encodes an absence, "a feeble shadow of the original conceptions of the poet." Of the original "evanescent visitations of thought and feeling," which upon dissolution produce "desire and regret," only "traces" remain. Experience can be reconstructed from these traces, but only partly: "A word, a trait in the representation of a scene or a passion, will touch the enchanted chord, and reanimate, in those who have ever experienced these emotions, the sleeping, the cold, the buried image of the past" (Shelley, 511).[8] Like the *Memoranda*, such an account grounds the representational function itself in typification (a single word or trait standing for all).

Shelley's theory does not invoke the inexpressibility topos to interdict representations of horrific or violent events. Horace—following Aristotle (*Poetics*, 1453b)—had long since legislated on this question, declaring that the poet ought not dramatize repulsive scenes such as Medea slaying her children because "anything that you thus thrust upon my sight I discredit and revolt at" (71). Insofar as Horace's remark is prescriptive it addresses the volitional aspect of the problem. But the question of interdiction is a formal one as well, for it turns on the convention that representations of horrors are not to be believed. Representation is thus regulated by the generic constraints shared by the audience of the drama who know what is conventionally discreditable. Horace does not deny the reality of violence nor try to exclude it from the *text*; but he holds that it can only be described rather than represented by actors in the drama.

In manuscript notes from 1855–60 in which Whitman develops a theory of language—published posthumously as *An American Primer* (1904)—he seems to refuse any appeal to the inexpressibility topos, even in cases of violence.[9] Whitman collapses Horace's distinction between enacted and textual representations, characterizing words as living embodiments of a poet's intentions: "A perfect writer would make words sing, dance, kiss, do the male and female act, bear children, weep, bleed, rage, stab, steal, fire cannon, steer ships, sack cities, charge with cavalry or infantry, or do anything, that man or woman or the natural powers can do" (16). It is striking how many of the potential acts of words are acts of war.[10] Whitman's antebellum poetics seem to meditate on an impending war—as in the 1855 preface, according to which, "In war [the poet] is the most deadly force of war. . . . He can make every word he speaks draw blood" (*LG 1855*, 8, ellipses added). Such a poetics refuses interdiction—indeed, Whitman describes a new American language, "a medium that shall well nigh express the inexpressible" (23). And yet by foregrounding violence to the body it threatens to destroy itself by prescribing violence to the source of one of its central tropes, embodiment.

In the *American Primer* Whitman claims that verbal representation is always possible if it is necessary. His argument against interdiction, however, is haunted by the thought of inexpressibility: "Of words wanted, the matter is summed up in this: When the time comes for them to represent any thing or any state of things, the words will surely follow. The lack of any words, I say again, is as historical as the existence of words. As for me, I feel a hundred realities, clearly determined in me, that words are not yet formed to represent" (21). The formal obstacle to perfect representation is the existence of a large fraction of unrepresented experience, words for which are deferred indefinitely ("not yet"). Despite (perhaps because of) this temporal gap between experience and formal representational structures, Whitman calls for a peculiarly American realignment of verbal and political representation: "In America an immense number of new words are needed, to embody the new political facts, the compact of the Declaration of Independence, and of the Constitution—the union of the States . . . stating all that is to be said in modes that fit the life and experience of the Indianian, the Michiganian, the Vermonter, the men of Maine" (*AP*, 9). The realignment Whitman envisions in 1855–1860 contains a harbinger of the coming war. In his catalogue of typical American "experience[s]"—which does not mention any "life" south of Mason and Dixon's line—certain political "facts" or "modes" are interdicted. The South is absent; perhaps it is to be regarded as atypical. Whitman's text not only seems to predict the Southern states' attempts

53

to remove themselves from a system that interdicted their politics, but also problematizes the textual representation of the Civil War as the political event that reincorporated those states into the structure of the Union.

The trope Whitman uses for representation here, as in the passage on the "perfect writer," is not mimesis but embodiment. Under normal political circumstances, this trope effaces its status as a structure of mediation: the lived political experience of human bodies is said to be transformed into a system of representation in the very terms of that experience. But when the "new political fact" to be represented is a corpse on a battlefield—the form of the body emptied of experiential content under peculiar circumstances—any notion of representation as embodiment is problematic.

Whitman's argument against interdiction anticipates the problems of representing the impending war. His rhetoric depends, as it so often does, on the trope of embodiment: "The blank left by words wanted, but unsupplied, has sometimes an unnamably putrid, cadaverous meaning" (*AP*, 20). From this passage it is clear that Whitman would not take easy refuge in the inexpressibility topos. A failure of representation is as abhorrent and recriminatory as a rotting corpse. In the case of the *Memoranda*, such corpses comprise a good deal of the reality of war, which remains underrepresented or even unrepresented. The sign that would refer to the corpse is often absent from the text. And yet, according to the theory of representation developed in the *American Primer*, the absence of the sign produces a meaning similar to that which the sign itself would produce.

The representational problem Whitman faces is how to transform the "unnamably putrid, cadaverous meaning"—produced by both the rotting corpses on the field and the absence of representation in histories of the Civil War—into ideologically productive signs. In this transformation he counts heavily on his readers—not only on what they know and can be expected to supply in place of these absences, but also on what they do not know. When Whitman asserts "words will surely follow" where they are needed, he is discussing the problem of reference (*AP*, 21). However, he also recognizes the importance of affect, claiming that the reader shares the responsibility for the production of representation, as in the following passage from *Democratic Vistas*:

> In fact, a new theory of literary composition . . . is the sole course open to these States. Books are to be call'd for, and supplied, on

the assumption that the process of reading is not a half-sleep, but, in highest sense, an exercise, a gymnast's struggle; that the reader is to do something for himself, must be on the alert, must himself or herself construct indeed the poem, argument, history, metaphysical essay—the text furnishing the hints, the clue, the start or frame-work. (*PW*, 2:424–25)

From early on in his career, Whitman regarded the role of the reader as a significant aspect of the problem of representation:

Latent in a great user of words, must actually be all passions, crimes, trades, animals, stars, God, sex, the past, might, space, metals, and the like—because these are the words, and *he who is not these*, plays with a foreign tongue, turning helplessly to dictionaries and author-ities.—How can I tell you?—I put many things on record that you will not understand at first—perhaps not in a year—but they must be (are to be) understood. (*AP*, 17, emphasis added)

The experience that grounds representation is often latent and vicarious. Whitman's description of the characteristics of a "perfect writer" implies a similar conclusion—since as far as we know Whitman never bore a child, fired a cannon, or sacked a city (*AP*, 16). Whitman claims the authority to represent death because death—even the death of the "typic" soldier—is "latent" in him, although he has not experienced it. He can hope that his readers understand because death is latent in them as well, although the doubt evident in the final sentence may apply to those who are not "great user[s] of words."[11] In claiming that "he who is not" the "passions, crimes" and the like which are to be represented "plays with a foreign tongue," Whitman is proposing lived experience as the ground of representation. This move shifts the burden of representational re-sponsibility onto the reader. Those who have not experienced the Civil War can thus be supposed to embody the reason why "the real war . . . will never be written" (*M*, 5).

But this shift only increases the burden of representing the war. Relatively few readers can have witnessed the death of any soldier, much less know if he were the "typic" one; none, obviously, can have *experienced* another's life or death. There seems to be no mutual ground for com-prehension. Given his model of reading as a strenuous, self-productive experience, Whitman counts on the ideology of Union, as disseminated, for example, in American texts such as *Leaves of Grass* (including its prefaces), to define such a mutual ground by producing a single, cohesive

55

community of readers. This interpretive community is responsible for prescribing the representational possibilities for the war and all other events in American history. As he writes in the preface to the 1876 edition of *Leaves*,

> the true growth-characteristics of democracy in the New World are henceforth to radiate in superior literary, artistic and religious expressions . . . . Estimating the American Union as so far . . . in its yet formative condition, I bequeath poems and essays as nutriment and influences to help truly assimilate and harden, and especially to furnish something toward what the States most need of all . . . namely, to show them, or begin to show them, themselves distinctly, and what they are for. (*PW*, 2:465, 469)

What is necessary for an American, democratic readership and polity is a common ground of experience that can be solidified into a single representational paradigm. Ideologically this entails, according to Whitman, the "necessity and centrality of Oneness—the national identity power—the sovereign Union, relentless, permanently comprising all" (465). Whitman's aesthetic reflection on this ideological necessity leads him to describe the "general object" of *Leaves of Grass* as a *memorandum* for the American experience: he intends "to make a *type-portrait* for living, active, worldly, healthy personality, objective as well as subjective . . . for the use of the United States" (470, emphasis added). This project of developing a prescriptive typification of American experience (a political poetics of "the sovereign Union") suppresses difference. As carried out in the *Memoranda* the project typifies death—rather than analyzing the material and political causes and circumstances of individual deaths (the "real war"), for these are said to be inexpressible—in order to guarantee meaning and ideological coherence.

II.   *The Corpse and the "Roses Sweetscented"*

The ground of the typical experience that Whitman imagines in the passage on the death of the "bravest soldier" was already inscribed in American ideology, in the form of the pastoral ideal.[12] We are asked in the *Memoranda* to read this death—and, by a typifying synecdoche, the whole of the war—as a violation of pastoral harmony and tranquillity. On this reading of the war, the corpse may produce an absence of meaning, but the landscape within which it is framed recovers that absence: "Likely, the typic one of them . . . crawls aside to some bush-clump, or ferny tuft, on receiving his death-shot—there, sheltering a little while, soaking roots, grass and soil, with red blood. . . . And there, at last, the Bravest Soldier crumbles in the soil of mother earth, unburied and unknown" (16). In contrast to the almost capricious behavior of the battle as it "flits" from the scene and the more gradual disappearance of the body of the soldier as it decays, the landscape itself remains permanent, a fixed point of reference. If the soldier is "unknown," the metaphor of the earth as our "mother" is familiar to all. The Civil War interrupts the scene, but it seems that the naturalizing power invested in the nurturing land itself covers the traces of that war.

The tendency of the pastoral has been to marginalize the representation of death. Originally (in Theocritus) Death asserted its presence. But by the time of the Renaissance, shepherds had Arcadia to themselves; the unwelcome presence had been erased, as signified by a displacement of the key phrase, "et in Arcadia ego," from the signature of Death to the characteristic speech of a shepherd.[13] By framing the corpse with a natural scene, Whitman epitomizes the conflict between representation and interdiction that had been played out in the history of the pastoral genre. A related passage also foregrounds this conflict, describing "the red life-blood oozing out from heads or trunks or limbs upon that green and dew-cool grass" (M, 14). The rhetoric of nature that locates the violated bodies in the scene (almost turning them into trees, placing them on soothing, "dew-cool grass") produces a strange idyll.

These passages develop images of blood dripping on leaves of grass; they evoke, even as they disrupt, the universal harmony of the first edition of *Leaves of Grass*, thus demonstrating the threat that the war poses to Whitman's antebellum poetics. Whitman opens the 1855 *Leaves* with a pastoral gesture, which he invites his readers to share:

> I celebrate myself,
> And what I assume you shall assume,
> For every atom belonging to me as good belongs to you.
>
> I loafe and invite my soul,
> I lean and loafe at my ease . . . . observing a spear of
> summer grass.   (*LG 1855*, 25)

The poet, speaking in the eternal (lyric) present, reclines on the solid, fertile ground of America. In this setting ideology (what we "shall assume") is not at all problematic; we can get on with the leisured, poetic activity of celebrating the nation as it is—that is to say, of celebrating our selves as represented in the poet's paradigmatic self. Perhaps no poem effects the characteristically pastoral operation of "giv[ing] an impression of dealing with life completely" (Empson, 27) more thoroughly than does "Song of Myself," as it proceeds to inventory American experience.

Of the many images that flow from this opening reverie, a relevant one in the present context locates death specifically within the organic cycle of nature:

> And as to you corpse I think you are good manure, but that does
>   not offend me,
> I smell the white roses sweetscented and growing,
> I reach to the leafy lips . . . . I reach to the polished breasts
>   of melons.
>
> And as to you life, I reckon you are the leavings of many deaths,
> No doubt I have died myself ten thousand times before.
> . . . .
> I bequeath myself to the dirt to grow from the grass I love,
> If you want me again look for me under your bootsoles.   (84, 86)

A corpse and "roses sweetscented" coexist harmoniously, before the war, in the same visual frame. Leaves of grass are fertilized by the "manure" of the corpse. The fact of death often frames the pastoral; in "Song of Myself" it is an object of affirmation, rather than grief or sentimental evasion. It does not matter if the death is unknown—since Whitman does not particularize the corpse, nor does he differentiate any particular death or manner or cause of death. Death is "typical" of everyone, not excluding the poet himself; thus it can be represented in the abstract. But in the case of Whitman's representations of the war, which raise the question of the ideological signification of death, it *does* matter that the deaths of soldiers are unknown: it matters that "no picture gives them" (*M*, 16).

The pastoral cannot easily accommodate the facts of war because death in war is an unnatural intrusion into the scene. While the pastoral is of course an artificial structure, it is "natural" by its own convention; war is "unnatural" by this convention. Responding to this convention in *Drum-Taps*, Whitman dissociates his poetics from the pastoral topos. The pastoral scene appears occasionally in the volume, but its ideological power as an image of America is attenuated by the war. In contrast to the expansive scenes of the antebellum *Leaves* we find the minimal, constrained image of "A farm picture," a poem of only two lines:

Through the ample open door of the peaceful country barn,
A sun-lit pasture field, with cattle and horses feeding.   (*DT*, 46)

The inclusion of the formal frame within the poem emphasizes the attenuation and argues for the transformation of the pastoral, during the war, from a popular poetic mode (as practiced by Bryant, Whittier, Longfellow, and the like) to a minor one. Whitman's usual gesture is simply to see, to ignore the mediation of vision implied by a restrictive frame. A third line was added at the end of the poem for the 1871 edition of *Leaves*: "And haze and vista, and the far horizon fading away" (*LGV*, 2:497).[14] This ending restores the poem, but only after the war, to Whitman's accustomed, expansive vision—perhaps straining against the imposition of the frame in the first line—while yet preserving the initial sense of the poem that during the war the pastoral topos was distant and attenuated, ideologically ineffective.

The next poem in the *Drum-Taps* volume, "Give me the splendid silent sun," goes on to explore the act of marginalizing while preserving the pastoral. This poem does not begin with the consciously framed perception of "A farm picture," but instead locates us at the outset in the open air, in the pastoral scene itself. Alluding structurally and thematically to "L'Allegro" and "Il Penseroso," the poem goes on to describe a renunciation of pastoral quietism with the coming of the war. Milton's pastoral pair delineate a movement from the joys of activity and society to the greater, more intellectual satisfactions of contemplation and solitude. Whitman reverses Milton's thematic movement and adds spatial movement as well, opposing the pastoral scene to an urban one.[15] The pastoral in "Give me the splendid silent sun" is the site of contemplation and solitude which, while not as isolating as Milton's "mossy Cell," is antithetical to the social and ideological milieu of Manhattan. Like Milton, Whitman begins by affirming pleasures that he will go on to renounce:

> Give me juicy autumnal fruit, ripe and red from the orchard;
> Give me a field where the unmow'd grass grows;
> Give me an arbor, give me the trellis'd grape;
> Give me fresh corn and wheat—give me serene-moving animals,
>   teaching content;
> Give me nights perfectly quiet, as on high plateaus west of the
>   Mississippi, and I looking up at the stars;
> Give me odorous at sunrise a garden of beautiful flowers, where
>   I can walk undisturbed;

Give me for marriage a sweet-breath'd woman, of whom I should
    never tire;
Give me a perfect child—give me, away, aside from the noise of
    the world, a rural domestic life;
Give me to warble spontaneous songs, reliev'd, recluse by myself,
    for my own ears only;
Give me solitude—give me Nature—give me again, O Nature,
    your primal sanities!   (47)

The penultimate line of the quotation refers especially to the epiphanic
moment of "Out of the Cradle Endlessly Rocking"—the mutual projection
of bird-song and poetic voice—thus connecting the persona of the first
half of the poem to Whitman's antebellum images of himself as the poet
of nature and the rural scene.

The "spontaneous songs" that the poet sings "aside from the noise
of the world" give way in the second half of the poem to an "endless
and noisy chorus"; the lyric voice is silenced by the wartime ideology
of the "world" represented by Manhattan. The poet finds that he must,
in spite of himself, turn away from pastoral topics and desires. "Rack'd
by the war-strife," he announces, "O city . . . you hold me enchain'd."[16]
The pastoral nostalgia is maintained ("O I see what I sought to escape")
yet temporarily displaced by the strenuous affirmation of new desires
(as exclamation points replace semicolons):

Keep your blossoming buckwheat fields, where the Ninth-month
    bees hum;
Give me faces and streets! give me these phantoms incessant and
    endless along the trottoirs!
Give me interminable eyes! give me women! give me comrades and
    lovers by the thousand!
. . . .
(The soldiers in companies or regiments—some, starting away,
    flush'd and reckless;
Some, their time up, returning with thinn'd ranks—young, yet
    very old, worn, marching, noticing nothing;)   (48)

Such a "life" may be "full to repletion, and varied," and yet there is
something unnatural about the "phantoms incessant" that haunt the city
and about these young soldiers, returned from the front, who are old
before their time.

The pastoral in general locates the human body in nature in such a way as to guarantee wholeness and integrity. The first half of the poem is filled with figures of wholeness: the harmony of man and woman, domesticated animals, and cultivated land, and the integral subject whose marital union with one woman produces "a perfect child." In contrast the experience of the city described in the second half disrupts the normal boundaries of the body:

> Manhattan streets, with their powerful throbs, with the beating
> drums, as now;
> The endless and noisy chorus, the rustle and clank of the muskets,
> (even the sight of the wounded;)
> Manhattan crowds with their turbulent musical chorus—with
> varied chorus and light of the sparkling eyes;
> Manhattan faces and eyes forever for me.   (49)

Detached from their status as definite individuals, the city-dwellers are configured in grotesque bodies that "throb" in the streets. Disembodied, they are reduced to faces and then, in the final image of the poem, to mere "eyes." In the rest of *Drum-Taps*, these bodily attributes often disappear completely into ideological figures.

The antithetical terms—the displacement of nature's "primal sanities" by the frenzied movement of Manhattan—preserve the pastoral even as they question its ideological efficacy during wartime. In the city the wounded are visible, although the poetic parenthesis (like a convalescent hospital) does what it can to minimize their offensive presence. It is significant that this poem does not locate the wounded in the scene where wounds are actually inflicted, in the "blossoming buckwheat fields," but rather at the locus of ideological recuperation—which is the city, whose voice is the "endless and noisy chorus" of patriotic songs and poems. Whitman goes to the city, to the convalescent hospitals, during the war, where he literally nurses the wounded and writes poetry that attempts figurally to recuperate the wounds in a way that makes them ideologically meaningful. The rural field, as he represents it in "Give me the splendid silent sun," is a site of nostalgia rather than action and of a wholeness of life rather than any consciousness of violence or death. Preserved pure and intact, the pastoral scene is a repository of a fictional antebellum harmony. The language of the renunciation—"Keep your fields of clover and timothy"—encodes the pastoral nostalgia in two ways: "keep" it because now the poet cannot want it, but also "keep" it in the sense of "preserve and maintain it."

The pastoral corpse in "Song of Myself" produced no hermeneutic void and thus posed no threat to the poetics of *Leaves of Grass*. But the problem of attributing meaning to deaths and wounds of the war requires Whitman to find ideological significance in the corpse, rather than merely to give evidence of the organic cycle of nature (the harmonious relation of the "corpse" and the "roses sweetscented"). The ideological recuperation of death obscures it as a historically structured fact. The passage on the death of the bravest soldier effects this disappearance of death from history in two ways—first, by attaching the corpse to a rhetoric of heroism (as if, somehow, the soldier's bravery is what makes the account of his death important). Second, by drawing a pastoral frame around the corpse, the passage locates the death of the soldier in the context of Whitman's antebellum poetics of democratic adhesiveness by placing it in a special contiguity with the pastoralism of *Leaves of Grass*.

Adhesiveness and pastoralism organize the representation of a prototypically American experience in the edition of *Leaves of Grass* published prior to the war. For example, images of America as a new Eden appear often in the 1860–61 edition, in the "Enfans d'Adam" cluster. Whitman seems to dismiss the fall, with its introduction of sin and toilsome labor into the landscape, as irrelevant for American mythology, concentrating instead on nonlapsarian images of "the new garden the West" or "The Garden the World" (*LGV*, 2:363, 352). "In the New Garden" erases the conventional pastoral difference between nature and the city. And here, prior to the Civil War, death need have no ideological significance; it can be "indifferent":

> In the new garden, in all its parts,
> In cities now, modern, I wander,
> Through the second or third result, or still further, primitive yet,
> Days, places indifferent—though various, the same,
> Time, Paradise, the Manhatta, the prairies, finding me unchanged,
> Death indifferent—is it I that lived long since? Was I buried
>   very long ago?   (*LGV*, 2:362)

Everything partakes of pastoral harmony, everything "though various, the same." This poem appears only in the 1860–61 edition. Its removal from *Leaves* with the 1867 edition suggests that after the war Whitman no longer found death "indifferent," no longer found vast assertions of *discordia concors* quite so easy to manage, and needed the interdictive power of the pastoral to rationalize death. The war, as I have been arguing, raised the problem of the ideological signification of death—the question of differentiating between the "natural" death assimilable to pastoral harmony (especially in the conventions of the elegy) and the "political" death which in the *Memoranda* invokes an absence of representation. The *Memoranda* accommodate such a differentiation only by means of figures of inexpressibility.

It is sometimes remarked that the 1860–61 edition of *Leaves of Grass* has a darker mood than the previous editions. Death is an important theme, especially in the "Calamus" cluster and "Out of the Cradle Endlessly Rocking." Nature frames the fact of death, but this death is undifferentiated and so completely "typical" that the poet can only affirm its omnipresence—as for example in the apostrophe to death that concludes the second poem in the "Calamus" cluster, "Scented Herbage of My Breast":

> Give me your tone therefore O death, that I may accord with it,
> Give me yourself, for I see that you belong to me now above all,
>   and are folded inseparably together, you love and
>   death are,
> Nor will I allow you to balk me any more with what I was
>   calling life,
> For now it is convey'd to me that you are the purports essential,
> That you hide in these shifting forms of life, for reasons, and
>   they are mainly for you,
> That you beyond them come forth to remain, the real reality,
> That behind the mask of materials you patiently wait, no matter
>   how long.   (*LGV*, 2:367)

Death, the poet affirms, is a transcendental sign, eliding difference and providing a certainty of meaning.

"Of the Terrible Doubt of Appearances," another of the "Calamus" poems, begins by doubting the easy certitude of the pastoral experience, questioning the harmony of human subject and landscape:

> May-be the things I perceive, the animals, plants, men, hills,
>   shining and flowing waters,
> The skies of day and night, colors, densities, forms, may-be these
>   are (as doubtless they are) only apparitions, and the real
>   something has yet to be known,
> . . . .
> May-be seeming to me what they are (as doubtless they indeed but
>   seem) as from my present point of view, and might
>   prove (as of course they would) nought of what they

63

> appear, or nought anyhow, from entirely changed points
> of view.   (377)

The poetic line threatens to degenerate into an inferior species of phi-
losophical prose, as the poem moves from a simple, pastoral perception
of nature to a metaphysical speculation on essences. The trope of adhesiveness—always Whitman's figure for his faith in representation—
permits a recovery of the poetic line and with it the pastoral attitude:

> When he whom I love travels with me or sits a long while holding
>   me by the hand,
> When the subtle air, the impalpable, the sense that words and
>   reason hold not, surround us and pervade us,
> Then I am charged with untold and untellable wisdom, I am silent,
>   I require nothing further,
> I cannot answer the question of appearances or that of identity
>   beyond the grave,
> But I sit or walk indifferent, I am satisfied,
> He ahold of my hand has completely satisfied me.   (377–78)

When adhesiveness displaces death from the privileged position of transcendental sign, the poet no longer desires to see beyond the surface
appearance of the landscape. The structure of this poem suggests not so
much a turning away from the epistemological questions raised in "Scented
Herbage" as a claim for a deeper understanding of the trope of typification.
For "death" in "Scented Herbage" is an abstraction; there are no concrete
signs of death, no represented indices such as corpses. The thoughts of
the poet avoid the material signifier of death in both poems, for it is
the most terrible appearance of all, producing the most terrible doubt.

In Whitman's experiences of army hospitals, the adhesive love that
had made his poetic self "completely satisfied" in the "Calamus" poems
had to find its object in the violated bodies of soldiers. Reassuring images
of nature—such as the phallic sign of the seed-cluster of the calamus
plant which had guaranteed the naturalness of Whitman's sexuality (see
Kaplan, plate 33)—no longer surround the poet and his lover. The wartime
context still admits a pastoral theme, however: many of Whitman's descriptive passages take the form of a lament for a beautiful youth dead
before his prime, which places them in the tradition of Milton's "Lycidas"
and Shelley's "Adonais." Such passages are inflected by the language of
homoerotic desire that animates the "Calamus" poems. Whitman speaks
thus in a description of a youth, "shot through the lungs—inevitably
dying," who now lies in a hospital bed,

64

with his frame exposed above the waist, all naked, for coolness, a fine built man, the tan not yet bleach'd from his cheeks and neck. . . . I often come and sit by him in perfect silence; he will breathe for ten minutes as softly and evenly as a young babe asleep. Poor youth, so handsome, athletic, with profuse beautiful shining hair. One time as I sat looking at him while he lay asleep, he suddenly, without the least start, awaken'd, open'd his eyes, gave me a long, long steady look, turning his face very slightly to gaze easier—one long, clear silent look—a slight sigh—then turn'd back and went into his doze again. Little he knew, poor death-stricken boy, the heart of the stranger that hover'd near. (*M*, 16–17)

The language of "Calamus" returns in the adhesive, ideologically re-cuperative moment in the poetics of *Drum-Taps*. In this passage, Whitman's description of the reciprocal gaze attempts to prolong and preserve this moment. It enacts the textual operation of a *memorandum* by representing only some (favorable) aspects of an event while interdicting others (such as what motivated the youth to place himself in the situation where he received his wound). The form of the youth is typified as a desirable object: he is said to be "a fine *specimen* of youthful, physical manliness" (16, emphasis added). Typification and Whitman's overriding concern with the adhesive moment suppresses the youth's history and his subjective experience of pain, as it does in the passage on the death of the bravest soldier. Instead the youth functions as a type; his relation to the interior "history" of the war is prescribed by the *Memoranda*'s governing trope.

By means of typification, the adhesive moment, and the pastoral framing of the corpse, Whitman attempts to cover the ideological loss threatened by potentially meaningless violence. "Give me the splendid silent sun" had seemed to preserve, by marginalizing, the ideological power of the pastoral topos; but the return to the pastoral in the *Memoranda* requires the recognition that it has been a site of violence. In this violated state its power to naturalize death, and thus to remove individual deaths from the domain of history, is weakened (although still somewhat effective when supplemented by other tropes). But in closing the *Memoranda* Whitman attempts a thoroughgoing restoration of the pastoral scene, the integrity of which the war had deconstructed:

As I write this conclusion—in the open air, latter part of June, 1875, a delicious forenoon, everything rich and fresh from last night's copious rain—ten years and more have pass'd away since that War, and its wholesale deaths, burials, graves. (*They* make indeed the true

Memoranda of the War—mute, subtle, immortal.) From ten years'
rain and snow, in their seasons—grass, clover, pine trees, orchards,
forests—from all the noiseless miracles of soil and sun and running
streams—how peaceful and beautiful appear to-day even the Battle-
Trenches, and the many hundred thousand Cemetery mounds. Even
at Andersonville [a notorious prison camp], to-day, innocence and
a smile. (57–58)

Nature restores itself even as Whitman writes. It has recovered its pastoral
power to marginalize death and is now in the process of effacing the
"true Memoranda of the War." Like the "blood-stain[s]" on Whitman's
wartime notebooks that invoke "associations never to be possibly said
or sung" (PW, 1:2), the real war survives here only in "mute" traces
which thwart textualization. Thus Whitman dramatizes the renewed
ideological power of the pastoral conception of nature—which *can* be
textualized, and is in this passage from 1875—to marginalize death and
evade the explicit representation of suffering.

When the text of the *Memoranda* was reprinted for mass distribution
in *Specimen Days*, Whitman concluded with an even more emphatic restoration of the pastoral. He affirms its complete dissociation from the
war:

Without apology for the abrupt change of field and atmosphere—
after what I have put in the preceding fifty or sixty pages—temporary
episodes, thank heaven!—I restore my book to the bracing and
buoyant equilibrium of concrete outdoor Nature, the only permanent
reliance for unity of book or human life. Who knows . . . but the
pages now ensuing may carry ray of sun, or smell of grass or
corn . . . to denizens of heated city house, or tired workman or
workwoman? (PW, 1:120)

The text locates the war as a spatial and temporal rupture. There is no
mediation between the pastoral and the war, only an "abrupt" change
of topos. No longer concerned with the problems of representing the
war, the text gives up the struggle to rationalize the presence of blood
and corpses in the pastoral scene. The recovery of the pastoral is enabled
by interdicting all traces of war; and yet this interdiction can only be
effected by proposing a radical discontinuity. Whitman's first reconstruc-
tive move in this passage is to deny that there has been any important
loss: the violent scenes of the war were only "temporary episodes,"
whereas the pastoral exists permanently and ahistorically, as something

which can always be "carried" poetically to those who live within a world structured by the forces of history (here industrialization, abetted by the war, and urbanization). In the absence of war and the presence of nature, the activity of producing a text—which is thematized so often in the *Memoranda*—is not at all problematic: "I find the woods in mid-May and early June my best places for composition," writes Whitman in *Specimen Days* as he turns away from the scenes of war (*PW*, 1:119). Following the summary comment on the war material ("the real war will never get in the books"), the section titles generally denote pastoral topics, suggesting how thoroughly history and politics have been interdicted.[17]

Even adhesiveness is transformed from a relation between man and man into an apolitical relation between the individual and nature. The ground of representation, as always, is experience; but the experience produced by nature, unlike that produced by war, is supposed to be permanent and invariant:

> Nature remains; to bring out from their torpid recesses, the *affinities* of a man or woman with the open air, the trees, fields, the changes of seasons—the sun by day and the stars and heaven by night. . . . Dear, soothing, healthy restoration hours . . . after the long strain of the war, and its wounds and death. (*PW*, 1:120, emphasis added)

Where, in the "Calamus" poems, pastoral nature had been the backdrop for the adhesive moment—a backdrop temporarily changed for the hospital ward in the *Memoranda*—here, after the war, the pastoral scene becomes in itself the object of the desiring "affinity." Whitman elaborates this emotional displacement, from the human object to the landscape, in his pastoral elegy "When Lilacs Last in the Dooryard Bloom'd."

III. *"Our Permanent Part, Our National Homestead"*

The pastoral evasion of history dictates Whitman's representation of an event of such great symbolic import that ordinary historical discourse could not contain it. In a lecture on the death of Abraham Lincoln delivered in the 1880s, Whitman argues that "the main things come subtly and invisibly afterward, perhaps long afterward—neither military, political, nor (great as those are) historical. I say, certain secondary and indirect results, out of this Death, are, in my opinion, greatest." (*DL*, 11).[18] These "indirect" results are to be felt in the "senses finally dearest to a na-

67

tion . . . the literary and dramatic ones": the "incalculable value" of Lincoln's death was that it "should so condense . . . a Nationality" (11, 12). The literary conventions that effect this unification of the American people are not those of history, but of myth (as Whitman's recurrent references in the lecture to classical Greek poets and tragedians suggest).

The origin of American, of Whitman's own, mythology was in the landscape, the scene of the transformation of nature into culture. As Leo Marx argues, a pastoral conception of the landscape permitted the naturalization of American material culture and ideology. Thus Whitman locates the event of Lincoln's death in a curious and yet predictable context:

> So the day, as I say, was propitious. Early herbage, early flowers, were out. (I remember where I was stopping at the time, the season being advanced, there were many lilacs in full bloom. . . . I find myself always reminded of the great tragedy of that day by the sight and odor of these blossoms. It never fails.) . . . The main thing, the actual murder, transpired with the quiet and simplicity of any commonest occurrence—the bursting of a bud or pod in the growth of vegetation, for instance. (*DL*, 6–8)

As does "When Lilacs Last in the Dooryard Bloom'd," this lecture frames not only Lincoln's death, but also Whitman's response, with a pastoral scene.[19]

Whereas the *Memoranda* explore the representation of death in war, the question posed in "When Lilacs Last in the Dooryard Bloom'd" is specifically elegiac: How shall mourning be represented? Whitman's poetics prescribes that his answer be nationally representative. In this context he searches "the boundaries of representation . . . for an instrument of sociability that does not produce the disappearance of its object" (Grossman, 200–201); that is, he must represent the loss of the loved comrade (which is the represented relation between poet and president) and preserve, rather than repress, his memory and the nation's. Yet his very choice of genre seems calculated to interdict certain aspects of national memory or history, especially as regards the war that was the context and the impetus for the assassination of Lincoln.

"Lilacs" exhibits the self-reflexivity conventional to the pastoral elegy; much of the poem concerns itself with the discovery or recovery of an appropriate voice.[20] At the moment the poet receives his voice— his ability to represent mourning—he has retreated into solitary communion with nature much like that represented in the pastoral half of

"Splendid silent sun." Before the war he had "warble[d] spontaneous songs, reliev'd, recluse by myself" (*DT*, 47); now he seeks a similar poetic experience from a "hermit" thrush:

> I fled forth to the hiding receiving night, that talks not,
> Down to the shores of the water, the path by the swamp in the
>   dimness,
> To the solemn shadowy cedars, and ghostly pines so still.
>
> And the singer so shy to the rest receiv'd me;
> . . . .
> And the voice of my spirit tallied with the song of the bird.
>
> (SDT, 9)

This moment, in which the poet's intention to sing a song of mourning is finally realized, apparently finds him "at the greatest distance from the social world in which alone his intention can have meaning" (Grossman, 201–202), in the company only of two abstract "comrades," "the knowledge of death" and "the thought of death." But Whitman's poetics dictate that there is more sociability in nature than at first appears. Although nature often seems to function as a place of escape from the historical constraints manifested in the social realm, "nature" is itself a cultural construct. This construct, especially in its pastoral configuration, provides a place from which a totalized image of the social can be envisioned. Briefly: the song the hermit thrush gives to the singer is the song that Whitman, the accomplished poet, brings with him.

The elegiac self-reflexivity which sets up the communion with the singer-thrush (in stanza 15) is most emphatic in stanza 10:

> O how shall I warble myself for the dead one there I love?
> . . . .
> And what shall my perfume be, for the grave of him I love?
>
> Sea winds, blown from east and west,
> Blown from the eastern sea, and blown from the western sea, till
>   there on the prairies meeting:
> These, and with these, and the breath of my chant,
> I perfume the grave of him I love. (SDT, 6)

This invocation of the geographical center of America allows Whitman to rephrase the question in stanza 11, the structural and ideological center of the poem:[21]

> O what shall I hang on the chamber walls?
> And what shall the pictures be that I hang on the walls,
> To adorn the burial-house of him I love? (7)

Developing the poem's opening scene—the dooryard of a farmstead framed by lilacs—Whitman answers that "Pictures of growing spring, and farms, and homes" are to be shown. Like the landscape paintings of George Inness or W. S. Mount, these pictures center the spectator in the idyllic, sun-drenched rural landscape, "with the fresh sweet herbage underfoot" (7). These pictures restore the poet and the poem to sociability, for they represent not the seclusion of the swamp (even supposing that all traces of culture could be eradicated from this experience of solitude) but an idealization of the material and social culture of America.

As if contemplating a pastoral landscape painting, we move from the middle ground of "ranging hills on the banks, with many a line against the sky," toward a corner of the scene.[22] There we observe

> the city at hand, with dwellings so dense, and
> stacks of chimneys,
> And all the scenes of life, and the workshops, and the workmen
> homeward returning. (7)

This part of the image suggests domesticity and social harmony, resulting from the material productivity of the factories and "workshops." We do not look long at the city, but draw back again to the broad vista to observe productivity and harmony on a grand scale:

> Lo! body and soul! this land!
> Mighty Manhattan, with spires, and the sparkling and burying
> tides, and the ships;
> The varied and ample land—the South and the North in the
> light—Ohio's shores, and flashing Missouri,
> And ever the far-spreading prairies, cover'd with grass and corn.
> Lo! the most excellent sun, so calm and haughty;
> The violet and purple morn, with just-felt breezes:
> The gentle, soft-born, measureless light;
>
> . . . .
> Over my cities shining all, enveloping man and land. (7)

Matthiessen suggests that although the poem apparently contains no biography of Lincoln or praise for his accomplishments (which would seem to be required by elegiac convention), Lincoln appears in the guise of the enigmatic image of the star in the west; the subsequent fall of the star invokes the pathetic fallacy (620). If so, the image of the star serves further to diminish the historicity of the poem by transporting it to the realm of myth. The implicit parallel with the star that signified Christ's birth hints at the popular representation of Lincoln as a martyr. Since Lincoln was the symbolic head of the body politic, his death was sometimes represented as a Christlike self-sacrifice that signified the re-surrection or rebirth of the Union (Rogin, "King's Two Bodies," 84–90). Melville entitled his poem on Lincoln's death "The Martyr," claiming it to be "indicative of the passion of the people" (*CP*, 93). But although, in his lectures in the 1870s and 80s, Whitman would allude to this rep-resentation—calling Lincoln the "first great Martyr Chief" of the United States (*DL*, 14)—in "Lilacs" he does not make very much of Lincoln's supposed martyrdom. Whitman had used the rhetorical topoi of sacrifice and the body politic to recover the meaning of the war in *Drum-Taps*, and found them to be somewhat problematic for that end. In "Lilacs" he refuses any explicit mobilization of these popular topoi. Instead, ideal-ized landscape views provide more significant images for the re-Union of America.

Whitman takes a historical fact—the journey of Lincoln's coffin homeward by train through "the yellow-spear'd wheat, every grain from its shroud in the dark-brown fields uprising" (4)—as a pre-text for a poem that is minimally about Lincoln's death as a historical event, and is scarcely at all about the Civil War. Instead, Whitman writes about the American landscape. The insistence on open landscape views through-out the elegy diffuses a potentially claustrophobic focus on coffin, "burial-house," and "dim-lit churches" (7, 5). More importantly, the very imagery of the poem retrieves an important aspect of Lincoln's ideology and bears on the questions of political representation over which the Civil War was fought.

Lincoln, too, saw a pastoral text written in the American landscape. In his "First Inaugural Address" he elaborates arguments against secession based on the Constitution and the principles of "organic law," bolstering these with an additional argument from geography: "Physically speaking we cannot separate. We cannot remove our respective sections from each other, nor build an impassable wall between them. A husband and wife may be divorced, and go out of the presence, and beyond reach of each other; but the different parts of our country cannot do this" (4:264, 269). Lincoln's metaphor may seem strange because it implies that, in view of the topography of the continent, Canada and Mexico ought to be part of the Union as well (although perhaps it is not all that strange, as the prosecution of the Mexican War had hinted).[23] The metaphor explicitly rejected here, of political union as marital union, would prove to be quite popular in later historical fiction about the Civil War, the romance plots of which often allegorized the political and military conquest of a feminine South by a masculine North (Diffley). But while the popular representation of gender roles provided an apt figure for Northern dominance, during the war Lincoln needed a figure for the Union that was more stable than marriage. Thus in his December 1862 "Annual Message to Congress," he clarifies the topographical figure of the "First Inaugural," developing it into a version of pastoral:

> Our national strife springs *not from our permanent part*; not from the land we inhabit; *not from our national homestead*. There is no possible severing of this, but would multiply, and not mitigate, evils among us. In all its adaptations and attitudes, it demands union, and abhors separation. In fact, it would, ere long, force reunion, however much of blood and treasure the separation might have cost. (5:529, emphasis added)

Lincoln's pastoral typification of the American experience privileges the representation of a particular segment of the population—the independent farmer with a small plot of ground, who "labors with satisfaction, and saves himself the whole fruit of his labor" (3:475). Even with the outbreak of war, he follows the conventional, agrarian opening of the Annual Message to Congress inherited from his predecessors: "In the midst of unprecedented political troubles, we have cause of great gratitude to God for unusual good health, and most abundant harvests" (5:35).[24] While the farming interest, Lincoln suggests, is at this time "so independent in its nature as to not have [*sic*] demanded and extorted more from the government," nevertheless he asks Congress to "consider whether something more cannot be given voluntarily with general advantage." The outcome of this proposal was the establishment of the Department of Agriculture in 1862, which increased and formalized the political representation of the agricultural interest (5:46). Late in the war Lincoln refers to the USDA as "peculiarly the people's department" (8:147–48). The Homestead Act, granting public land to a settler after five year's residence, was also passed by the Republicans in 1862; the secession of the Southern states had eliminated opposition to the bill in Congress (McPherson, 450).

Even before the war, Lincoln claimed to want to remove any agriculture not conducted according to a model of free, independent labor from the economic base of the country. This included not only plantations operated by slaves but also large, corporate farms operated by wage-laborers; prior to the war he argues against the supposed inefficiency of such farms in a speech to the Wisconsin State Agricultural Society (3:471–82). The pastoral image of the small, independent farm seemed to him both economically and politically preferable: "Our abundant room—our broad national homestead—is our ample resource. Were we as limited in territory as are the British Isles, very certainly our population could not expand as stated. . . . But such is not our condition. We have two millions nine hundred and sixty-three thousand square miles" (5:532). The Jeffersonian perception of the landscape, from which Lincoln's vision derives, assumes that "any democratic politics or democratic poetics would require an underlying, everyday context of an undifferentiated democratic social space"; this ideological paradigm was manifested in the use of a Cartesian grid, based on the assumption of forty-acre, single-family farms, to organize the space of the entire continent (Fisher, 66). The Homestead Act increased the size of the standard farm to 160 acres (simply quadrupling the forty); but this did not change the basic conceptual map on which each farmer got an identical, symmetrical piece of America. For Jefferson, this model was a means to promote a decentralized federal government. Lincoln, however, needs to argue for a strong central government, es-pecially during the war. He does so by reading Jefferson's map as the site of a *single*, typified "national homestead," a synecdoche by means of which one pastoral scene, inhabited by the one body politic of the Union, represents the entire sociopolitical organization of rural America and guarantees an end to the divisions represented by secession and the war. Slave labor could be removed from this site of Union by a plan of compensated emancipation followed by colonization; this plan for a 'separate but equal' pastoral would free the slaves, reimburse their owners for economic losses, and remove them from North America to "new homes . . . in congenial climes, and with people of their own blood and race" (Lincoln, 5:535–36).

Lincoln's agricultural economics mobilizes the pastoral aesthetic—incorporating its subgenre the georgic. This aesthetic is progressive (argues Leo Marx) and yet pastoral all the same; it promoted the rural scene as a site of independence, virtue, pleasure, and Americanness. In his address to the Wisconsin Agricultural Society, after the panegyric on small, independent farms and free labor, Lincoln describes this aesthetic:

No other human occupation opens so wide a field for the profitable and agreeable combination of labor with cultivated thought, as agri-culture. I know of nothing so pleasant to the mind, as the discovery

73

of anything which is at once *new* and *valuable*—nothing which so lightens and sweetens toil, as the hopeful pursuit of such a discovery. . . . Every blade of grass is a study, and to produce two, where there was but one, is both a profit and a pleasure. (3:480)

Lincoln finds in the aesthetic-economic culture of leaves of grass a predictive, eternal text of "individual, social, and political prosperity and happiness, whose course shall be onward and upward, and which, while the earth endures, shall not pass away" (3:482). Like Whitman, he was confronted with a potential historical rupture of this text during the war. Also like Whitman, he reiterates the pastoral ideal in the hope that it will restore itself and end the war.

In "Lilacs," Whitman invokes Lincoln's own rural origins with the journey of the coffin in stanza 5. Lincoln returns in death to the origin of his own political image—the homely rail-splitter, special representative of the small-farm interest that he sentimentally proposed as the paradigm of America. Thus the journey recalls Lincoln's promotion of the American pastoral ideal. There is more at stake here than the elegiac convention that Lincoln, too, dwelt in Arcadia: at the time of his death the pastoral topos needed to be recuperated and its attendant ideals reaffirmed after the material and ideological crises of the war. Lincoln attempts to demonstrate this recuperation throughout the war in his speeches; for example, he marks the progress of "our arms" by stating that the "liberat[ed] regions" of "Missouri, Kentucky, Tennessee and parts of other States have again produced reasonably fair crops," now that the land is under Federal control (8:148).

The images of harmony and plenty that adorn the walls of the burial chamber in "Lilacs" represent what had been Lincoln's own vision of America, as well as Whitman's. Lincoln's texts exclude the corpse from the pastoral topos: the image of "our national homestead" is located in opposition to the war, in hope of guaranteeing an eventual end to violence and disruption. When Lincoln does literally place himself in the rural landscape, during the Gettysburg Address, his text follows the rhetorical paradigms that Whitman had used to produce the meaning of the war in *Drum-Taps*; he does not invoke the pastoralism of the Annual Messages to Congress. Lincoln's assertion that the Union soldiers "gave their lives that that nation might live" and experience "a new birth of freedom" combines the tropes of the body politic and the exchange of life for ideology; the assertion that they "gave the last full measure of devotion" mobilizes the trope of sacrifice (7:23). These recuperative moves are re-

quired because of the violence of the war that is Lincoln's reason for
dedicating the cemetery—because the pastoral did not supply the pacific
power that Lincoln attributes to it in other speeches.

In "Lilacs" the hymn to death, which the poet finds in his communion
with the thrush, begins with homage to a view of the rural scene that
is, like Lincoln's version of pastoral, sympathetic to the harmony of the
Union. The material presence of the corpse does not disrupt this scene,
as it had threatened to do in the *Memoranda*. From his viewpoint in the
secluded swamp Whitman envisions a social totality, all life in harmony
with the landscape:

> From me to thee glad serenades,
> Dances for thee I propose, saluting thee—adornments and feastings
> for thee;
> And the sights of the open landscape, and the high spread sky,
> are fitting.
> And life and the fields, and the huge and thoughtful night.
>
> (*SDT*, 10)

Whitman does later permit an attenuated image of the war to intrude
on this scene:

> I saw battle-corpses, myriads of them,
> And the white skeletons of young men—I saw them;
> I saw the debris and debris of all dead soldiers. (11)

The image of debris dehumanizes the corpses, making the representation
less horrific than it could have been (the scene much less horrific than
it actually was during a battle). The generalized assumption that many
died in the recent war is the image's only concession to history. History
is being effaced by the power of nature. The bodies of the "young men"
are disappearing into the landscape as the forces of nature bleach and
intermingle their bones; they have already disappeared into the ideological
discourses of Whitman and Lincoln.

Yet in terms of Whitman's antebellum poetics, the image of "debris"
even in this generalized form threatens the possibility of representation.
It returns to the fragmentation of all semiotic systems that Whitman had
contemplated in 1860, in "As I Ebb'd with the Ocean of Life." Thus
in its intertextual connections the "debris and debris" of the dead potentially distracts from the construction of national harmony that Whitman has achieved, up to this point in the elegy, through the pastoral
framing of Lincoln's death. To recover representation completely and

75

account in some way for the violence of the war, Whitman develops a scene of mourning. A typified representation of universal suffering provides a common, potentially nationalist, experiential ground:

> But I saw they [the dead soldiers] were not as was thought;
> They themselves were fully at rest—they suffer'd not;
> The living remain'd and suffer'd—the mother suffer'd,
> And the wife and the child, and the musing comrade suffer'd,
> And the armies that remain'd suffer'd. (11)

This scene is conceived in such a way as to demonstrate that effacing the history of death in war and achieving the ideological significance that makes sense of death in war are a single operation. The commonality of experience, of every single person remaining and suffering in the same terms, perhaps suggests grounds for re-Union. And yet it may not be so, for suffering can produce isolation, an antisocial attitude of the sort represented in *Drum-Taps* in "Come up from the fields" (in which a mother withdraws from social intercourse at the news of the death of her son in battle). The "musing comrade"—from the pun on "muse," it could be the poet himself—suffers such a loss of comradeship.

At this juncture Whitman turns abruptly away from the scene of suffering. Like the other images of stanza 18 it had appeared, after all, in a phantasmagoric interlude, "as in noiseless dreams"—in contrast to the eternal stability of the pastoral landscapes shown earlier in the poem. Whitman has devised the answer to the question posed by elegiac convention—How shall mourning be represented?—by figuring it as dissipation, as "death's *outlet* song" (emphasis added). The formal structure of the poem—the very question of *mourning* itself—leaves little room for critique; the genre of pastoral elegy, within which Whitman writes, admits only a limited range of responses to the violence of war or political assassination. It seems too late to question the political origins of the "debris and debris of all dead soldiers" or of Lincoln's death. Interdiction, disguising itself as transcendent affirmation, is the ideological response prescribed by the genre:

> Passing the visions, passing the night;
> Passing, unloosing the hold of my comrades' hands;
> Victorious song, death's outlet song,
>
> . . . .
>
> Covering the earth, and filling the spread of the heaven,
> As that powerful psalm in the night I heard from recesses. (11)

The song of "Lilacs" has been "death's outlet song," inasmuch as the pastoral context of the elegiac expression of emotion has evoked scenes from the American landscape in which the mourning and suffering typified in the preceding stanza can dissipate. This song, like the Union victory, affirms the naturalization of the American empire by "Covering the earth."

In Whitman's poetics, as in Lincoln's politics, the pastoral provides a powerful, typifying structure of recuperation. Both Whitman and Lincoln represent America as but one harmonious and undifferentiated landscape. The land itself (places unspecified, time dehistoricized) becomes a sign of Union; its vastness implies the indefinite reproducibility of the pastoral topos as a cultural paradigm. This paradigm, according to Lincoln, was what was essential to America, transcending political conflicts and civil wars. Within the pastoral, the bodies covering the landscape did not die political deaths. Lincoln is dead but his fiction of an American political structure firmly grounded in the landscape has been restored. Whitman's version of pastoral reserves no space for politics; instead it invokes Lincoln's idyllic ideology, as encoded in American geography, to legitimate the outcome of the war and provide a vision of the future.

3. Photography and the Scene
of History

WHITMAN, saturated in the dominant ideology of his time, mobilized an organicist poetics to heal or hide the wounds of
the Civil War and to idealize the conservation of the Union
effected by the war. An analogous visual organicism, manifested
in the picturesque and the pastoral modes, came to be mobilized
by the Civil War photographers to naturalize the Union in a similar
way—thus making its operations, such as the prosecution of a bloody
war, seem unquestionably right.[1] Pastoralism was used to evade certain
historical processes and conflicts and to promote an idealized image of
"America." The picturesque, which valued the subordination of parts
to the unity of the whole, provided a formal, aesthetic analogy for Unionism. In this context war photography operated as a technology for
the appropriation and control of lands and persons.

I.   *Photography and Historiography*

Photography, suggests Alan Trachtenberg, is "the popular historicism of
our era" (1). In 1841, shortly after the invention of photography, Emerson
had asked, "And why not draw for these times a portrait gallery? . . . A
camera! a camera! cries the century, that is the only toy. Come let us
paint the agitator and the dilettante and the member of Congress and
the college professor . . . . So should we have at last if it were well done
a series of sketches which would report to the next ages the color &
quality of ours" (*JMN*, 8:126). If contemporary technology were able
to provide "color" as well as form and shading, the historical record
envisioned here would appear nearly complete. Yet in citing such an
absence in photographic representation, Emerson identifies a split between
the image and what it is supposed to "report to the next ages" (for if
color is supplied, the record also lacks motion, tactility, and so on). Only
two years after the invention of photography, its claim to document history
already appears problematic.

On the centenary of photography in 1939, Valéry formulates the
question that the photographic image puts to history: "Could such and
such a fact, as it is narrated, have been photographed?" The post-

photographic historical consciousness realizes that "history" has become a series of observed "moments" tenuously spliced together by "literature": "All that is left consists of those components of the narrative or of the thesis that originate in the mind and are consequently imaginary, mere constructions, interpretations, bodiless things by nature invisible to the photographic eye . . . so that they could not have been observed and transmitted intact" (195–96). Thus Valéry separates the idea of photographic objectivity, the structure of which dictates the narration of "fact," from ideological considerations which are "mere constructions" or "interpretations." Pure history, it seems, would have no thesis and provide no causal or intentional explanations.

Valéry can develop such a theory of historiography only by refusing to admit ideology into the domain of photographic representation. A photograph apparently bears no ideology because it seems simply to picture the world the way it was. But we might argue that the cultural sign systems within which photography is embedded have tended to efface the mediacy of the representation by providing viewers with an interpretive rhetoric of realism. That is, despite appearances, photographs do not just "happen": photography is a representational *practice*. The production and reception of the photographic image are heavily determined by texts, which "alone can specify its relation to localities, time, individual identity, and other categories of human understanding" (Hunter, 6). Without such texts a photographic image is historically meaningless (and often aesthetically impoverished). Textual structures of historical representation such as "mode of emplotment" and "mode of argument," Hayden White argues, always imply an ideological agenda (29). Fredric Jameson claims similarly that "history is *not* a text, not a narrative, master or otherwise, but . . . an absent cause . . . inaccessible to us except in textual form" (35). White's and Jameson's theses imply that photographic meaning is always a function of the historical context within which it is embedded.[2] If this is not the case, then what Valéry identifies as the photographic "moment" lies outside of history altogether.

Mathew B. Brady traded on the ideological value of photographic history when, in the late 1840s, he set about collecting daguerreotype images for his *Gallery of Illustrious Americans*. In 1850 the first volume of a projected two-volume edition was advertised as "containing portraits of twelve of the most eminent citizens of the American Republic since the days of Washington, all from the original daguerreotypes taken by Brady" (Horan, 14). Brady had no illusions about photographic objectivity in undertaking this project: the patriotic historical narrative of the events

79

that made these Americans "illustrious" determined which portraits could be included.

Brady's *Gallery* was a critical success but a commercial failure (the book was relatively expensive) and was never completed (Horan, 14).[3] But the war provided a new commercial opportunity for this entrepreneur and historian. By the late 1850s the technology of the wet-plate process permitted the large-scale, commercial production and reproduction of history. Photographic prints seemed to open an even clearer window onto history than did engravings taken from daguerreotypes; they promised a relation to the world in which human art did not intervene. Carrying his camera and equipment to the scene of the first battle of Bull Run, Brady is reported to have said, "We are making history now, and every picture that we get will be valuable" (Andrews, 88).[4] The "we" were both the soldiers on the field and the photographers who found that manuacturing and selling history was quite profitable. Both were "making" history; both were engaged in a single representational endeavor, which was the attempt to legitimate the political ideology of the Union.

II.   *Photography at Midcentury*

When Brady and his colleagues were learning their trade in the 1840s and 50s, three genres of photography were generally recognized. The portrait was commercially most important. The "view"—generally of a landscape, sometimes including human figures—was more artistic and commanded a smaller share of the market. "Genre" or "figure" scenes were also of artistic importance; if they did not sell as well as portraits and "views," they could still promote a photographer's reputation.

Photographic portraits were valued for their "sublime power . . . to catch the living forms and features of those that are so fondly endeared to us, and to hold them indelibly fixed upon the tablet for years after they have passed away" (Burgess, "Value"). Many people perceived a sort of magical quality about the daguerreotype, as if life itself inhered in the representation. There were occasional stories in photographic journals about customers who supposed that daguerreotypy had the power to recover images of persons already dead and buried, in a sort of visual séance. One work of fiction published in 1852 even fantasized a new form of the daguerreotype that would change its image to show what a subject was doing at any given moment (Rudisill, 218–19). In contrast to the popular tendency to invest the daguerreotype with life, Emerson found in its image "a portrait of a mask rather than a man" (*JMN*, 8:115–16). But even this critical response was conditioned by the rhetoric of presence and truth that structured the popular reception of the medium.

Photographic portraiture also influenced the perception of death. One journalist proposed that daguerreotype portraits ought to be affixed to gravestones, because "the green hillocks of the dead" would be more cheerful places if visitors could see "the living representative of the sleeper" on every stone ("Daguerreotypes on Tombstones"). The funerary daguerreotype, a subgenre of commercial portraiture which traded in a different way on the evasion of death, was quite popular in some areas of the country (Sobieszek and Appel, 48, 55; Rudisill, 217–20). Its purpose, according to one daguerreotypist, was "to retain a facsimile of the outline of the face to assist the painter in the delineation of the portrait" which would bear the living image of the deceased (Burgess, "Portraits"). Most commonly the subject of a funerary daguerreotype was an infant, posed as if he or she were sleeping peacefully; if a family could not afford to have a miniature portrait painted, they could at least retain the sentimental image in the daguerreotype.

Professional portraiture remained commercially important through the Civil War. The cheaply produced *carte-de-visite* (a tiny portrait pasted on cardboard) was enormously popular with soldiers, who wanted to be photographed in their new uniforms. E. and H. T. Anthony and Co., a large New York firm, produced as many as 3,600 *cartes-de-visite* per day during the war (Horan, 22–23). These were primarily valued for their personal, not historical, interest; soldiers bought them to give or mail to their families and sweethearts. Early in the war, however, more than a thousand prints per day were sold of a portrait of the first (Northern) hero of the war, Major Robert Anderson, who had commanded the besieged garrison at Fort Sumter (Newhall, *History*, 64).

Some portraits, as Emerson and Brady both realized when they proposed portrait galleries for the times, would come to be received as *historical* representations—just as, on a more local and personal level, the daguerreotype image affixed to a gravestone or displayed on a shelf might become a part of a family's history. A history organized around portraits, such as Brady's *Gallery of Illustrious Americans*, is intrinsically nonnarrative and obscures important material, economic, and social forces. (In the case of the *carte-de-visite* of a soldier, for example, the most one can hope to infer is that the subject saw military service of some kind.) According to the conventions of various photographic genres, the *individuality* of a "great man" was immortalized for a nation and for history in a portrait. The portrait of a middle-class soldier was also a sign of individuality, but only to a limited circle outside of which the portrait became simply another face (how interesting are pictures of other people's relatives?).

The working classes were represented not in portraits made for their own consumption but in "genre" photographs made for the middle and upper classes. Such images typified rather than individualized their referents. "Genre" scenes perhaps did not attain the status of art in America as fully as they did in England, where David Octavius Hill was photographing rustics, laborers, and sailors, Julia Margaret Cameron was posing her servants in classical or Shakespearean costumes, and Henry Peach Robinson was producing formal pastoral views and sentimental interior scenes by means of staging and composite printing. But they still held an important place in the repertoire of the American photographer. Trading on the contemporary appetite for "local color," like contemporary American genre paintings (for example, by W. S. Mount or Eastman Johnson), they tended to idealize and sentimentalize rural life (Rudisill, 158).

The difference between portraiture and "genre" photography bears implications for historiography. The portrait of a "great man" is read for signs of his biography. An impressive daguerreotype of Massachusetts Chief Justice Lemuel Shaw taken by Southworth and Hawes of Boston was said, for example, to express the "great power, splendid intellect, and mighty will" that Shaw was reputed to possess (Sobieszek and Appel, 10). Brady counted on this sort of reception for his *Gallery of Illustrious Americans*. In contrast, genre scenes representing working class types, such as George Barnard's "The Woodsawyer's Nooning" (fig. 2) effaced the individual histories of their subjects. A contemporary description of Barnard's daguerreotype, which depicts a man and a young boy having their dinner surrounded by tools of their trade, claims that the boy's face

> betokens by its abstracted air that his thoughts are absent. Perhaps his imagination is soaring in aerial flight, and enjoys a glance of improved destiny in the future. In this happy land—as he has learned, that rank and title are of no avail in running the race of life—that the lowliest can aspire to the highest attainments. His frank and manly countenance indicate [sic] his nature, and who knows but the boy of the wood-sawyer before us, may yet be a brilliant star in the constellation of his country's glory. (Rudisill, 158)

Perhaps the boy will one day prove himself worthy of inclusion in a volume such as Brady's *Gallery*. The prospective, patriotic biography cannot be written about the middle-aged man, because it is too late for

FIG. 2. George Barnard, "The Woodsawyer's Nooning" (1853). International Museum of Photography at George Eastman House.

him to gain a place in history by achieving "the highest attainments." If the boy does not grow up "in the constellation of his country's glory" he will be fit only to be a typical subject for a genre scene; he can only escape this generic representation by becoming a great individual like Justice Shaw.

As photography replaced daguerreotypy, landscapes and architectural views became increasingly popular. The technology of the daguerreotype enlarged the existing market for portrait miniatures; but the small size of the typical "sixth-plate" image (2.75 x 3.25 inches) made it less suitable for the representation of expansive views. During the 1850s the Boston firm of Southworth and Hawes made many aesthetically influential daguerreotypes of landscapes, seascapes, and harbor scenes, generally on expensive, 6.5-x-8.5-inch "whole-plates" (Sobieszek and Appel, 78–93). But in 1859 Oliver Wendell Holmes, Sr. (whose articles on photography for the *Atlantic Monthly* are among the most important early accounts of the medium in America), reported that the daguerreotype had "almost disappeared from the field of landscape, still life, architecture, and *genre* painting, to make room for the [wet-plate] photograph" ("Stereoscope,"

742). Larger plate sizes, up to 10 x 14 inches, permitted the construction of panoramic views; two or more negatives could be printed side-by-side to give an even broader view.[5]

Whereas each daguerreotype was a unique image, the wet-plate process enabled the photographer to produce an indefinite number of prints inexpensively from a single negative. Thus new photographic technology allowed middle-class Americans to embark vicariously on prepackaged photographic tours, as Holmes explains in an article in the *Atlantic*: "These sights, gathered from Alps, temples, palaces, pyramids, are offered you for a trifle, to carry home with you, that you may look at them at your leisure, by your fireside, with perpetual fair weather, when you are in the mood, without catching cold, without following a *valet-de-place* in any order of succession,—from a glacier to Vesuvius, from Niagara to Memphis" ("Sun-Painting," 16). Holmes proceeds to guide his readers on vicarious tours of the United States (starting, of course, with Niagara Falls) and Europe. Enterprising photographers would very soon be guiding another kind of tour—of the battlefields of a war-torn nation. The market Holmes identified continued to exist, expanded by patriotism and curiosity. Images of the war were brought home to be contemplated in comfort and leisure by consumers whose photographic taste had been educated, prior to the war, by landscape, portrait, and genre photographs and by photographic criticism in magazines such as the *Atlantic*.

Civil War photographers used the conventions of all existing photographic genres. In addition to portraits, photographic representations related to the war included landscape views, usually of important battlefields or landmarks, and genre scenes representing typical but interesting moments in the life of the officer or soldier. The idea of the documentary photograph was more or less inherent in the "truthful" representational capabilities of the medium itself, but the war played an important role in its emergence because now there was so much history to record. The advent of modern photojournalism is most reasonably dated from the invention of the half-tone screen circa 1885, which made the accurate reproduction of photographic images cheap enough for daily newspapers (Newhall, *History*, 251). But during the war American illustrated weeklies—especially *Harper's* and *Leslie's*—helped to create a market for photographic reportage of the war by publishing woodblock engravings derived from portraits or battlefield views.

What was genuinely new in Civil War photography was the representation of death. Although English photographer Roger Fenton made over 360 negatives (mostly portraits) during the Crimean War, American awareness of this enterprise was very limited. Some of the views were reproduced as woodcuts in the*Illustrated London News*. William Frassanito claims that "the better-informed American photographers were at least aware of their existence," and speculates that Alexander Gardner may have seen some of the woodcut reproductions before he left his native Scotland for America in 1856 (*Antietam*, 20, 22). None of Fenton's Crimean photographs represents a corpse. Although his private letters from the Crimea contain at least one gruesome image of mangled bodies, his photographic coverage excluded any such unpleasantness. Sent by Prince Albert on behalf of the government, Fenton knew that he needed to put the best face on an unwelcome war, to show sanitary conditions and pleasant "genre" scenes rather than dead Englishmen (Lewinski, 39–40).

In the context of the American Civil War, however, photographers began to find that images of the dead could serve a significant ideological function, especially when surrounded and controlled by other, more benign views of war. Traces of violence could thus be transformed into signs legitimating the Union. In response to the challenges of the subject of death in war, American photographers adapted the antebellum conventions of funerary portraiture, the view, and the "genre" scene to provide an archive that in its very vastness signaled the completeness of the photographic record. The picturesque and pastoral aesthetics proved especially influential. Genre scenes were common. Landscape views were even more prevalent: a view of a battlefield, with or without corpses, must necessarily be represented as some sort of landscape. Beyond this precondition, however, Civil War photography appealed to the repository of naturalized ideological values contained in the American landscape aesthetic. These images predicted that the destiny of the Union was inscribed on the face of the land itself. In order to analyze the means by which Civil War photography appropriated the corpse in the landscape for ideological ends and naturalized the history and politics of the Union, we will first need to examine the values attached to "nature" in the reception aesthetics of mid-nineteenth-century American photography.

III. *The Nature of Photography*

Early discourse (circa 1840) on the representational capacities of the photographic medium was organized in terms of "nature." Photography seemed closer to nature than did painting, drawing, or engraving; thus early discussions report on the best and most accurate ways to fix images directly from nature. William Henry Fox Talbot, inventor of the modern

negative-positive print process, reported that he failed to produce a satisfactory view of the landscape at Lake Como, in Italy, by tracing the
image formed by a camera obscura.[6] This failure of existing artistic
technology caused him to speculate on "how charming it would be if
it were possible to cause these natural images to imprint themselves
durably, and remain fixed upon the paper" (29). Thus in its conception
photography was thought to permit nature to be the means and agency
of its own representation. Although most of the early texts on photography
attempt to efface human and even mechanical agency, their metaphors
often belie this effacement. Daguerre, whose work in France was con-
temporaneous with Talbot's in England, wrote that "the DAGUERREOTYPE
is not merely an instrument which serves to draw Nature; on the contrary
it is a chemical and physical process which gives her the power to reproduce
herself" (13). As in Talbot's theory, nature is conceived as the object,
agent, and material means of representation. And yet Daguerre has inscribed his own ghost in (the name of) this machine. Apparently con-
tradicting his thesis, he reveals a trace of history in the "natural" image.[7]

Thoreau, in a journal entry from 1841, similarly avoids direct mention
of the place of the human agent in his comments on the photographic
process, but his metaphor reveals it: "It is easy to repeat, but hard to
originate. Nature is readily made to repeat herself in a thousand forms,
and in the daguerreotype her own light is amanuensis, and the picture
too has more than a surface significance,—a depth equal to the prospect,
so that a microscope may be applied to the one as a spy-glass to the
other" (7:189). According to the metaphor, natural light is the copyist
that transcribes nature. Although the photographer and the camera might
also be appropriately described as "amanuenses" of nature, Thoreau defers
to nature in the way that Talbot would when he entitled his first book
of calotype prints The Pencil of Nature (1846). In his essay "Paradise (To
Be) Regained," Thoreau finds in photography an instrument that might
further the Transcendentalist project of restoring humankind to the wholeness of nature: "How meanly and grossly do we deal with nature! Could
we not have a less gross labor? What else do these fine inventions suggest—
magnetism, the daguerreotype, electricity? Can we not do more than
cut and trim the forest?—can we not assist in its interior economy, in
the circulation of the sap?" (4:284). In the company of electricity and
magnetism the daguerreotype appears to be less an invented gadget than
a discovered, natural principle. However, although Thoreau suggests we
enter into an internal, "natural" relationship with nature, he himself gains
entry by means of the cultural metaphors. If nature has an "economy"

PHOTOGRAPHY AND THE SCENE OF HISTORY

then it invites human transaction. Even more important is the semiotic of landscape art and architecture: his journal entry of 1841 states that a daguerreotype has a "depth" and a "prospect." This language works against Thoreau's thesis, prohibiting his access to the interior of nature and situating him as a spectator of a framed "view" of the landscape. Emerson, perhaps recognizing more clearly than Thoreau the "external" nature of the semiotic relationship, is more skeptical of the power of the camera to integrate us into some essential natural property or principle. And yet he too thinks in terms of landscape, even when discussing daguerreotype portraiture:

> Were you ever Daguerreotyped, O immortal man? And did you look with all vigor at the lens of the camera . . . but [in the resulting image] unhappily the total expression escaped from the face and you held the portrait of a mask instead of a man. Could you not by grasping it very tight hold the stream of a river or a small brook & prevent it from flowing? (*JMN*, 8:115–16)

Thoreau, like Daguerre and Talbot, proposes that in the photograph nature controls and determines its own (self-) representation; the human subject is merely a witness to an unmediated transcription. But Emerson describes an attempt to control the representation of nature which produces only an artificial sign (a mask) rather than a natural one (the essence of the man, the flux of the stream of life). For Emerson the photographic process is outside of nature, producing images that are only poor resemblances.

Holmes also uses the critical vocabulary of landscape painting. Like Thoreau, he thinks in terms of the place of the human being in the natural semiotic. The stereoscopic photograph produces the same sublime effect as the immediate experience of nature:

> The mind feels its way into the very depths of the picture. The scraggy branches of a tree in the foreground run out at us as if they would scratch our eyes out. The elbow of a figure stands forth so as to make us almost uncomfortable. There is such a frightful amount of detail that we have the same sense of infinite complexity which Nature gives us. ("Stereoscope," 744)

Holmes thus suggests that the photographic medium has become the epitome of the aesthetic of realistic representation. Like Thomas Cole's picturesque-sublime landscapes, but even more powerfully, photographs instill a moral lesson by allowing us to contemplate the perfect plenitude of Nature: "theoretically, a perfect photograph is absolutely inexhaustible" (744).[8]

IV. *The Picturesque*

The early work of Thomas Cole provides a pre-photographic point of reference for the aesthetic of the picturesque that informed the reception of the photographic medium in the United States. Cole wanted to transform landscape painting into high art, capable of producing the moral effect of the sublime, "in order to justify its consideration in the same category with history painting" (Powell, "Picturesque," 116). In seeking this goal, however, he did not attempt to make the landscape "historical." Transforming the picturesque from a mode of representation that "merely makes you see" rather than think or feel, to one that produced the moral effect of "communion with God through a contemplation of the forms of nature," Cole came to emphasize the wildness of the American landscape as presenting an image of prelapsarian nature in which one might glimpse the possibilities of harmony and redemption (110, 116). The "impulse to naturalization" that characterizes especially Cole's early work "represented the defeat of an older mode of historical discourse" (that is, of Enlightenment historiography) (Wolf, 195). Bryan Wolf argues that in place of recoverable traces of an objective social history, Cole projects his own autobiography, structured as a *Kunstlerroman*, into the form of the image, "filling the silence of nonnarrative vistas with the clamor of self-discovery" (178). Cole's aesthetic is similar in this respect to that of John Constable. For Constable, "'landscape' is history painting with the history (or the literary myth, the human protagonists) removed." By divesting the form of history painting of its historical content, Constable was able to invest his canvases with "his personal image, a landscape of his affections," and yet to align his work with the dominant artistic tradition (Paulson, 134–35). Cole's displacement of history from the image involves more than a projection of his artistic struggles into the form of the image; additionally, it has implications for the politics of American nationalism. As his "Lecture on American Scenery" suggests, his paintings describe an ideal sympathy between the landscape and the individual. Freed from historical specificity, the image of the landscape became a space, occupied by God, in which the American national spirit could find itself (Rudisill, 7, 17–19). In its assumption that the landscape was a source of spiritual and political value, Cole's work provided one of the links that associated organicist aesthetics with American nationalism.

    In England the picturesque mode of painting was "an early ideological response to [the] decline of rural paternalism" in the late eighteenth and early nineteenth centuries. The naturalizing rhetoric of the picturesque obscured both the causes and effects of the ongoing transformation of the rural economy. It endorsed the new mode of agricultural production (now organized primarily in terms of a "cash nexus") at the same time that it "mystified the agency of social change so that fate, and not the economic decisions of the landowning classes, seemed responsible" (Bermingham, 74–75). By aestheticizing poverty and distancing the spectator from the represented object by means of an encoded nostalgia, which was proposed as the reality of the present, the picturesque assured the middle and upper classes that the English countryside remained as it had always been, regardless of economic transformations.

In nineteenth-century America, the version of the picturesque initiated by Cole and his contemporaries represented a similar aesthetic response to a different set of ideological categories. Important for the legitimation of politics since the Puritan days was a sense that American history was uniquely and divinely mandated. To this end, history paintings by John Trumbull and others, in conjunction with historical and biographical texts, created a usable American history of a struggle for freedom and the like. But landscape painting could also promote the legitimacy of the American political system, because the boundless landscape itself had been identified as a source of American values. The imperialist direction of American history was preinscribed in the name of the "*Continental* Congress" and was later written into the Constitution, in the form of instructions for the formation of new states from the territories of the continent. Leo Marx argues that in this apparent potential for the limitless expansion of the culture of the Colonies, "the topographical image of a fresh start lent an impetus to the revolutionary spirit, and . . . may help to account for the unusual character of the American Revolution" ("Revolution," 320). Later, picturesque landscapes painted by Cole and others made this image of a "fresh start"—that is, the land's own apparent endorsement of the ideology of the Republic—available even to those who had never been west of Philadelphia.

G. P. Putnam's popular collection *The Home Book of the Picturesque* offers several insights into the aesthetic of the American picturesque and its relationship to history and ideology. Published in New York in 1852, the *Home Book* includes, among others, essays by James Fenimore Cooper, William Cullen Bryant, and Washington Irving and engravings taken from landscape paintings by Thomas Cole, Frederick Church, and Asher Durand.[9] Two topics relevant to the present essay occupy the writers: the cultural value of the American landscape and the relations between art and politics.

The writers agree that topography often bears traces of history, but disagree on the extent to which history is inscribed in the *American* landscape. Cooper argues that, unlike European landscapes where we see "ample pages of the history of the country and the character of its people," the American land bears no important traces of history (Putnam, 55). Thus

> we concede to Europe much the noblest scenery, in its Alps, Pyrenees, and Apennines; in its objects of art, as a matter of course; in all those effects which depend on time and association, in its moments, and in this impress of the past which may be said to be reflected in its countenance; while we claim for America the freshness of a most promising youth, and a species of natural radiance that carries the mind with reverence to the source of all that is glorious around us. (69)

Bryant and Irving find it easier than Cooper to read history in the landscape. Irving uses an engraving of J. F. Kensett's "Catskill Scenery" as an object of association, alluding to the tales of Indians and early Dutch explorers he had included in his *History of New York*. Bryant, departing from "The Housatanic Valley" by Regis Gignoux, speculates on the differences in the landscape that Dutch, rather than British, political ascendancy would have produced:

> So far as concerns the fine arts, the dwellings would have been picturesque, comfortable Dutch houses with low roofs and spacious *stoops*, embowered in trees, instead of the grim, naked and tasteless habitations of the Yankees. The painters who sought their subjects among the inhabitants of the valley would have painted interiors in the manner of Teniers, or elaborate and highly finished landscapes, in which fidelity to nature was more regarded than the selection of objects, after the manner of Cuyp. (160)

Bryant, Irving, and Cooper all refer immediately to geography when discussing history or its absence; for them the landscape (either with or without signs of human habitation) is the essential bearer of the picturesque quality. The engraved reproductions of paintings get them to the physical topography and geography (and thence to historical significance), after which point the works of art no longer feature in the essays.

Susan Cooper (James's daughter) dwells on the evanescence of the historical reflection inspired by American scenery; she is more overtly interested than the other writers in the imaginative transformation of the bare perception of the landscape. Placing herself in a natural setting, she describes how with a wave of a sprig of witch-hazel she can produce visions of ancient mounds (like those in Bryant's "The Prairies") or castles, thus suggesting that the hold of American culture on the land is only tentative:

> It would be comparatively an easy work to remove from the earth all traces of many of the peculiar merits of modern civiliza- tion . . . . Look at our light suspension bridges, marvelous as they are, how soon could they be destroyed; look at . . . the wonders Daguerre has showed us . . . and see how speedily all traces of them could be removed. If barbarians [or American Indians?] were to sweep over the civilized world . . . as regards America, the chief proofs that eastern civilization had once passed over the country would then be found in the mingled vegetation, the trees, the plants, ay, the very weeds of the old world. (89–90)

Her essay thus makes explicit the relation of the picturesque mode of perception to historical representation that structures all the essays in the volume. The picturesque was valued because, as in the case of Con- stable's aesthetic, it was perceived as history painting without the historical content (Paulson, 134). The perceiver, enabled by the logic of eighteenth- century associationist psychology endorsed by theorists of the picturesque (Powell, "Associationism," 113–15), is free either to imagine a usable past or to make an unusable past disappear. Even "the wonders Daguerre has showed us" are not immune to this disappearance of history: if a picturesque image, perhaps supplied by a photograph, is an impetus to revery, that revery is capable of dissolving consciousness of its material, historical origin. Yet this evanescence of culture is also a demand for its solidification. If more people were to cultivate rural America, the "barbarians" could not so easily "sweep over" it.

The final essay in the volume, "Art in the United States," by George Bethune, is more theoretical in character than the others and includes a socioeconomic history of art. Bethune argues that the prospects for the American artist are now (in the 1850s) excellent. The early nationalist labor of colonizing the continent had left "neither time nor desire for the cultivation of those elegant pursuits which are the luxury of leisure, the decoration of wealth, and the charm of refinement." But that same labor produced a class of consumers who, now "intoxicated with sudden wealth . . . are eager to lavish it, yet know not how to do so elegantly and creditably" (171, 179). Bethune's ideological position is clear from the repetition of phrases such as "the principles of our government" and "the vital necessity of union" (170) in his history of the market for the visual arts. The education of taste he proposes must be politically motivated.

Bethune argues that "the moral power of Art is best exerted on the popular mind" in the form of history paintings reproduced for mass consumption, and that refinement and elegance in this case are less important than the dissemination of a nationalist ideology: "We can well pardon the awkward multitude of legs in Trumbull's picture, when we know that it has carried to every dwelling of our people a perpetuation of the sublime assembly, which declared our national independence" (185). Next to history painting, Bethune states, "the painter of landscapes has met with the most general favor" (186). *The Home Book of the Picturesque*, which made reproductions of landscape paintings readily available, is itself an example of the popularity of the genre. Precisely with the introduction of the topic of landscape art, however, Bethune's essay loses touch with the political and historical topics it had previously engaged. A vague sort of history as divine ordination may be seen entering by the back door in the requisite discussion of Cole, who is praised for "his tribute to the surpassing beauties, which the hand of nature has scattered so lavishly and on so grand a scale over the mountains and valleys of our native land" (187). But Durand gives us primarily "delicious traces of a calm, chastened spirit," and by the end of the brief survey, we find that Church (who, it must be remembered, was still fairly young) is merely said to produce "creditable landscapes."

In Bethune's concluding remarks, political questions have been thoroughly reformulated in the guise of aesthetics: "Our art has not passed the period of its youth, nor acquired sufficient boldness or self-reliance. With more maturity, we may expect more originality. It were strange indeed if, with so many new lessons from Nature, the great teacher, our artists should content themselves with doing only what has been done before" (187). This aesthetic implies that American nationalism will best be represented not only in paintings with identifiable historical referents (such as Trumbull's), but also more subtly in the compositional form of the picturesque. Such representations, unlike history paintings, disguise their ideological agenda—the "boldness or self-reliance" that promoted an expropriative attitude toward the land—in an appeal to "Nature." As in Cole's wilderness paintings, the landscape becomes a space into which the American spirit (in its Emersonian manifestations) projects itself endlessly.

By the time of the Civil War, boldness and self-reliance had become ambivalent values in the maintenance of the American nation-state. The American Revolution had required these political values, as had the westward expansion and the first war for empire (the Mexican War). But the doctrines of popular sovereignty, states' rights, and secession were also theoretically justified in terms of the self-reliance of territories and states. In this ideological context J. E. Cabot, an art critic writing for the *Atlantic* in 1864, offered a definition of "the picturesque" that emphasized the beauty of totality and ordered subordination of individual elements to a unified whole:

> The modern ideal is the Picturesque,—a beauty not detachable, belonging to the picture, to the composition, not to the component parts. It has no favorite; it is violated alike by the systematic glorification and the systematic depreciation of particular forms. . . . Claude's or Turner's figures may be absurd, when taken by themselves; but the absurdity consists in taking them by themselves. . . . Each must have felt that anything that should call attention to the figures would be worse than any bad drawing. (326)

According to this theory, picturesque art does not merely transcribe nature but develops an image that completes nature's intention toward the beautiful which is "everywhere implied, but nowhere expressed" (190).

Cabot's ideas on the picturesque motivate him to protect the territory of landscape painting from recent encroachments by photographers: "It is a very general opinion that photography has made painting superfluous,—or, at least, that it will do so as soon as further improvements in the process shall enable it to render color as well as light and shade" (183). Painting is superior to photography as a picturesque mode of representation, Cabot argues, because photographs do not have the power that even mediocre paintings or drawings have to produce a contemplative experience on repeated viewings: "The landscape-photographs that we have lately had in such admirable perfection, however they may overpower our judgement at first sight, will, I believe, be found not to *wear* well; they have really less in them than even second-rate drawings, and therefore are sooner exhausted" (318). For Cabot, the photograph is at once "too full and too empty" (319)—too full, because "we stop at the outside, the material texture" (318); too empty because this surface texture is said *not* to be the result of an organizing aesthetic perception. The significance of surface detail is soon exhausted, whereas the compositional form of a painting reveals the deeper intentional form and significance of nature.

Holmes, however, had argued that "theoretically, a perfect pho-

93

tograph is absolutely inexhaustible" ("Stereoscope," 744). Whereas Holmes has no difficulty reading photographs as art, Cabot's ideas on high art have made him resistant to such a reading.[10] Yet Cabot's argument against photography is directed not at its place in the market, but against the historical specificity of photographic representation. He proposes Claude's paintings of Rome as counter-examples to the aesthetic claims of photography. The beauty of these paintings consists not in their fidelity to historical incidents or epochs but in the associations they inspire of a sort of vague or typified experience of "generation after generation of pilgrims": "Is it not that the place seems set apart from the working-day world of selfish and warring interests? that here all manner of men, for once, lay aside their sordid occupations and their vulgar standards, to come together on the ground of a common humanity?" (322). Photographic objectivity seems not to produce the vague and idealizing response of painterly subjectivity. For Cabot, minute representational fidelity to the accidents of nature prevents the realization of transcendence because it captures nature in a moment of imperfect or unrealized intention. He assumes that the viewer does not generalize the photographic index-icon to produce the symbolic value he attributes to the picturesque.[11] We have seen, however, that Thoreau and Holmes *do* find transcendental signs in the photographic image—because they also find transcendental signs, fully complete and significant, *in* nature prior to human perception or intervention. Unlike Cabot, they are willing to treat photographic representations of nature seriously. Cabot in contrast finds "transcendentalism" characteristic only of painting (and, to a lesser extent, Classical sculpture) (186).

The disagreement between the positions represented by Holmes and Cabot over the artistic status of photography turns on the values attributed to the landscape itself, prior to the production of images. If one's conceptual geography finds ideological significance in the landscape, one is prepared to accept a photographic landscape as art. Whether or not Cabot realizes it, the aesthetic he describes is more than a label for a genre of painting. "The picturesque" is a set of instructions for reading the landscape and the human figures who populate it. Cabot suggests that not everyone can read in this way, and that those who deserve to be called artists are persons skilled at imposing totality and unity on a visual field in order to produce a representation in which "a visible dependence of each part, by its partiality declar[es] the completeness of the whole" (327). By extension, this sense of the picturesque became the core of the semiotic of landscape and genre photography—in spite of the protests of high-culture critics such as Cabot, who would have reserved such aesthetic perceptions for an elite. Thus photographers were inspired to produce images that *did* provide material for a contemplative experience.[12]

The organicist aesthetic that structured this experience proved to be conducive to the ideology of Unionism. In the context of the secession of the Southern states, the aesthetic that Cabot describes in 1864 seems to bear ideological significance:

> The picturesque has its root in the mind's craving for totality. It is Nature seen as a whole; all the characteristics . . . such as roughness, wildness, ruin, obscurity, the gloom of night or of storm; whatever the outward discrepancy, wherever the effect is produced, it is because in some way there is a gain in completeness. (327)

The structuring operations of organicism thus became manifest on the two parallel levels of art and politics. For the ruins of the war, there would be an analogous compensatory "gain in completeness" in the subsumption of the Southern states within the organic Union.

V.   Pastoralism

A review in the *New York Times* of photographs of the Civil War exhibited at Mathew Brady's gallery identifies a trace of the mechanic force of war in a pastoral landscape:

> A simple Virginian farmhouse, with its low walls, its high and sloping roof. Under the tall, gaunt trees, which shade its rustic doorway, (for porch it has none) stands a table, and around the table is gathered a group of country people—the natural Arcadians of the soil. There is nothing in this scene to suggest the throes of war . . . . Turn to the title and what do you read: "Battle-field of Cedar Mountain. House in which Gen. CHARLES WINDER was killed." Over this commonplace corner of the Old Dominion . . . the red light of battle has fallen. Never again shall the new glow depart from the scene. ("Brady's Photographs")[13]

The red light of the war-machine, counterpoised to the natural sunlight of "Arcadia" (by which the photographic image was taken), radiates from the Satanic fires of industrial furnaces that had begun to appear in the landscape and in literature (Marx, *Machine*, 265–319). The glow of technology that the *Times* reviewer imagines in the landscape image indicates the "signet which history sets upon nature." But that glow is not recorded

FIG. 3. Thomas Cole, *Consummation of Empire,* from *The Course of Empire* (1833–36). The New-York Historical Society, New York.

by the camera. This pastoral photograph "of war" does not in itself represent "the war"; the caption locates the image in history and allows the reviewer to imagine the battle that has taken place.

The opposition to which the *Times* appeals, between pastoral and historical modes, invites a reexamination of American pastoralism in relation to history and to visual representation. The most comprehensive work on American pastoralism is Leo Marx's *The Machine in the Garden,* a study of the incorporation of images of technology into representations of the American pastoral ideal of the "new garden." The pastoral mode, which Marx claims constructed an idealized image of America as early as Shakespeare's *The Tempest* and Michael Drayton's "To the Virginian Voyage," was still available in the nineteenth century as a mediating category that could resolve a perceived opposition between nature and technology. This resolution was often accomplished by means of a verbal and visual "rhetoric of the technological sublime" (195) which transformed the conventionally nostalgic pastoral mode (with its anti- or ahistorical impulses) into a beneficent "progressivism" that soothed American anxiety about technology. The central trope of this rhetoric was naturalization, by means of which the factory and the railroad were represented as belonging organically to the landscape. Yet the factory and railroad were more than signs of a mercantile-industrial economy; additionally (or, perhaps, identically) they were signs of the forces of history. Both the capitalist economic system and a "progressive," nationalist interpretation of history were being naturalized and incorporated into the conceptual landscape of America.

The Civil War, because of its vast effects on American politics, economics, and technology, was an important test case for the mediating capabilities of the pastoral mode: the presence of the war machine in the garden of America strained the capacity of the culture to assimilate images of mechanic force into the ideal of the pastoral "middle land-scape."[14] The camera, a technology that was reproducing images of the antebellum American landscape, is especially interesting in this regard. This machine, unlike the railroad engine or the steam mill, was absent usually from images of the garden. As a cultural object, a camera could be photographed like anything else; but when it was used as a repres-entational technology it did not record the history of the act of producing representations. The "mirror with a memory," as the daguerreotype was popularly called, did not reflect itself. Perhaps the reason that Marx does not mention attitudes toward the technology of photography in his study is that photography effaced itself as a technology. It caused no anxiety because its images seemed wholly natural.

As in the case of the picturesque, the work of Thomas Cole provides a pre-photographic point of reference for the evasion of history effected by American pastoralism. Although Cole spent much of his career at-tempting to recover prehistorical states of experience relevant to the American mythos of a new Eden—the domain of the picturesque—he also represented human society in several paintings. Each of the five canvases in the series *The Course of Empire* (1833-36) typifies a different kind of social organization within a particular configuration of the land-scape. None, however, proposes to represent a specific historical event or time. Rather, the series is organized in terms of a conflict between "nature" and "history." The central scene, "The Consummation of Em-pire," contains practically no greenery; what vegetation there is has been transplanted in urns (fig. 3). The scene is replete with signs of history, in the form of mythical and heroic statues. An interesting detail is the sculpture of Diana and her nymphs in the hunt, represented on the ped-iment of the temple, which recalls the actual hunt in the first painting

97

Fig. 4. Thomas Cole, *The Pastoral State,* from *The Course of Empire* (1833–36). The New-York Historical Society, New York.

in the series, "The Savage State" (Baigell, 52). In contrast, the primitive temple represented in "The Pastoral State" (which seems to be an allusion to Stonehenge) is devoid of any ornamentation whatever, for the discourse of history has not yet entered human consciousness (fig. 4). This detail and others signify that in the state of empire (allegorically, the modern state), human activity has come to be represented in historical texts, emphasizing the conceptual difference between action and the representation of action that produces history. Yet in the opposition between nature and history set forth in the series, nature maintains primacy. In "Desolation," the final canvas, nature is shown effacing the traces of history. Nature restores its primacy by covering with vegetation the architectural remains of the empire, the course of which was but an interlude.

Thus *The Course of Empire* presents itself not as a series of history paintings, but rather as a historiographical generalization. Yet Cole is not interested in exploring the historical conditions of empire—namely, that military conquest is necessary to establish and maintain it. War, as represented in the "Destruction of Empire," is something that happens *to* an empire; but in the entire series it is not something that the empire engages in willingly. The story of *The Course of Empire* is the one narrated (although more optimistically) by Leo Marx—of technological progress without militarism.

It is Cole's pastoralism that has partially blinded him to the origins of history and empire. When Cole paints the "middle landscape"—that is, rural, not wild, nature—he does so with a pastoral nostalgia. Other paintings by Cole, such as "The Old Mill at Sunset," "View on the Catskill, Early Autumn," or "Dream of Arcadia," construct idealized visions of America, scenes and times that never existed. They represent not the awareness structured by a historical consciousness, but a nostalgic sentimentality. Images of the technologies that characterize a given state of sociopolitical organization can be found in these scenes (for example, the rude stone temple in the background of "The Pastoral State"). But these technologies are not represented as having any direct relation to the human figures that populate the landscapes; that is, the figures are never shown in the acts of using technology or even in contemplating its results. The geometer drawing figures in the dirt in "The Pastoral State" suggests that there is ample leisure time to explore pure, abstract philosophy, but the labor that produces such leisure remains unexamined. "Consummation of Empire" similarly represents only leisure. The scene is transformed, but the pastoral attitude remains.[15] However, this does not seem to be a warning against the pastoral attitude, for the final two panels—"Destruction of Empire" and "Desolation"—argue only for the naturalness and inevitability of the fall of empire. The series as a whole represents social transitions as stages in an organic cycle.

Nineteenth-century American genre paintings were generally structured by a version of pastoralism in which human figures occupy a more emphatic position than they do in Cole's pastorals. Yet both versions traded on the pastoral effacement of history. The idealized and yet "realistic" vision of Eastman Johnson's "Old Kentucky Home" (fig. 5) provides a good example of the interdiction of history in the pastoral mode. The artist claimed that this painting, first exhibited in Washington in 1859, represented "negro life in the South" (Prown, 84). But only one person in this image works, and she seems more interested in the attentions of the man leaning toward her than in her sewing. A reminder of labor is present in the ax lying on the ground; but it has been cast aside in this relaxed (if not quite festive) atmosphere. The slaves—at least we assume they are slaves from the date of the painting—are all physically attractive; and their culture of leisure is attractive, also, to the genteel

FIG. 5. Eastman Johnson, *Old Kentucky Home* (1859). The New-York Historical Society, New York.

white woman who observes the picturesque qualities of the scene from its edge. "Old Kentucky Home" proposes that the American land supports a beneficent slave system and implies that there is no reason to intrude an economic or political analysis on the rural scene. Indeed, the presence of the white woman merely hints at the issue of race relations, and then only to suggest there is harmonious coexistence in the social realm (the separation of two races necessitated by the subjugation of one). Her uncertain posture as she enters the scene through the door in the garden wall suggests that she is not in her social place here. There is nothing in the scene to suggest the imminence—or even the possibility—of war or any other form of conflict, because it is an image displaced by its mode of representation from historical time and the unpleasant aspects of social reality.

Holmes's essays in the *Atlantic* show that the pastoral evasion of history structured the reception of photographs as well as paintings; for example:

In the lovely glass stereograph of the Lake of Brienz, on the left-hand side, a vaguely hinted female figure stands by the margin of the fair water; on the other side of the picture she is not seen. This is life; we seem to see her come and go. All the longings, passions, experiences, possibilities of womanhood animate that gliding shadow that has flitted through our consciousness, nameless, dateless, feature-less, yet more profoundly real than the sharpest of portraits traced by a human hand. ("Stereoscope," 745)

Holmes cannot read the figure in the photograph as a particular woman in a concrete, temporal situation, but instead constructs a type, a reification of idealized, "dateless" feminine attributes. The difference between the images of the two plates of the stereograph (for one plate evidently depicts the woman at the edge of the image where the other does not) induces Holmes to dwell on the evanescence of the particular, and to recuperate a potential absence by means of an appeal to universals. And in this case, the play between the presence and the absence of the woman's image suggests to Holmes that the lack of substantiality or wholeness signifies femininity. The semiotic of truth in photographic representation thus rein-forces the cultural codes that define (upper-middle class) "womanhood" for the Victorian Holmes. For all we know, the particular woman depicted here may have been an artist or a political activist, but the double mediation of photograph and text prevents us from reading her history. Holmes describes precisely, if unwittingly, the idealizing, potentially dehistori-cizing effects of photographic representation.

By finding in this photograph a representation of certain supposedly universal constituents of the human condition, Holmes is in effect reading it as a version of pastoral. The precise nature of the pastoral varies from critic to critic; but attention to its dehistoricizing tendency is a common feature of most accounts. Renato Poggioli theorizes that "the psychological root of the pastoral is a double longing after innocence and happiness, to be recovered not through conversion or regeneration but merely through a retreat. By withdrawing not from the world but from 'the world,' pastoral man tries to achieve a new life in imitation of the good shepherds" (1). Pastoral poetry is effective because it assumes a perspective on "the world" that is apart from it. In this imaginative realm the individual is, for example, "the opposite of *homo oeconomicus* on both ethical and practical grounds" (4). Historical analysis is inappropriate because the motivating impulse of the genre is to escape from history. Empson characterizes this feature of the genre as "the pastoral process of putting the complex into the simple" (23). Pastoralism, argues Empson, is in-compatible with radical ideology because, by representing a natural har-mony of class relations, it conserves the existing class system; Gray's "Elegy," for example, "compar[es] the social arrangement to Nature" and in doing so "makes it seem inevitable" (4). Holmes finds a similar inevitability in the "profoundly real" photographic image of a woman in a landscape: "This is life" ("Stereoscope," 745). The stability achieved by means of such a naturalization of the status quo dehistoricizes the structure of the social relations that make the woman appear in the landscape in the way she does.

White's thesis on historiography would suggest that the naturalizing power of the pastoral inheres in a structural affinity between an organicist mode of historical argument and conservative ideology (29, 163–90). My claim here is not that pastoralism is *inherently* conservative (although this argument could probably be sustained). Rather it is that the links between a totalizing, organicist aesthetic and a totalizing, conservative political ideology were culturally forged in the United States prior to the Civil War.[16] The mobilization of organicism, at this particular cultural moment, was possible because analogously totalizing tropes were employed in the rhetorics of visual and political representation. The appropriative nature of photographic technology, which produced images of the garden of America without representing its own relation to the production of these images, aided this mobilization.

VI. *Photography as a Technology of Appropriation*

Photographic "realism" masked its objectification of "nature" and "his-tory" as categories to be inscribed in and thus mastered by representation. By transporting the landscape to galleries in Boston, New York, and Washington, the camera wrote a predictive text of the technological and economic appropriation of nature—while seeming merely to reproduce nature in all its pristine clarity, without simultaneously recording traces of the production of the image. The practice of photography seemed not to disrupt the pastoral or picturesque harmony of the landscape. Of all representational media, photography was the most prone to efface its own status *as* representation (it has since been superseded in this respect by documentary film and video); hence the rhetoric of "truth to nature" in which early accounts of the medium were shrouded. But in the system of the production and exchange of images, photography became yet another instrument of knowledge which aided the exploitation of the wilderness. Viewing a photograph, suggested Holmes in a fanciful but revealing metaphor, produced the feeling that one controlled not only the representation, but the referent as well: "We steal a landscape from its lawful owners, and defy the charge of dishonesty" ("Sun-Painting," 13).

Daguerreotypes documenting the appropriation of the American wilderness—for example, from the early mining settlements in California—represent overtly the American mythos of struggle with and mastery over the land, in images of loggers or miners busy at work or resting surrounded by the evidence of their labors.[17] Wolf reads the recurrent motif of the pioneering woodsman as Cole's image for the landscape artist. Sometimes represented by the figure of a woodchopper, sometimes only as an abandoned ax wedged in a log, this motif always invokes a sense of "the woodsman as an image of power, his mastery and view contingent upon an act of despoliation. As a surrogate for the artist, he expresses at what is presumably a preconscious level the painter's sense of struggle with nature for mastery" (182). Artistic photography also treated the motif of the woodsman. In Barnard's genre scene "The Woodsawyer's Nooning" (fig. 2), all the tools of despoliation are present, momentarily unused, but ready; the sawyer's cart forms his table, the sawhorse, his seat. In such photographs the basis of American culture in the appropriation of the wilderness seems more real, less symbolic than in Cole's painted visions. Both painting and photography, however, indicate a similar attitude toward the landscape—a culture of mastery. Cole's tropes of mastery have broad ideological implications which are relevant to a consideration of the Civil War as, fundamentally, one of a series of American wars for empire.[18] During and after the Civil War, the aesthetic exemplified by Cole's work was mobilized to legitimate the establishment of political control over tracts of land that had been under the control of another government (for example, the C.S.A. or the Sioux).

Holmes and Cole were both fascinated by the power of photography to provide a repertoire of pure forms readily available to the appropriative forces of culture. Cole speculates in a notebook entry that "the invention of Daguerre and Talbot" will cause the demise of "those things called views"—that is, of landscapes intended to be direct and literal transcriptions of particular scenes, as opposed to landscapes created by the imagination and structured according to the rules of picturesque composition. Photography could aid the creative activity of composition (of inventing, rather than transcribing, a scene) by providing the artist with "a rich mine from which to select materials for the structure and embodiment of his most beautiful and sublime conceptions" (Powell, "Picturesque," 114). Holmes envisions similar possibilities, proclaiming that photographs will provide an encyclopedia of forms that can be selected and manipulated at will: "*Form is henceforth divorced from matter.* In fact, matter as a visible object is of no great use any longer, except as the mold on which form is shaped. Give us a few negatives of a thing worth seeing, taken from different points of view, and that is all we want of it. Pull it down or burn it up, if you please" ("Stereoscope," 747, Holmes's italics). Rather than instilling a respect for the domain of wilderness that was yet outside of history, Cole's aesthetic predicted the destruction of natural referents by seeming to preserve them in images. Holmes's logic is similar: once the image is owned and catalogued by culture, its referent is no longer important. The blankness of nature in some of Cole's paintings—the seeming absence of history from the represented wilderness—invited history to write itself on the landscape in the form of a display of technological power. Of course the very intrusion of the painter or photographer begins to transform the landscape; the natural scene is compromised as Cole mixes his paints. The selection and composition of specific images, proposed by Cole's compositional aesthetic, are the mechanics of control.

The representational possibilities of photographic technology inspire Holmes to envision a structure of control more direct than Cole's, and more efficient for the technological appropriation of form: "The consequence of this [proliferation of photographic images] will soon be such an enormous collection of forms that they will have to be classified and arranged in vast libraries, as books are now" ("Stereoscope," 748). As an aid to this encyclopedic project, Holmes proposes a standardized system of photographic representation, including "a stereographic *metre*, or fixed standard of focal length for the camera lens, to furnish by its multiples or fractions, if necessary, the scale of distances, and the standard power in the stereoscope-lens. In this way the eye can make the most rapid and exact comparisons" (748).[19] Motivating this obsession with order is a fear of the possibility of the chaotic, random production of images.

Holmes also wants war to be contained and controlled in this photographic encyclopedia: "The next European war will send us stereographs of battles. It is asserted that a bursting shell can be photographed. The time is perhaps at hand when a flash of light, as sudden and brief as that of the lightning which shows a whirling wheel standing stock still, shall preserve the very instant of the shock of contact of the mighty armies that are even now gathering" (748). Practical technology was at least thirty years behind Holmes's vision of stop-action photography. But the location of his prediction within the context of the call for an encyclopedia of photographic forms is significant. The assumption that in 1859 pictures of war—of "the mighty armies that are even now gathering"—are very soon to be gotten from Europe strikes the modern reader as a mistaken insight. On the eve of the Civil War, Holmes regards photographic history to be a European, not an American, project. The firm of Brady & Co., however, was ready.

Both the Union and the Confederacy came to embrace the position that war was the only way to resolve questions of political representation and control of the American land. This position required the transformation of violence into ideological signs. When the corpses of soldiers were textually or visually represented within the scene of the landscape, they became objects appropriated by the state no less than the land itself over which they fought. The dead soldier—Northern or Southern—was the sign of an individual whose autonomy was surrendered to the ideology of the Union. As Scarry argues, no matter what political beliefs are held by an individual soldier, his death or injury is a referentially unstable sign that is appropriated by the discourse of war to legitimate the ideology of the victor state (117). During and after the Civil War, photographic representation of corpses in the landscape was an important mechanism of the legitimation by means of appropriation.

VII. *The Political Import of American Scenery*

Three important features characterized the semiotics of visual representational media in mid-nineteenth-century America. The pastoral evaded historical processes and conflicts in favor of an idealized image of "America." The picturesque located value in the subordination of parts to the unity of the whole. Photographic representation became part of an efficient technics of control and appropriation of nature and persons. Relations between political conservatism and these tenets and consequences of the organicist aesthetic were historically constructed in such a way that organicism could be effectively mobilized in the legitimation of the American nation-state in the postbellum years.

To extrapolate from aesthetics to politics is often difficult, especially when the artifact or aesthetic theory under examination does not display a manifestly "political" content.[20] The picturesque as such is not inherently "Unionist." The pastoral may be conservative in a general sense; but the important questions are, what is conserved and what is interdicted?

TRACES OF WAR

The values these aesthetics place on formal, organic unity and harmony can and did bolster a nationalism theorized in terms of a totalizing model of the state—a model that assumed that the state was indivisible and that its citizens must kill and die in order to maintain this indivisibility. We have seen how Whitman's organicist poetics, including pastoralism (an ideal he shared with Lincoln) and tropes of embodiment and typification, encoded the Northern Unionist ideology at a crucial historical moment. The picturesque visual aesthetic was suited to a similar ideological operation. In structuring the representation of the Civil War it promoted the preservation of the Union as inscribed by Federalist tradition in the Constitution. The value placed by the nineteenth-century American picturesque on a particular form of representation that subordinated parts to the whole, and the naturalizing rhetoric that legitimated this sort of subordination, became readable, within the political context of mid-nineteenth-century America, as predictive signs of Union. To use Fredric Jameson's term, these are instances of "transcoding," by means of which political values and aesthetic values appear contemporarily in homologous forms of ideological representation (40).

The nationalistic theory of the American picturesque proposed that

American Scenery has an import of the highest order. The diversified landscapes of our country exert no slight influence in creating our character as individuals, and in confirming our destiny as a nation. Oceans, mountains, rivers, cataracts, wild woods, fragrant prairies, and melodious winds, are elements and exemplifications of that general harmony which subsists throughout the universe, and which is most potent over the most valuable minds. (Putnam, 3)

But because "national intellect receives a prevailing tone from the peculiar scenery that most abounds" (4), the political project of ensuring a unified nationalism requires that the diversity of the landscape be subject to a totalizing image. There is an implication that if the sceneries of different geographical regions were too individualized or "peculiar" they would produce radically diverse "national intellects," which could lead to the fragmentation of a coherent national ideology. The complex harmony of the American landscape ("the book of nature, which is the art of God" [5]) came to signify the naturalness of the complex harmony of the Union of States. Civil War photographers mobilized these values to control the landscape and to naturalize the body of the soldier as a pastoral feature of that landscape. In this way they justified the use of violence as a means to maintain a political structure.

106

4. Some Versions of Pastoral:
Brady and Gardner

TO THE modern eye, one of the most remarkable features of Civil War battlefield photography is its uniformity.[1] The compositional repertoire available to the Civil War photographer involved the position, angle, and distance of the camera relative to the objects, the choice of the focal length and aperture of the lens, and the sensitivity to light (in modern terms, the "speed") of the emulsion coating the negative plate. The technology of the wet-plate process, which required that each plate be prepared in the field in a transportable darkroom and then be exposed for at least several seconds, limited the photographer's capabilities. But aesthetic conventions were also important in determining the appearance of the image. Adherence to conventions that derived from the contemporary landscape aesthetic produced a set of regularized representations—an archive of straight-on shots and compositionally balanced images taken at middle to long distances. The camera was nearly always placed at normal eye level, usually angled slightly or moderately downward. Except for portraits, the horizontal dimension of the image is greater than the vertical dimension, as in contemporary landscape paintings.[2]

Photographers sometimes rearranged the objects to be photographed, in order to compose the image for aesthetic or narratival purposes. Such intervention is obvious in a photograph of a mutilated corpse by Alexander Gardner (fig. 6). Its title in Gardner's 1863 catalogue reads, "War, effect of a shell on a Confederate soldier at Battle of Gettysburg" (26). Even without this explanatory text it is clear that the image is composed to display cause and effect—note the artillery shell above the right knee. The musket across the knee directing our attention to the shell, the severed hand beside the trigger of the musket, and the canteen near the head of the corpse are additional signs of the photographer's intervention. It would seem that in the absence of such deliberate composition, the image of the violated corpse would have fully spoken for itself—for nothing but an artillery shell was likely to produce such damage (and if the destruction had some other immediate cause, would it matter?). However, the photographer was impelled to control the trace of violence by carefully inscribing signs of a narrative in the image he was producing, rationalizing

FIG. 6. Alexander Gardner, "War, effect of a shell on a Confederate soldier at Battle of Gettysburg" (1863). Library of Congress.

its horror in terms of an orderly assertion of cause and effect (shell and wound). Gardner's self-conscious photographic artistry thus represents an impulse to control images of rupture by subordinating them to the visual unity of the composition—much in the way that Whitman's organicist political and poetic ideology transformed traces of violence into signs of Union. Perhaps Gardner realized that the technics of control could not be entirely successful in "War, effect of a shell": he included no such powerful trace of violence in his historical album, *Gardner's Photographic Sketch Book of the Civil War* (1866).

Single images, regularized by means of generic conventions, self-conscious manipulation, and explanatory captions, were catalogued beginning early in the Civil War. Prints could be purchased directly or by mail from firms such as E. and H. T. Anthony of New York and

Gardner's gallery in Washington.[3] The organizing categories of these catalogues were primarily geographic location and military structure (company, regiment, and the like); thus they subsumed individual images under a single "emergent totality" that gave meaning to the parts (Trachtenberg, 3). In spite of this appearance of the completeness of the archive, most of the photographs are distanced from the interior of the war—especially from actual combat—and show only limited aspects of its history. Trachtenberg points out that Gardner's *Sketch Book* underrepresents the experience of the common soldier by privileging the perspective of the officer who sees only "the mass of soldiers filling in the scene" rather than a group comprised of individual men (23). It especially underrepresents the horrors of war by excluding views such as "War, effect of a shell."

One important condition regulating Civil War photography proscribed any representation of the borderline between life and death. The dead were fit subjects of memorialization—especially if the bodies appeared relatively intact, as they do in the photographs of the dead included in Gardner's *Sketch Book*—but the wounded were not memorialized in this way. Technological limitations were significant. It was impossible with bulky cameras, long exposure times, and the cumbersome wet-plate process to produce images such as Robert Capa's famous photograph from the Spanish Civil War of a soldier falling at the moment he is hit by a bullet.[4] But certain technologically possible kinds of representations of death and other repulsive subjects were also proscribed. Confederate dead appear far more frequently than Federal dead.[5] The bodies of the dead soldiers are nearly always shown intact. Few photographs exist of amputees, and none were published in Gardner's or Barnard's albums. Hospital scenes were primarily architectural views, sometimes populated by stewards, ambulance drivers, and the like—those who are *not* wounded. In those hospital interiors that show patients, signs of wounds such as bandages or crutches are minimally represented.[6]

The photographic archive contemporarily ascribed to Mathew Brady was in fact the combined work of several other photographers; of these, Alexander Gardner, George Barnard, Timothy O'Sullivan, and James Gibson are most important. Brady himself was an entrepreneur who only occasionally worked in the field. At the beginning of the war he employed Gardner and Barnard as his chief field operatives. Both men later resigned to accept military appointments. Gardner's official duties as photographer to the Army of the Potomac under General McClellan were limited to the photographic reproduction of maps and documents; at this time his battlefield photography was a private sideline. When McClellan was dismissed, Gardner's military appointment lapsed and he operated as a private entrepreneur. Barnard, whose *Photographic Views of Sherman's Campaign* will be discussed in Chapter 5, held a post as attaché to the Corps of Engineers of the Military Division of the Mississippi under General Sherman. His official duties, unlike Gardner's, included the taking of views (Milhollen and Mugridge, xi). While neither Timothy O'Sullivan nor James Gibson (both of whom worked first for Brady and later for Gardner) ever held a military appointment, obviously they too received the approval and cooperation of the officers at the sites where they operated, sometimes photographing the dead while army burial details worked nearby.[7] Thus Federal military authority exercised considerable but not complete control over the formation of the Brady archive. While newspaper reports were often censored by the War Department (Andrews, 648–50), no research to date has suggested any government interference with the commercial operations of photographic galleries. It is necessary here to distinguish between physical control and ideological directive, both of which structured the production of war photography.[8]

Representational possibilities were prescribed not only by military authority, but also by the traditions of the visual arts that came to be mobilized in support of the Unionist ideology: namely, the pastoral simplification or evasion of history, the organicism of the picturesque mode of visual representation, and the use of visual representation as a technology of appropriation. Within the aesthetic context of organicist realism, the conventions of the pastoral mode came to be employed to read the photographic traces of death in war. But representations of wounded men (who exist precariously on the border between life and death) could not be recuperated so easily by means of pastoralism. Images of intact, dead bodies show that death in general is "natural"; in contrast, wounds appear to be "unnatural." The interdiction of the wound effaces consciousness of the central activity of war, which is injuring, and thus functions to naturalize the historical and political forces that demand this activity. The life of the soldier can be described as a necessary "expenditure," his death as a "by-product," thus marginalizing the physical events of war that transform life into death.[9] In this way, the photographic archive obscured the place of violence in history.

I. *Pastoralism and the Formation of the Brady Archive*

In Gardner's *Photographic Sketch Book of the Civil War*, a photograph captioned "Stone Church, Centreville, Va., March, 1862" is accompanied by a text that describes the war as a violation of the pastoral harmony of a small town and the surrounding countryside:

> Perched upon the gentle slope of the ridge that bears its name, and looking across the fertile fields to the mountains that rise up grandly hiding the West, Centreville had smiled on many generations . . . . There was always an odor of wild roses and honeysuckles about it, and a genial hospitality to welcome the stranger. War crushed it, piled earthworks upon its ruins to protect hostile camps, built cantonments in its gardens. Scarcely a vestige of its former self remains. Redoubts and riflepits stretch along its knolls; graves, half hidden by the grass, tell where the dead of both armies slumber, and the spot now only interests the visitor because of the wreck that has come upon it. (4)[10]

In the photograph (fig. 7) the primary evidence of war appears in the figures of Federal soldiers who are posing for the camera, not in the sort of disfiguration of the land described in the text. The landscape itself looks much as it would have on any March day prior to the war. This land, the text goes on to suggest, is hardy and restorative; its permanence contrasts with the momentary disruption of the pastoral scene effected by the war:

> Through all of these scenes a few of its people have lived and suffered, faithful to their homes. Others are turning back from uncertain wanderings to the resting place of their fathers, and, with returning peace, the husbandman finds that nature has not forgotten its fruitfulness in the years of war and devastation. (4)

Trachtenberg argues that we can "accept" the pastoralism of Gardner's explanatory text "only as long as we repress a troublesome question: what does the only determinate act recorded in the image—the making of the photograph itself—have to do with Gardner's metaphor? The most immediate fact registered by the image is the presence of a camera at this particular scene. Why is it there?" (16). Trachtenberg describes the relations between the photographs and their accompanying explications, finding the pastoral explication of the photograph of "Stone Church, Centreville" to exemplify the relations between text and image throughout the *Sketch Book*: "In almost all instances the picture can be turned against the text." Such contradictions reveal "Gardner's effort to contain the image, to suffuse or saturate its quiddity with ideological import" (16). Trachtenberg does not pursue the topic of pastoralism,

Fɪɢ. 7. "Stone Church, Centreville, Va., March, 1862," *Gardner's Photographic Sketch Book of the Civil War*, plate 4. Library of Congress.

concentrating instead on the ways in which the archive of Civil War photography reinforces two important ideological lessons of the war— that the technological superiority of the North assured its victory and that the victory was aided by rigid obedience to a hierarchy that subordinated common soldiers to officers and blacks to whites. These lessons are the reasons that Gardner's camera is "there," recording a given scene.

However, the question of pastoralism is not confined to Gardner's image and text representing the church at Centreville. It is central to all battlefield photography of the Civil War. As early as July 1862, a review in the *New York Times* posed the question of pastoralism in relation to war photography. The brief history of photography that opens the review suggests that the Civil War is a disruption of pastoral harmony:

Photography came to us smilingly and trippingly, fragrant with meadows and beautiful with landscapes, seemingly the handmaid of Peace. She had a bucolic air. Vague rumor, it is true, stated that she was not the pastoral maid that the popular imagination painted her; that she used gun-cotton liberally in the making of her toilette, and indulged in vitreous acids and sulphuric mixtures with unbecoming freedom. But such rumors floated unheeded by, or were but noticed to be stamped as slanders. Consequently, one may be pardoned for starting with surprise when she suddenly flashes from the clouds, helmeted, plumed, and be-belted, at once the Minerva and the Clio of the war. ("Photographic Phases")

The transformation of photography from pastoral maid to patroness of commerce and muse of history is more than a comment on the emergence of the new genre of documentary photography ("Minerva" is relevant because this was a commercial enterprise). By finding a trace of war— "gun-cotton," the main ingredient in collodion—in the photographic process itself, the reviewer suggests that the pastoral mode of antebellum photography attempted to elide a certain intrinsic violence.[11] From the vantage point of 1862, that is, even the apparently apolitical representational medium of photography becomes a harbinger of (in the words of Seward) the "irrepressible conflict." Yet that photographic trace of violent rupture also contains the means to repair itself: collodion had only two common uses in the nineteenth century—as a vehicle for the light-sensitive chemicals in a photographic emulsion, and as a surgical dressing for wounds and burns. A metaphorical bandage, the pastoral photographic text attempted to hide and heal the wound even while marking it.

This review allegorizes an opposition between two ways of organizing the nationalist ideology: the ground of "American" experience was sometimes proposed as pastoral agrarianism (whose figure is the pastoral maid), sometimes as progressive, mercantile, or industrial capitalism (whose figures are Minerva and Clio). Leo Marx argues that in the reconciliation of this opposition a progressive version of pastoralism emerged as the dominant cultural mode, able to recuperate the newly emerging economic and technological structures of life.[12] In wartime the pastoral impulse to naturalization eased more overt anxieties about politics, violence, and death. The trace of war that the *Times* reviewer finds in Brady's photography may reveal that American pastoralism was a failed project; and yet the nostalgia encoded in the pastoral also bespeaks an impulse to recover that project. As we have seen in the case of Whitman's

FIG. 8. "Scenes on the Battlefield of Antietam," *Harper's Weekly,* 18 October 1862, pp. 664–65. University of Virginia Library, Special Collections Department.

texts, the close of the war brought with it attempts to reconstruct the pastoral ideal and to mobilize it in healing the rupture in history produced by the war. For these reasons, the pastoral maid is a figure no less appropriate, contemporarily, than Clio for much of the photography of the Civil War.

Since it was written before the photographic record of the aftermath of Antietam, this review does not mention any photographs of the dead.

When such photographs did become publicly available, they seemed at once similar to and different from the landscape views with which nineteenth-century Americans were familiar. Within this aesthetic context, battlefield photographs invited a consideration of their relationship to the pastoral mode of visual representation—partly because they were landscape views and partly because of the prevalent narrative of the war in general as a violation of the American pastoral ideal. If the war was a rupture, the landscape itself was represented as having a restorative power that could be mobilized by the photographic medium.

"Brady's" series from Antietam, exhibited at his New York gallery in October 1862, included the first photographic representations of corpses on the battlefield ever seen by the American (or any other) public.[13] Journalists paid more attention to these photographs than to any others made during the war (Frassanito, *Antietam*, 17). They were reviewed by the *New York Times* (20 October 1862) and discussed by Oliver Wendell Holmes, Sr., in the *Atlantic*. A few were reproduced as wood engravings in *Harper's Weekly*, but these engravings minimize the importance of the representation of corpses (18 October 1862, 664–65). The focal point and by far the largest image in the two-page layout is a picturesque view of Burnside Bridge; the figure in the top-center image evokes a contemplative view of the neatly aligned corpses that are represented (fig. 8).

The reviewer for the *Times* begins by imagining the reaction of New York civilians if one morning they found "a few dripping bodies, fresh from the field, laid along the pavement" of Broadway. The usual method of reporting casualties was to publish a list of names, but "our sensations might be different if the newspaper carrier left the names on the battlefield and the bodies at our door instead." The body is a more palpable sign than the text; thus the reviewer announces the *reality* of the photographic image as his primary topic. Photographs are said to have a force, more powerful than written reports, to make the war seem actual to those who are removed from it: " Mr. Brady has done something to bring home to us the terrible reality and earnestness of war. If he has not brought bodies and laid them in our dooryards and along the streets, he has done something very like it" ("Pictures of the Dead"). Yet this account of the power of the images depends on an experiential gap between the civilian milieu and certain events of the war, which representation cannot bridge. Even the most realistic representation of war (supposing Brady had transported actual corpses to the streets of New York) is not equivalent to the "terrible reality and earnestness of war" as experienced by the soldiers, even though the photographs are credited with bringing the war home.

But through its mystified claims for the palpability of the photographs, the *Times* review identifies a genuine and seldom noticed absence in Civil War photography: "There is one side of the picture that the sun did not catch, one phase that has escaped photographic skill. It is the background of widows and orphans, torn from the bosom of their natural protectors by the red remorseless hand of Battle. . . . All of this desolation imagination must paint—broken hearts cannot be photographed" ("Pictures of the Dead"). The allegorical figure of Liberty may grieve at the bier of Lincoln in Thomas Nast's famous engraving for *Harper's* (29 April 1865), but in photographs mothers, fathers, siblings, wives, and children are never shown mourning their loved ones killed in battle. (Very occasionally a grieving woman is represented in an engraving; but there are no war-related photographs analogous to, for example, H. P. Robinson's sentimental photograph "Fading Away.")

The knowledge produced by the photograph "can, finally, never be ethical or political knowledge . . . [but] will always be some kind of sentimentalism, whether cynical or humanist" (Sontag, 24). Brady's Antietam series supplied the knowledge that death is one result of war. This obvious fact may have been news to the civilian public, accustomed as they were to the heroic rhetoric of history paintings and engravings that evaded the issue by glamorizing death—and by showing very little of it. (Most Americans had never heard of Goya, nor seen his horrifying series *Los desastres de la guerra*.) But even in the case of photography, as Susan Sontag argues, "the camera's rendering of reality must always hide more than it discloses" (23). That is, although Brady's photographs document deaths resulting from war, they do not represent death in war; they do not produce any significant (that is, unsentimental) political or ethical knowledge of the relations between the Unionist ideology and the presence of corpses on a battlefield. There are only images of lifeless bodies—from which the experiences of dying in (or living through) battle cannot in any important sense be inferred, and which cannot reveal the politics that demanded these experiences.

If photographs are to serve any political purpose, Walter Benjamin argues, they must be captioned in such a way as to control the viewer's "free-floating contemplation" (226). Thus the distance between the unrepresented effects of the war on the civilian population and the photographic trace of the effect of war on the soldiers' bodies induces the *Times* reviewer to appeal to pastoralism (which he found in his first review to be characteristic of antebellum photography) in an attempt to control the traces of war that appeared in photography in 1862. He begins by comparing the photographs of the dead to bodies "fresh from the field," suggesting a pastoral conceit that Gardner and O'Sullivan would also adopt: a "harvest of death." The times would not allow the author to draw, from the proposition that death is a necessary feature of war, the conclusion that the Civil War ought to have been prevented, or ought now to be stopped. Instead, a melancholic, contemplative attitude is called for—a meditation on the desolation of the landscape and of the bodies within it:

> They are taken as they fell, their poor hands clutching the grass
> around them in spasms of pain. . . . The ground whereon they lie
> is torn by shot and shell, the grass is trampled down by the tread
> of hot, hurrying feet, and little rivulets that can scarcely be of water
> are trickling along the earth like tears over a mother's face. It is
> a bleak, barren plain and above it bends an ashen sullen sky; there
> is no friendly shade or shelter from the noonday sun or the midnight
> dews. ("Pictures of the Dead")

There are several dewy notes here. The description develops a sentimental,
even beautiful scene—and does so despite the announcement of realism
as the primary topic of the review. The reviewer (and, one assumes,
most of the readers of the *Times*) does not consider realism and sentimental
pastoralism to be separate aesthetic categories.

The reviewer affirms the pastoral rhetoric of the image, which
inscribes politics in the landscape only as a natural fact. Rather than making
something of the historical significance of the first photographic representations of battlefield dead in human history, he informs his account
with the pictorial conventions of the established genre of pastoral landscape. The corpses and the terrain harmonize to present a unified image
of desolation. The inversion of the pastoral does not produce antipastoral,
but preserves the essential conventions of the mode, one of which is the
invocation of the pathetic fallacy. The landscape is in sympathy with
man as mother earth sheds tears for her children. Thus the reviewer's
acceptance of the war as a fact of nature becomes the strongest possible
endorsement for its inevitability and necessity.

Two conclusions are proposed for this strange idyll, one imagined,
the other real, but neither pointing in the direction of political consciousness. First, the reviewer describes a funeral according to the conventions
of the pastoral elegy, in which the "corpse should be strewn with the
rarest flowers that Spring brings or Summer leaves." But this Arcadian
funeral is acknowledged to be a fantasy, because in reality the corpses
had probably been put by "rude hands" into "a shallow trench, hastily
dug." The second ending mitigates this harsh reality by recounting the
theology of the Rapture in some anonymous lines of verse: "With pealing
of trumpets and beating of drums, / These trenches shall open—the Son
of Man comes." We ought not let the comic effect (on the modern reader)
of the poetic meter distract from the way in which this Christian piety—
the appeal to the teleology of the Apocalypse—provides a contemporarily
satisfying end to the scene of grief. This narrative pulls the spectator
out of the elegiac reverie. However, the teleology of the Apocalypse

refers not to history but to the end of history. Thus it enables the evasion of the particular moral and political issues—of autonomy, of choice, of representation—which could easily be raised in response to these images of corpses on a battlefield. By announcing the topic of photographic realism and then ignoring it to sentimentalize the photographic images, the text performs a pastoral operation—suggesting that the forces that placed these victims at Antietam need not be examined.

Oliver Wendell Holmes, Sr., one of the most important photographic critics in nineteenth-century America, also reviewed Brady's Antietam series, in an essay in the *Atlantic* which otherwise ignores the fact that a war is presently taking place. Appealing, like the *Times* reviewer, to the "dread reality" of the photographs, Holmes proclaims: "Let him who wishes to know what war is look at this series of illustrations" ("Doings," 11). But whereas the announced purpose of the *Times* reviewer is to display this "reality," Holmes's impulse is to remove it from sight. Holmes himself had been near the scene of a battle some months earlier in searching for his wounded son and described this experience for the readers of the *Atlantic* in "My Hunt after 'The Captain.'" These photographs evoke memories of that frantic time before he found that his son was not seriously hurt and was recovering well: "It was so nearly like visiting the battle-field to look over these views, that all the emotions excited by the actual sight of the sordid scene, strewed with rags and wrecks, came back to us, and we buried them in the recesses of our cabinet as we would have buried the mutilated remains of the dead they too vividly represented" ("Doings," 12).

Trachtenberg identifies, beyond Holmes's emotional response, an additional reason why the photographs must be "buried"—which is that Holmes finds a "potential fissure" in his Brahmin ideology: "The seeable represented the unspeakable: was the Union worth the cost?" (10). And yet Holmes's reading of the photograph does not depend on economic metaphors; in order to recuperate the traces of violence, he appeals, like the *Times* reviewer, to an organic system of visual and political representation. Holmes employs two of the tropes that Whitman favored to organize the meanings of the war, subsuming the trope of ritual sacrifice ("martyrdom") under the master-trope of the body politic:

> The sight of these pictures is a commentary on civilization such as a savage might well triumph to show its missionaries. Yet through such martyrdom must come our redemption. War is the surgery of crime. Bad as it is in itself, it always implies that something worse has gone before. Where is the American, worthy of his privileges,

who does not now recognize the fact, if never until now, that the
disease of our nation was organic, not functional, calling for the
knife, and not for washes and anodynes? ("Doings," 12)

Whitman never explicitly calls for "the knife," but in other respects his
political semiotic shares much with that of Holmes. For both, the meaning
not only of "America" but also of "civilization" in general consists in
the health of a body politic into which the bodies of individuals disappear,
especially in wartime.

Holmes attempts to cancel the representation of the dead not simply
by burying their photographic traces in his cabinet, but also by writing
over those traces an organicist text representing the war as the removal
of the cancers of slavery and rebellion from the single body of the Union.
While the *Times* review remains largely within the "apolitical" discourse
of the pastoral mode, Holmes brings the photographs into contact with
political discourse. Both, however, like Whitman, recuperate traces of
violence with appeals to a naturalizing, organicist mode of representation,
the functioning of which depends on a simplification that produces internal
harmony and unity.

II. *Gardner's "Harvest of Death"*

In 1866 Alexander Gardner published *Gardner's Photographic Sketch Book
of the Civil War,* a two-volume album of one hundred 7-x-9-inch prints,
each accompanied by an explanatory text. It was too expensive (at $150)
to be widely popular, but it did find a small market in legislators and
other officials in Washington, where Gardner's gallery was located (Cobb,
127). The title of the album problematizes the relationship of photography
to the history of the war, seeming to anticipate Valéry's observation that
history in the age of photography has become a series of disconnected
"moments": "All that is left consists of those components of the narrative
or the thesis that originate in the mind and are consequently imaginary"
(195). Gardner's preface to the *Sketch Book* argues for the superiority of
photographs over texts for the purpose of historical representation: "Verbal representations of . . . places, or scenes, may or may not have the
merit of accuracy; but photographic presentments of them will be accepted
by posterity with an undoubting faith." Texts, according to Gardner,
are *re*-presentations; photographs are "presentments." This unusual choice
of word invokes the authority of legal or ecclesiastical usage (these are
the most prevalent senses given by the *OED*), suggesting that the sense

FIG. 9. "Ruins of Stone Bridge, Bull Run, Va., March, 1862," *Gardner's Photographic Sketch Book of the Civil War,* plate 7. Library of Congress.

of "presentness" conveyed by the photograph is an undeniable, even metaphysical truth supported by tradition and faith, rather than a cultural construct open to critical evaluation. The usage seems particularly ironic because early photographs (more obviously than the "action" shots of modern photojournalists) could only record the aftermath of a battle, days or years after it was fought.

Gardner's claim for the presentness of the photographs is especially interesting in regard to the first battle of Manassas (an embarrassing defeat for the Union army, witnessed firsthand by many Washington civilians who went out to watch the nearby battle). Although the battle took place in July 1861, the photographs of the area reproduced in the *Sketch Book* are dated March 1862, when Jackson's forces retreated toward Richmond to regroup with Lee and the Federal army gained control of the ground, thus permitting the locale to be photographed. (Federal forces lost the ground again in August, with the second battle of Manassas.) No photographs exist of the events of First Manassas. Mathew Brady was the only photographer who claimed to be on the scene during the battle. But although *Humphrey's Journal,* a contemporary trade magazine for photographers, claimed that Brady had documented the panicked Union retreat from the site and thus "fixed the cowards beyond the possibility of a doubt" (Horan, 39), it is doubtful that he did get any such photographs, or that the editor of *Humphrey's* saw any, because none were offered for sale in Brady's or any other gallery's catalogue (Frassanito, *Antietam*, 30).

Gardner's *Sketch Book* reproduces eight views of the locale: three from Manassas Junction, three from Centreville (including "Stone Church, Centreville," fig. 7), and two from Bull Run.[14] One of the texts mentions the Union retreat; it supplies, if we recall Valéry's formulation, a great deal more historical narration than the photograph, "Ruins of Stone Bridge, Bull Run" (fig. 9), seems to demand:

> The fighting had nearly ceased [in the first battle of Manassas], and Gen. McDowell was expressing his thanks to some of his officers for their services, when Johnston's reinforcements from Winchester suddenly appeared in the rear of our right, and threw our lines into utter confusion. A feeble attempt was made to repulse the attack, but the regiments rapidly broke to pieces, and forming a mass of terror-stricken fugitives, rushed from the field down across the bridge, which soon became obstructed with wagons, and to prevent pursuit by the enemy was destroyed. (7)

The photograph does not evoke this event. The formal, picturesque qualities of the image restore order to the chaos suggested by the narrative—as does the last sentence of Gardner's text: "A portion of this ground was fought over in the battles of Gen. Pope in 1862, and hundreds of acres still bear evidences of those fearful scenes." (There is no mention that the Federal army lost this battle.)

The viewer is left with a sense of pastoral melancholy, from which Gardner's minimal military history does not distract. This pleasant, contemplative experience is incompatible with the horror of battle. The land itself, rather than the experiences of the men who fought and died on it, is the only subject of the image. The fallen trees and ruined bridge do "bear evidences" of the battle. But the scene is composed according to the conventions of the picturesque landscape, in which stone ruins are only remnants of some long-forgotten human presence. The contemplative figure in the middle distance asks the viewer to meditate on the picturesque qualities of the view, not on the retreat of the "terror-stricken fugitives" mentioned in the narrative. The bridge functions, as it conventionally does in picturesque landscapes, as an integrative compositional device, ensuring the harmony of the image and the land it represents.

FIG. 10. "Fortifications on the Heights of Centreville, Va., March, 1862,"
Gardner's Photographic Sketch Book of the Civil War, plate 5. Library of
Congress.

Bridges figure similarly in Gardner's selection from "Brady's" Antietam series. Views of the two bridges, along with one of Dunker Church,
one of a Signal Corps tower, and one of Lincoln's visit to the battlefield,
comprise the record in the *Sketch Book* of what would come to be called
"America's bloodiest day."[15] In the *Harper's* reproduction of "Brady's"
photographs from Antietam (fig. 8), a view of Burnside Bridge (the more
picturesque of the two bridges), peopled with two soldiers and a horse-
drawn wagon so as to imitate a pastoral composition, occupied the center
of a two-page layout. It is surrounded by smaller views, some of which
represent corpses. The composition indicates the ideological center of
the pastoral view of war. Nothing can be done to efface completely the

photographic traces of death; but the aestheticized landscape is the center of attention, marginalizing the dead.

Gardner's texts repeatedly reinforce the pastoralism of his images by suggesting that the land itself possesses a restorative power; where there were once earthwork fortifications, there are now (after the war) fertile fields, because "The soil composing [the earthworks] is of a light character, and washes away in every rain, filling up the ditches and reducing the sharply defined works to sloping mounds, over which the farmer's plow is already turning the furrow" (11). Nature is recomposing itself according to the pastoral landscape aesthetic. Gardner counts on this recomposition to efface even those traces of war that his camera had recorded. But he also equates the Federal army with this restorative force. Noting the devastation caused by the battle, he writes that later "Federal camps were established, and with the return of spring much of that which disfigured the landscape utterly disappeared" (10). The identification of Federal occupation of the land with the restoration of the pastoral landscape remains a significant theme throughout the album.

Demonstrating his awareness of the reception of photography as a pastoral or picturesque mode, Gardner often shows more interest in the landscape than in military history. Rather than narrating the history of the "Fortifications on the Heights of Centreville, Va." (fig. 10), the text describes the scene with an artist's judgment:

> The view from the crest of the works was very fine. To the east was a wide area of undulating country, covered with dense woods, and with grassy hill-sides, here and there smiling to each other over the forests. Looking west the eye rested on a fertile valley, watered by countless streams, dotted with farm-houses and herds. . . . All this section was devastated by the armies, and is [now a] wilderness, overgrown with bushes, rank weeds, and running briars. (5)

The war has, according to the text, transformed the middle landscape of agrarian America into a forbidding waste; yet the artist's imagination, which perceives the view to be "very fine," is not disturbed by the wilderness. The relation of the soldiers and fortifications occupying the foreground of the image to history and also to the landscape is now uncertain. Why do they guard the wild overgrowth mentioned in the text—which in any case we cannot clearly see? In the middle of this desolate expanse, they seem removed from history. One of the soldiers plays with a dog, but none seems connected to anything or to anyone else—their gazes are locked on the camera lens, except for one who stares off to the left, refusing even the strange form of social contact offered by the presence of a camera. But as we have seen, other texts from the Manassas series suggest that these Federal soldiers stand guard over nature in the process of restoring itself, preventing Confederate troops from despoiling the land and transforming it yet again into waste land. The camera constructs their relation to this recuperative process.

Many other of Gardner's texts are equally conscious of pastoralism. Plate 36 of the *Sketch Book* (fig. 11) is entitled "A Harvest of Death." This title and the title for plate 37 (fig. 12), "Field Where General Reynolds Fell," may have been inspired by an engraved reproduction in *Harper's* of a two-plate, composite print attributed to Brady, "Wheat-Field in Which General Reynolds Was Shot." "Brady's" image depicts a pond bordered behind with a rail fence; a human figure (apparently a civilian) stands with his back toward us surveying the field and woods behind the pond. The figure is most likely Brady himself (Davis, 3:394–95). The only hint of battle is that one section of the fence has been opened. The engraving reproduces the composite view quite accurately, subtracting nothing of interest and adding only a few spears of grass to define the edge of the pond more clearly (*Harper's Weekly*, 22 August 1863, 532). The scene has a bucolic air, suggesting that these events of the war are closely connected to the agrarian middle landscape. General Reynolds was in fact shot, and died, in McPherson's woods, visible in the background of "Brady's" view (Frassanito, *Gettysburg*, 225). But Gardner evidently accepted the authority of Brady's caption, magnifying the error by writing a short history of the battle:

> The cavalry had just taken up the last available line of defense beyond Gettysburg, when, at eleven o'clock, General Reynolds arrived with the 1st corps on a double-quick. . . . Appreciating the importance of holding the seminary ridge, [he] rode out into the field, and directed the posting of troops, and while engaged in this work, received a shot in the neck, falling lifeless to the earth. (37)

Gardner may not have had access to a detailed, authoritative history. Or perhaps he felt that to be shot in a woods was not quite heroic enough for a general.[16]

Although the captions and texts were "in all probability written by Gardner himself," we cannot be certain (Newhall, Introduction, iii). The caption, "A Harvest of Death," remained unchanged from its first publication in Gardner's gallery catalogue from 1863 (Frassanito, *Gettys-*

FIG. 11. "A Harvest of Death, Gettysburg, July, 1863," *Gardner's Photographic Sketch Book of the Civil War,* plate 36. Library of Congress.

burg, 228, 234). It is not known who invented the caption—whether Gardner or Timothy O'Sullivan (who made the negative) or someone else. The identification of the site of Reynolds's death was added to the caption of plate 37 when it was reproduced in the *Sketch Book,* perhaps in imitation of Brady's earlier caption (which is only assumed to have been invented by Brady himself). It seems fruitless to speculate about the origin of these captions, since the relevant records have been lost. What is clear, amid this uncertainty about authorship, is that those involved in the production and distribution of war photographs found something compelling in the relation of agrarian metaphors to these photographs of the dead.

The text of the *Sketch Book* often seems to be of two minds. The immediate referent of the caption, "A Harvest of Death," is the Grim Reaper; the political context suggests that the represented Confederate dead are the fruit of the rebellion cut down in the field and left to

FIG. 12. "Field Where General Reynolds Fell, Gettysburg, July, 1863," *Gardner's Photographic Sketch Book of the Civil War*, plate 37. Library of Congress.

decompose into the land. The photograph thus becomes a symbol of the death and decay of the Confederacy that fertilizes the new growth of the Union (fig. 11). In the case of the image of "our own men," however, the text represents an impulse to revitalize the dead of the war, to imagine that the reaper has not harvested a crop of bodies (fig. 12): "The faces of all were pale, as though cut in marble, and as the wind swept across the battle-field it waved the hair, and gave the bodies such an appearance of life that a spectator could hardly help thinking they were about to rise to continue the fight" (37). The power of nature, present in the wind blowing over the wheat field, is the alibi for the imagined resurrection— although photographic representation in general necessarily excludes the possibility of motion (and even its conventional sign, a static blur, is absent from this image). And yet in this text there is something manifestly "unnatural," which derives from a clash of modes. Statues ("cut in marble") may not come to life except in romance. The pastoral generally does not revitalize, but sentimentalizes or marginalizes death. This particular text displays (albeit unwittingly) the *rupture* in the organicist ideology effected by the violation of bodies: it momentarily gives up the "realistic" pastoral in favor of pure fantasy.

The first sentences of the text accompanying "A Harvest of Death" locate the scene at sunrise. In this setting the lack of clarity in the background of the image can be attributed to fog, whereas in fact it is a function of lens aperture. The comparatively shallow depth of focus compels the viewer to concentrate on the presence of the corpses in the field of flattened stalks of wheat. This aspect of the composition was undoubtedly a conscious choice on O'Sullivan's part, since he could easily have chosen a smaller aperture ring (and lengthened the exposure time accordingly) in order to produce a greater depth of focus that would emphasize the standing and mounted soldiers in the background. The text capitalizes on the composition of the image, invoking the supposed sympathy of nature to the tragic event: "Slowly, over the misty fields of Gettysburg—as all reluctant to expose their ghastly horrors to the light— came the sunless morn, after the retreat of Lee's broken army. Through the shadowy vapors, it was, indeed, a 'harvest of death' that was presented" (36).

Gardner restores a deadly force to the formula "et in Arcadia ego." The text, with its exhortations against the "devilish" motivations of the Confederates, recalls the oldest version of pastoral—the garden of Eden. The original rebellion of the Fall and the rebellion of the seceded states are thus both violations of the serenity and fertility of the garden. They interrupt the moral purpose of nature to provide signs of God's bountiful providence. At Gettysburg, nature is "all reluctant" to reveal the signs of death, and reacts in a sentient, human way to a violation of law, as Milton had imagined in *Paradise Lost*: "Earth felt the wound, and nature from her seat / Sighing through all her works gave signs of woe" (IX.782– 84). At the same time that Gardner imagines the presence of death in Arcadia, he finds that nature is in sympathy with the law—which permits him to invoke nature's restorative powers.

The two images of corpses on the battlefield of Gettysburg reproduced in the *Sketch Book* (both made by O'Sullivan) are noticeably similar; yet one is said to represent Confederate dead, the other, Union dead. Frassanito argues that the two views in fact represent a single set of corpses. In photographing the "Union" dead, the camera was evidently relocated to a position roughly 135 degrees counterclockwise from its position in photographing the "Confederate" dead (*Gettysburg*, 222–28). Even to contemporary viewers, who were no doubt willing to accept the claims of

FIG. 13. "A Sharpshooter's Last Sleep, Gettysburg, July, 1863," *Gardner's Photographic Sketch Book of the Civil War,* plate 40. Library of Congress.

Gardner's texts, the two images must have seemed remarkably similar in both style and representational content. How strange, then, that only one of the two texts claims that "the rebels represented in the photograph are without shoes. These were always removed from the feet on account of the pressing needs of the survivors. The pockets turned inside out also show that appropriation did not cease with the coverings of the feet" (36). The text accompanying the image said to represent Union dead does not mention the practice of stripping the dead of their valuables, even though the medium-close distance of the shot shows clearly that the corpses of "our own men" (37) have no shoes and empty pockets. (And those who strip the dead are usually those who control the field, in this case, the Federal troops.) These photographs are evidence of a practice common in all wars, and yet the explanatory texts reinforce a mythology of want and deprivation resulting from the South's violation of the beneficent harmony of the Garden of the Union. The scene of "rebel" dead is said to have a "devilish" quality. They "paid with life the price of their treason, and when the wicked strife was finished, found nameless graves, far from home and kindred" (36). The implication is that secession, like the original rebellion of Satan, disrupted the divine harmony of the world. In this photograph, the image reinforces the text; there is something sinister about the open mouth and the darkened features of the only clearly visible face. On the following page we read that the Union dead, on the contrary, "wore a calm and resigned expression, as though they had passed away in the act of prayer" (37).

The unifying, organic interpretation is difficult to sustain in the face of photographic evidence of violent death; thus Gardner must appeal to theological justification in the texts accompanying plates 36 and 37. However, two other images of the dead at Gettysburg are more easily re-cuperated by means of the sentimental rhetoric characteristic of the pas-toral mode. The visual composition of plate 40 permits it to be captioned "A Sharpshooter's Last Sleep" (fig. 13). By contrast, it would be hard to suggest that the life of the disemboweled body represented in "War, effect of a shell on a Confederate soldier" (fig. 6) was rounded with a sleep. Gardner made this negative at Gettysburg as well, obviously taking a great deal of care to arrange the scene to rationalize its violence with an inscription of cause and effect. He did not, however, include it in the *Sketch Book*. Although it seems calculated to have an "explanatory" value that would suit the purposes of a history of war, the image finally refuses any sentimental or pastoral narrative—when the body is not whole it cannot easily be said to sleep in death—and probably for this reason was not reproduced in the *Sketch Book*.

"A Sharpshooter's Last Sleep" is directly followed by "Home of a Rebel Sharpshooter" (fig. 14). Here, as in the other representations of the dead at Gettysburg, Gardner's art intervenes in the recording of the image. The corpse has been carried some forty yards and arranged within the frame provided by the stone wall, the musket carefully placed near where it would have been last fired—and yet only by calculating the im-probability of the position of the musket could the viewer conclude that this image was arranged (Frassanito, *Gettysburg*, 191).[17] The caption suggests that the soldier was at "home" in this stone structure and the protective rock walls are amenable to the metaphor. Yet it is also clear that this "home" was not his natural one, failing as it did to protect him from the hostile forces of the world. "There was no means of judging how long he lived after receiving his wound, but the disordered clothing shows that his sufferings must have been intense" (41). Perhaps realizing that the image does not immediately support such a text, Gardner reorients the narrative, turning away from the scene of suffering and drawing instead on associ-ations made possible by the protective rock walls that surround the body:

Did death come slowly to his relief, while memories of home grew dearer as the field of carnage faded before him? What visions, of

130

FIG. 14. "Home of a Rebel Sharpshooter, Gettysburg, 1863," *Gardner's Photographic Sketch Book of the Civil War,* plate 41. Library of Congress.

loved ones far away, may have hovered above his stony pillow! What familiar voices may he not have heard, like whispers beneath the roar of battle, as his eyes grew heavy in their long, last sleep! (41)

The text, like many of Gardner's, is of two minds. It wants the rebel to have suffered, unlike the Union dead who "wore a calm and resigned expression, as though they had passed away in the act of prayer" (37). But it also wants to evade this suffering and death—because one realizes that it was common to the Union dead as well—and so appeals to the sentimental icons of home and loved ones.

Thus the "rebel" is an ordinary American like the Union soldiers whose graves Lincoln consecrated at Gettysburg. But he is also different, because he did not die on native ground. Gardner writes that only the rebels died "far away from home and kindred" (36)—even though, for example, a Minnesotan would be much farther from home than a Virginian at Gettysburg. He argues that even the corpses of the Southerners belong at home:

> On the nineteenth of November, the artist attended the consecration of the Gettysburg Cemetery, and again visited the "Sharpshooter's Home." The musket, rusted by many storms, still leaned against the rock, and the skeleton of the soldier lay undisturbed within the mouldering uniform. . . . "Missing," was all that could have been known of him at home, and some mother may yet be patiently watching for the return of her boy, whose bones lie bleaching, unrecognized and alone, between the rocks at Gettysburg. (41)

This report is obviously fictionalized, because the corpse would not have been overlooked by the burial detail and the rifle would most likely have been taken by a soldier or a civilian (Frassanito, *Gettysburg*, 192). The relation of text and image to an organic model of nationalism is complex here. Farmers, hunters, and herdsmen seem not to live and die in history; soldiers do. And yet the soldier was perhaps also a farmer and a hunter— a modern Cincinnatus who goes from killing the deer that inhabit his land to killing Northern soldiers, supposedly in order to protect that land. His "natural" place, especially now that the war has ended, is at home in the South. He is an alien in the Pennsylvania landscape, unlike the Northerners who are supposed to be such an integral part of this land that they seem to draw their strength from it, and can be imagined to be "about to rise to continue the fight" (37).

Perhaps images of the dead at Gettysburg elicited such extensive attempts at pastoral recuperation because the battle was perceived in retrospect as a turning point of the war. Gettysburg was the northernmost point ever occupied by Confederate troops. With the battle, the Confederate offensive was halted; Southerners no longer occupied Northern land and began to retreat homeward. Thus it could be perceived as the first sign of the restoration of the natural balance of the Union. After the war, Whittier singled out this of all battles of the war for memorialization. Alluding in "The Hive at Gettysburg" to Samson's riddle about finding a beehive filled with honey in the carcass of a lion (Judg. 14.8–18), Whittier writes:

> Just on the spot whence ravening Treason crept
> Back to its lair to die,

Bleeding and torn from Freedom's mountain bounds,
    A stained and shattered drum
Is now the hive where, on their flowery rounds,
    The wild bees go and come.
Unchallenged by a ghostly sentinel,
    They wander wide and far,
Along green hillsides, sown with shot and shell
    Through vales once choked with war.   (348)

Samson's riddle—"out of the eater came forth meat"—invites Whittier
to affirm this image as a sign of "union, peace, and freedom plucked
away / From the rent jaws of wrong." The hive is not found in a corpse
of a Confederate soldier, as we might expect, but in a snare drum. Even
so, the image indicates Whittier's attempt to recuperate the violence of
the battle by showing how nature is effacing its traces. The rhetoric argues
that the Union resulting from the war is both divinely ordained and in
harmony with the natural scene, much in the way that Gardner had
mobilized both theodicy and pastoralism to give ideological meaning to
his photographs of corpses.

While Gardner's conscious manipulation of the image significantly
determines the representation of the dead in the *Sketch Book*, it is also
quite evident in photographs not directly concerned with death. The two
scenes representing blacks also exhibit the photographer's artistry on their
surfaces. A genre photograph entitled "What Do I Want, John Henry?
Warrenton, Va." (fig. 15) represents a black servant in the act of responding
to a white officer's "query" with "the only appropriate prescription that
his untutored nature could suggest," a jug of liquor (*Sketch Book*, 27).
This view is composed according to the antebellum conventions of the
pastoral genre scene. Trachtenberg argues that the "theatricality of the
image itself discloses, albeit unconsciously . . . how racism represents itself
in the staging of roles, roles self-proclaimed as artificial and theatrical"
(28). That is, John Henry's understanding of his master's demand for an
"appropriate prescription" is an allegory of the structure of race relations
itself. Like Eastman Johnson's genre painting "Old Kentucky Home" (fig.
5), the realism and compositional form of the photograph naturalize the
allegory. The uniforms indicate that the white soldiers are representatives
of the Union. The black man is clothed similarly, but by no structure
of authority does he represent the Union, for the text tells us that he
is not a soldier but the private servant of the officer. Uniforms, like civil
rights, are external; from this image it is apparent that both can easily

FIG. 15. "What Do I Want, John Henry? Warrenton, Va., November, 1862," *Gardner's Photographic Sketch Book of the Civil War,* plate 27. Library of Congress.

FIG. 16. "A Burial Party, Cold Harbor, Va., April, 1865," *Gardner's Photographic Sketch Book of the Civil War,* plate 94. Library of Congress.

be stripped away if, for example, the black man does not please the white man who occupies the seat of power. Without his uniform, John Henry retains only his "untutored *nature*" (*Sketch Book*, 27, emphasis added).

"A Burial Party, Cold Harbor, Va." (fig. 16) represents a somewhat less stable allegory of race relations. In this georgic of the aftermath, the blacks who do not look at the camera are actively working as field laborers. Their postures appear realistic, unstaged, and natural. Against this background, another black man poses (but not quite "theatrically") for the camera. Presumably the individuals in the photograph are not slaves but freedmen, and yet there is little in the image to mark that distinction—just as there was very little in the politics of emancipation and Reconstruction that signified to the blacks that they had the rights of free individuals. The image associates blacks in a significant way with the violence of the war, for they are engaged in digging up its unpleasant memories (Trachtenberg, 29). The politically unstable sign of black labor (is it free or slave?) is juxtaposed, in the image, with the even less stable sign of the violated body. The signification of both is anchored by the power structure that emerged after the war, legitimated by its result, and represented in the image by the pastoral structure of race and labor relations.

Gardner seems to refuse to recognize the force of his own image, using the accompanying explanatory text instead to castigate the residents of Cold Harbor, Virginia, for allowing the Union dead to remain unburied and thus preventing their natural return to the land. When *Harper's* reproduced this photograph in 1866, it was given a slightly different caption: "Collecting the Remains of Union Soldiers for Re-Interment in National Cemeteries." This new caption reinforces the ideology of Gardner's text. As Antigone had argued long ago, proper burial is an eternal, natural law.[18] By implication, the Southerners of Cold Harbor have exhibited an unnatural response to death in war (as rebellion had itself been characterized as "unnatural"). With the postwar Federal control over the land symbolized by this group of laborers, law is once again in harmony with nature.

In preparing the engraving, *Harper's* introduced a subtle change in the image, but one that extends the force of Gardner's pastoralism. In the photograph, the attitude of the central figure toward his labor is ambiguous. He has shadows for eyes that make it hard to read his face. His expression could indicate weariness, intensity, or even resentment; his darkened eyes play off the eye sockets of the skull, adding more tension. These features threaten to subvert the georgic representation of labor. Unlike the corpse, which has no choice in how it appears to the camera,

FIG. 17. "Collecting the Remains of Union Soldiers for Re-Interment in National Cemeteries," *Harper's Weekly,* 24 November 1866, p. 740.

the worker seems (albeit in a limited way) to resist his photographic appropriation with the only available means, his facial expression. The engraver, however, eliminates much of the capacity of the image to evoke uncertainty and uneasiness (fig. 17). The eyes are restored, and even a suggestion of a smile appears. In a *Harper's* engraving one almost never sees any unusual treatment of the eyes. The engraver has adjusted the image to the prevailing representational conventions. But in doing so he has also produced one of the few surviving contemporary interpretations of a Civil War photograph. His interpretive code called for regularity in visual representations and de-emphasis of traces of discord and conflict. Thus *Harper's* effaces the unsettling, potentially symbolic gaze of the black man, reiterating and reinforcing the pastoral conventions that structure Gardner's album.

Let me make it clear that in discussing the conscious manipulation of images, either in their initial composition or in their reproduction, I am not criticizing Gardner or *Harper's* because they tampered with "the facts." All photographs are composed. In the staging of "What Do I Want, John Henry?" Gardner reveals a good deal about the contemporary structure of race relations.[19] And in 1866 the idea of "objectivity" had not yet become one of the preconditions of photojournalism. Mid-Victorian documentary photographs (by, for example, Roger Fenton, David

Hill, and Robert Adamson) were usually overtly staged and otherwise manipulated, in imitation of the conventions of portrait, landscape, and genre paintings. Holmes claimed that a photograph shows "such a frightful amount of detail" that "theoretically, a perfect photograph is absolutely inexhaustible"; he attempted to control this potentially bewildering capacity by proposing a photographic encyclopedia of useful forms ("Stereoscope," 744). Civil War photographers attempted to control the viewer's associative reception of photographs by means of regularized compositional forms (as specified by the pastoral and picturesque modes) and by means of pastoral, yet overtly ideological, interpretive texts. In this sense, Mathew Brady and Alexander Gardner had a better understanding of the medium than many later photojournalists.

In Gardner's visual aesthetics, as in Whitman's poetics, organicism masquerading as an unmediated recovery of the real is the governing ideology of representation. As manifested in the semiotics of the pastoral mode, the organicist aesthetic subordinates traces of violence to the unifying power of the compositional whole. In reading this formal subordination as a sign of the affirmation of the status quo enforced by the war—the Unionist ideology—it is necessary to remark by way of qualification that there is no inherent connection between the organic unity of an artifact and the organic unity of a political structure. But within a given historical context it is reasonable to say, for example, that Fenton's artistically composed, compositionally balanced images of the Crimean War indicate a conservative ideology, or that the fragmented forms of Goya's etchings that make up *Desastres de la guerra* seem appropriate to the expression of a radical, pacifist agenda. Northern Unionism was not an egalitarian ideology (particularly in the context of Reconstruction) even though "democracy" was sometimes said to be the preeminent American value. Aesthetic and political organicism both operate by means of hierarchy and subordination. In terms of *realpolitik* this meant the control and selective mobilization of "Southern" values (the value of hierarchy and the like), and it also meant the swearing of loyalty oaths by Southern congressmen. In visual art, organicism implied an analogous operation of control. "The picturesque," wrote an art critic for the *Atlantic* in 1864, "has its root in the mind's craving for totality. . . . On this condition everything is welcome,—without it, nothing" (Cabot, 327). In the context of the northern United States in 1866, the organicist representational aesthetics of Gardner's war photography reflects the organicism of the Unionist perspective on the representational politics of the war. In this way traces of war were mobilized as signs of Union.

5. Barnard and the American Picturesque

UNLIKE Gardner's *Photographic Sketch Book of the Civil War*, George Barnard's *Photographic Views of Sherman's Campaign* is organized on its surface as a conventional military history. Although the images in the *Sketch Book* are sequenced according to a rough chronology of the events they are supposed to document, the structure of that album is archival rather than narrative. The arrangement of images constructs relatively few historical relationships and continuities. Only rarely in the *Sketch Book* does the "event" that dictates the inclusion of a particular image in the album seem to appear "in" that image (for example, in a photograph documenting Lincoln's official visit to the Antietam battlefield [plate 23]). Barnard, too, had to work within the existing technological limits that prohibited the photographic representation of actual combat or the moments of destruction themselves; his subject also is the aftermath. But Barnard mobilizes traces of war in the service of a concrete narrative of specific, ordered events. His project has a fairly narrow scope—a small and very linear segment of the war. Thus his album has a continuity that distinguishes it from a merely archival organization.

The history illustrated by Barnard's *Views* was preinscribed as a simple narrative, with a single protagonist (General Sherman), readily identifiable antagonists (Generals Hood and Johnston), and a clear conflict and resolution (the surrender of the Confederate forces). The original edition of the *Views*, containing sixty-one 10-x-14-inch prints with captions denoting locations, was prefaced by four maps denoting the movements of Sherman's troops from the consolidation of Federal forces at Nashville to Johnston's surrender at Raleigh.[1] In addition, Barnard published an accompanying pamphlet, entitled "Sherman and His Generals," which was to serve as both a prospectus and an explanatory text for the album (Newhall, Preface, vii).[2] The text is a military-historical account of Sherman's operations that supports a narrative reading of the photographic archive. Even without Barnard's text, the narrative sequencing of the prints would have been recognizable to readers familiar with newspaper accounts of the military operations of the war. Barnard stops short of the final scene of military victory, however, ending his story symbolically in Columbia, South Carolina, the original seat of secession. The scene of Johnston's surrender near Raleigh, North Carolina, is not documented. (This may well have been for lack of available photographs. There is no evidence that Barnard followed Sherman any farther than Columbia.) The narrative ends on a contemplative, rather than a decisive note among the ruins of Columbia and Charleston. And yet the symbol of the destruction of these sites of Southern economic and cultural power probably provided a more satisfying ending for the Northern Unionist than any allusion to Johnston's surrender: the great symbols of Lee and Appomattox were outside the sphere of Sherman's and Barnard's operations. Barnard thus gave his story more ideological force than he might have, for it was Lee's surrender, rather than any capability of Sherman's army to defeat Johnston's army, that forced Johnston's surrender.[3]

Although in sequence the images imply a narrative, individually each invokes the associative, contemplative logic of the picturesque in mid-nineteenth-century America. A brief glance through the album shows the extent to which the composition of the photographs derives from the contemporary aesthetic of the picturesque. Barnard gives us broken trees and ruined buildings and invites the kind of contemplative reverie that these signs inspire within the context of the picturesque. Given the viewer's (limited) freedom to invest the landscape associatively with history, Barnard naturalizes the war by providing an *organic* structure within which that history must be inscribed. His use of the idea of organicism is more sophisticated than Brady's or Gardner's, and is similar in some respects to Whitman's. Whitman's poetics of typification led him eventually (in "Lilacs") to revitalize the pastoral mode as an ideology conducive to postwar reconciliation and to the restoration of a unified image of America. Given the temporal specificity of the photographic image, Barnard must dwell on the aftermath of destruction rather than on the coming Reconstruction. Yet his album also contains a program for re-Union, the cultural power of which derives from his representation of the Southern landscape as an object of appropriation. For Whitman, the power to restore the Union lies in a pastoral representation of the land. For Barnard, the power to restore the land to its antebellum pastoral state lies in the authority of Northern Unionism lately legitimated by the war. His picturesque treatment of the devastation of the South during Sherman's campaign reveals the imperialist impulse that motivated Unionism and required the Northern prosecution of the war.

The view of history inscribed in the picturesque stalls the surface-level historical narrative of Barnard's album. Military history assumes a continuous narrative that ends, decisively, in victory or defeat; it describes actions (of officers, if not common soldiers). The picturesque, on the other hand, represents history only as a potentially or partially recoverable trace, readable in the compositional structure of the scene. Actors are displaced by an observer, who is sometimes explicitly represented in the image (as the contemplative figure in the middle distance) and sometimes implicitly located outside of the frame by compositional devices such as perspective. The two contrasting ways of organizing the representation of history—narrative versus picturesque—pull Barnard's album in different, if not precisely opposite, historiographical directions. Thus finally, in spite of its narrative structure, the volume emerges as an important example of the American picturesque. As a representation of the war, Barnard's picturesque album has an ideological function, no less important than the more obvious ideological function of the military-historical narrative it illustrates. The aesthetic theory that valued organic unity and complex harmony corresponds in a significant way to the politics of Unionism and the postwar attitude in the North that represented the South as an object of economic and political appropriation.

Barnard was among the first professional photographers in the United States. He opened a profitable daguerreotype gallery in Oswego, New York, in 1843 (Newhall, Preface, iii). In 1853, still working in Oswego, he made several spectacular daguerreotypes of a burning grain mill that are among the first American "news" photographs (Newhall, *History*, 39). While he was one of the first to exploit the documentary potential of the medium, Barnard seems primarily to have been interested in its aesthetic possibilities. Before the war he made genre scenes such as "The Woodsawyer's Nooning" (fig. 2); for this daguerreotype he won an honorable mention in a competition sponsored by E. and H. T. Anthony (a photographic firm that dominated the New York market in the 1850s) (Rudisill, 158).

In an invited paper read before the New York State Daguerrean Association on the subject of "Taste" (published, in 1855, in the *Photographic and Fine Art Journal*), Barnard argued that while the "true Daguerreotypist" should be skilled in chemistry, optics, and "the theory of color, last but not least he should be a cultivated artist."[4] For Barnard photography transcends mere technics; it is an *artistic* medium capable of disseminating the values of humanistic high culture:

I would see science wedded to Art, with Truth and Beauty as their Handmaids and our profession soaring above the merely mechanical

position which it now holds, aspire to a place among the higher
branches of employment and the Daguerrean ranked as he deserves
among the noble, intellectual and humanizing employments of the
age. (159)

The photographer's "acquisition of Taste" requires the "acquisition of
graces which unite the True with the Harmonious and the Beautiful"
(158). Of course, "the True" had been recognized as photography's special
province since the invention of the medium; so Barnard is more interested
in what progress can be made toward the other two aesthetic values of
beauty and harmony. He claims that the best photographs, like the best
painted portraits, "have an intrinsic value even after the name and history
is [sic] lost" (159). The argument—that the cultural value of photography
inheres not so much in its unique, apparently unmediated relation to the
referent of the representation, but in the purely pictorial qualities of the
image—appeals to the aesthetic of the picturesque.

The aesthetic value of a photographic portrait, according to Barnard,
"is shewn in the depth and power of light and shade; in . . . relieving
sharp features, emboldening round ones, revealing with exquisite grace
the beauties of the elegant form, hiding with adroit skill the inelegancies
of the clumsier; varying the light with various complexions, subduing,
emboldening, changeful as the sunbeams, but beautiful in all" ("Taste,"
159). Although he devotes some of his lecture to the recently exhibited
"striking views of the Crystal Palace" in London, he does not discuss
landscape photography in any detail. (His audience would have been
primarily interested in his advice on portraiture, the most commercial
photographic genre.) But we can infer his ideas on the representation
of landscapes from his portrait aesthetic. For Barnard, as for other theorists
of the picturesque, the power of the image is determined by its compositional form rather than by the historicity of its referent. Barnard's
discussion of portrait technique suggests that he took a self-consciously
artistic approach to photography in general. This is consistent with his
view of the cultural function of his art: "How much does the multiplication
of pictures tend to enlighten and unite the Human family! Read and
understood by the infant and the aged; scattered from the hovel of the
poor to the palace of the great, it extends a humanizing influence where-
ever it goes" (158). His agenda is vague, but he seems to be arguing that
the artistic photograph transcends specificity to promote mutual understanding among diverse cultures. It has the capacity to do so because
the representational codes of photography can be understood easily by

all. The codes Barnard himself proposes—manipulating light and shadow, smoothing the rough and "emboldening" the smooth so as to depict everything in its best light—are supposed to be universally readable as signs producing "enlighten[ment]" and "virtue." The idea that photographs, composed according to these picturesque codes, have a capacity to "unite the Human family" would serve Barnard as an appropriate aesthetic for the representation of a war fought in the name of political and ideological unification.

The *Photographic Views of Sherman's Campaign* show that when Barnard left the employ of Brady & Co. in order to take a post as an army photographer, he did not put aside his artistic aspirations. But he was now responsible not only to "art," but to "history" as well. The taking of views was "an integral part of his duties" as photographic attaché to the Military Division of the Mississippi (Milhollen and Mugridge, xi). Sherman assumed supreme command of the Division of the Mississippi in 1864, at which time Barnard began to take orders from Sherman's chief engineer, Colonel E. M. Poe (who, among other accomplishments, engineered the destruction of Atlanta, Columbia, and Charleston). Barnard was thus in an excellent position to document military history. By his own admission, he did not follow Sherman every step of the way. Nevertheless he claims to present complete documentation: "The rapid movement of Sherman's army during the active campaign rendered it impossible to obtain at the time a complete series of photographs which should illustrate the principal events and most interesting localities. Since the close of the war the collection has been completed" (*Views*, xviii).

After the war Barnard sought approval to publish his photographs from Sherman, who responded that "I now have [seen] a great part of the series and believe that in connection with the Maps, they will be very interesting and instructive to the General [*sic*] reader" (Newhall, Preface, vi). Sherman may not have intended the pun, but it is likely that civilian readers and army commanders found different kinds of interest and instruction in the *Views*. *Harper's Weekly* commented that while the volume was an important piece of military history,

> for the care and judgement in selecting the points of view, for the delicacy of execution, for scope of treatment, and for fidelity of representation, they surpass any other photographic views which have been produced in this country—whether relating to the war or otherwise. . . . Although, from its expense, the book can not be popular, those who can afford to pay one hundred dollars for a work

of fine art can not spend their money with more satisfactory results than would be realized in the possession of these views. (Rev. of *Photographic Views*)[5]

Harper's evaluated the photographs not only as documentation, but as "art." Barnard's artistic sensibilities must have been gratified by the claim that his photographs were aesthetically superior to all others; they evidently conformed to his own criteria of "taste."

Painting has long collaborated with military history to provide heroic and romantic images of war. Formally, Barnard's *Views* have little in common with such images. Instead, they take the form of "history painting with the history . . . removed," as Ronald Paulson remarks of Constable's picturesque aesthetic (134). A heroic narrative forms a pre-text for Barnard's *Views* (albeit Sherman's campaign was somewhat less "heroic" than others). But the visual form of the individual images tends to pull the reader away from a "historical" or "heroic" reading. Pictorial and narratival modes each inscribe histories of the war, but they are by no means homologous; in combination they imply that there can be no totalizing historical account of Sherman's campaign—and so, by extension, no full history of the war.

Most insistently excluded from historical representation in the *Views* is the experience of the common soldier. In the prefatory text Barnard follows the conventional military-historical representation of war which (as Scarry argues) removes the central fact and act of injuring from the discourse on war. Barnard's text, as Trachtenberg points out, "opens with a Homeric (or Bancroftian) listing of generals under Sherman"; it follows such conventions as "always identif[ying] armies and smaller units by the name of their commanding officer." Thus the trope of embodiment, which Whitman also favored in his poetic representations of the war, subsumes the thousands of persons who make up an army or division or corps under a single name, reinforcing "the importance of hierarchy, of subordination and obedience, one of the war's significant subliminal lessons" (Trachtenberg, 25). Instead of the myriad stories of individual hardships and sufferings, military history in this mode becomes "a mythology of giants lumbering across rivers and stalking through forests" (Scarry, 70)—similar to Whitman's "Years of the unperform'd" (*DT*, 53–54). Barnard no doubt found tropes of embodiment appropriate to his subject because the Atlanta, Savannah, and Carolina campaigns of 1864–65 seem to be a coherent, single-minded enterprise.[6] One episode in the campaign is still popularly embodied as *Sherman's* "March to the Sea."

Unlike Grant's lengthy siege of Petersburg, Virginia (which was also taking place in 1864–65), the Savannah and Carolinas campaigns seem naturally to assume a linear form in historical representation—a vigorous march, rather than, say, a game of chess that threatens to stalemate.

Sherman's *Memoirs* emphasize the preparation for this swift, linear movement of the campaigns:

> [In order] to make these troops as mobile as possible, I made the strictest orders in relation to wagons and all species of encumbrances and impedimenta whatever. Each officer and soldier was required to carry on his horse or person food and clothing enough for five days. To each regiment was allowed but one wagon and one ambulance . . . . I doubt if any army ever went forth to battle with fewer impedimenta, and where the regular and necessary supplies of food, ammunition, and clothing, were issued, as called for, so regularly and so well. (2:15, 22)

The narrative organization of Barnard's album often reflects Sherman's own intentions for the operations under his command, and his own attitudes about the importance of mobility, efficiency, and ruthlessness. But it does not do so directly, by documenting the differences between the usual encumbered, relatively inefficient army and Sherman's streamlined organization. In fact battle-ready troops and materiel are entirely absent from the photographs. Barnard represents the rapid movement of the troops by means of a sequence of images that proposes the camera lens as a substitute for the eyes of a commanding officer. The sequencing implies the efficient movement of Sherman and his forces. When the narrative pauses, it is in locations where Sherman's troops paused, in Atlanta, Savannah, and Columbia. There are two scenes of a pioneer camp, but in general Barnard pays minimal attention to any living human presence in the scenes. Furthermore he completely excludes the dead from photographic representation. This depopulation serves to bolster the ideology that the experience of the common soldier is irrelevant to military history (Trachtenberg, 25). It further suggests that the experience of the white Southern civilian or the newly liberated slave required no photographic comment whatever.

One strange feature of the album is that it contains no illustrations of the notorious "March to the Sea," but moves immediately from scenes of Atlanta to scenes of Savannah. Barnard's elision of the most famous episode in the history he is nominally documenting betrays an insistent appeal to an aesthetic of the picturesque that would efface some unpleasant aspects of the war. The review of the *Photographic Views* in *Harper's Weekly* refers to the expected sequence of episodes in the campaign without mentioning that the march to the sea went unillustrated: "61 imperial photographs, embracing scenes of the Occupation of Nashville, the Great Battles around Chattanooga and Lookout Mountain, the Campaign of Atlanta, March to the Sea, and the Great Raid through the Carolinas." But the album moves immediately from a photograph of Atlanta to one of the "Savannah River, near Savannah, Ga.," thus omitting what is now a very famous part of Sherman's operations. If Barnard counted on his audience to fill this gap in his visual narrative, the notice in *Harper's* is evidence that they did so. The lack of representation seems not to have mattered at the time; perhaps viewers would have extrapolated from the other photographs, assuming that the march to the sea was simply more of the same.

Contemporary representations of the march to the sea were rare, even though the illustrated weeklies sent their best artists to observe a campaign that must have promised to be much more exciting than the siege of Petersburg. During the march from Atlanta to Savannah, the only available reports came from Georgia papers; Northern editors refused to reprint these (when they were available) for obvious political reasons, trading instead on pure speculation (Andrews, 580). Theo Davis, a field artist for *Harper's*, followed Sherman from Atlanta to Savannah, sending to New York several sketches of Federal troops pillaging and looting—but none of these was published. Neither *Harper's* nor *Leslie's* ever published a sketch of Sherman's "bummers," the specially designated details that became notorious for their ingenuity at foraging and looting. The publishers may have feared the War Department's censorship, or they may not have agreed with Sherman's ideas about the new method of "total warfare" which affected civilians to an unprecedented degree (Thompson, 158–62). Barnard's album similarly minimizes the representation of the march (and the other parts of the campaign) on the civilian population.

Sherman himself regarded the march to the sea as "a means to an end, and not as an essential act of war" (2:220). (On the following page of his *Memoirs* he gives a casualty report.) He argues that acts of robbery and plundering were "exceptional and incidental" and that he "never heard of any cases of murder or rape" (2:182–83). But despite his appeals to the necessities of military efficiency, Sherman's account of the devastation has a moralizing tone. For example, he orders the total destruction of an estate because it is known to belong to a Confederate general, and

FIG. 18. "'The Halt'—A Scene in the Georgia Campaign," *Harper's Weekly*, 30 June 1866, p. 401.

reports that "the whole army is burning with an insatiable desire to wreak vengeance upon South Carolina. I almost tremble at her fate, but feel that she deserves all that seems in store for her . . . . I look upon Columbia as quite as bad as Charleston, and doubt if we shall spare the public buildings there as we did at Milledgeville" (2:228).

One of the few contemporary visual representations of the march, "The Soldier's Halt," a genre painting by Thomas Nast, appeals similarly to the supposed moral superiority of the Northern troops, implying that no unjust devastation occurred. Nast's painting was reproduced as an engraving in *Harper's* (30 June 1866). To judge from this picture, the march to the sea was quite a decorous affair (fig. 18). A Federal soldier, having received a cup of water from a local resident, now plays with the baby she holds; young children look up at her while another soldier sits on the ground playing with a dog. The image is remarkable, in relation to the larger historical context of the march to the sea, for its peaceful, domestic tone. The woman and children are well dressed, the house and grounds neatly maintained. Her downcast eyes perhaps suggest a measure of resentment at even this small act of hospitality (and rightly so, we should think), yet the soldiers are almost submissive before this icon of

146

FIG. 19. "View from Kenesaw Mountain, Ga.," Barnard, *Photographic Views of Sherman's Campaign*, plate 32. Library of Congress.

domesticity. Thus Nast not only effaces any recollection of the destruction and looting that characterized the campaign, but suggests that the soldiers who participated in it upheld respectable moral and behavioral standards in the face of their awareness that they were in enemy lands. Such representations probably held little if any authority with Georgians, who knew better either from personal experience or from the newspapers. Sherman characterized the Southern newspaper accounts as "false publications" that "represented the conduct of the men of our army as simply infamous; that we respected neither age nor sex; that we burned every thing we came across—barns, stables, cotton-gins, and even dwelling houses; that we ravished the women and killed the men, and perpetrated all manner of outrages on the inhabitants" (2:236). But to Northerners who read jubilant accounts of the march and of Sherman's supposed popularity in Savannah (Andrews, 583–84), Nast's painting provided reassurance that Federal troops treated the land and its residents with respect, suggesting that whatever destruction occurred was inevitable and, perhaps, regrettable.

Even in the relative absence of visual representations of the march to the sea, the contemporary audience could be expected, in their im-

147

mediate response, to fill the gap in Barnard's *Views* because the narrative
of the album constructs a single, coherent perceiving subject whose point
of view regularizes the "experience" of war (analogous to Whitman's
recuperative transformation of individual soldiers into larger bodies). But
Barnard's depopulated images often suggest that the historical subject
of Sherman's campaign is split, and that its history is not simply a single-
plotted narrative. In describing the battle of Kenesaw Mountain, the
prefatory text traces the withdrawal of Confederate forces from Pine
Mountain to a stronger, more heavily fortified position on Kenesaw, the
ensuing battle, and the subsequent Confederate withdrawal to the south
bank of the Chattahoochee River. A contiguous sequence of four images
traces a similar movement:

> Plate 30 "Pine Mountain"
> Plate 31 "The Front of Kenesaw Mountain"
> Plate 32 "View from Kenesaw Mountain"
> Plate 33 "South Bank of the Chattahoochee"

One might conclude from this image sequence that the figure of Sherman—
the embodiment of the entire Military Division of the Mississippi—occupied Kenesaw Mountain and thus gained possession of the view represented in plate 32 (fig. 19).[7] In the panoramic view from the peak, log
fortifications function, in the place of the conventional stone ruins of
the picturesque, as an integrative device to harmonize foreground and
background.

But at this point, the panoramic "View from Kenesaw Mountain,"
the photographic and verbal narratives diverge. Barnard's text reports
that the Federal troops marched *around* Kenesaw:

> The failure of these attacks to break through the rebel line [of
> fortifications on Kenesaw Mountain] determined General Sherman
> to execute a flanking movement to the right, which was completely
> successful, Johnston being forced to abandon the Kenesaw line and
> retire behind the Chattahoochee river. The army at once advanced
> to the north bank of the Chattahoochee, Marietta being made the
> temporary depot for supply. (*Views*, xiv)

A very few Federal soldiers did see the view from Kenesaw Mountain;
Sherman, along with nearly all of the troops under his command, probably
did not. Once Johnston's forces had withdrawn toward the river, the
mountain lost its strategic importance and there was no longer any reason
for commanding the view from its peak. Sherman reports that as soon

as his spyglass revealed a few Federal soldiers running across the crest unmolested, he began preparations to pursue Johnston's forces toward the Chattahoochee (2:62). The framing effect of the spyglass is similar to that of a photograph. But Barnard's photographic sequence frames the views of two perceiving subjects: one who sees the panorama and one who, like Sherman himself, does not but instead moves directly from the point of view of plate 31, facing Kenesaw, to that of plate 33, looking over the river.

The photographic narrative pauses, unlike Sherman himself and unlike the soldiers who hurried over the crest, in order to linger on the view from the top of Kenesaw. The placement of this image within the sequence stalls the master-narrative of the relentless pursuit of Johnston. The viewer is invited to turn aside from Sherman's path in order to contemplate the scene—that is, to occupy a physical and experiential position, in relation to the view, prescribed by the aesthetic of the picturesque. Such an invitation suggests a general resistance to the nominal project of the album, the photographic illustration of military history. Barnard's album thus defines two kinds of aesthetics and implies two kinds of histories. There is, most obviously, the history to which this essay has attended so far—a contiguous narrative of Sherman's military operations prescribed by a heroic aesthetic. Trachtenberg's reading takes this form when he finds "a tightly structured march of images [that] generates the illusion of an unstoppable force thrusting itself through space, overturning everything in its path" (24). But there is also a history that lingers on the scene to contemplate the trace left by the relentless, forward-looking narrative. The former history tells of the war; it is teleological and claimed proudly by the Northern military and political establishment as a sign of power. The latter kind is marginalized by the perspective of the establishment to which it, also, belongs. It speaks not of the war or Sherman's military prowess, but of the imminent problems of reconstruction—of what the conquered territory of the South looked like after Sherman was done with it. And although Barnard's photographs allow this latter kind of history to be represented, they also engage in a certain form of interdiction: by constructing picturesque images of the traces of war, they reflect the nostalgic pastoralism that was often invoked (as for example in Whitman's "Lilacs") as a restorative version of history.

Barnard's elision of the march to the sea reveals a particularly insistent appeal to pastoralism. He thoroughly documents the locale from which the march began by providing eight views of Atlanta and the surrounding area. We find him next abruptly transported to Savannah. While there

FIG. 20. "City of Atlanta, Ga., No. 1," Barnard, *Photographic Views of Sherman's Campaign,* plate 45. Library of Congress.

is no possibility that Sherman's *Memoirs* influenced Barnard (since they were not published until 1875), his photographic treatment bears interesting parallels to Sherman's account. Sherman reports that before he entered the city of Atlanta, "Colonel Poe, United States Engineers, of my staff, had been busy in his special task of destruction. He had a large force at work, had leveled the great depot, round-house, and the machine-shops of the Georgia railroad and had applied fire to the wreck" (2:177). Barnard's "City of Atlanta, Ga., No. 1" (fig. 20) shows the round-house as Sherman may have seen it (after the destruction). After listing his personnel for the coming march toward the sea, Sherman describes his last view of Atlanta: "Reaching the hill, just outside of the old rebel works, we naturally paused to look back . . . . Behind us lay Atlanta, smouldering and in ruins, the black smoke rising high in the air, and hanging like a pall over the ruined city" (2:178). The next photograph

FIG. 21. "City of Atlanta, Ga., No. 2," Barnard, *Photographic Views of Sherman's Campaign,* plate 46. Library of Congress.

Barnard gives us—"City of Atlanta, Ga., No. 2"—is taken from a similar elevated perspective (fig. 21). It does not, however, have the force of Sherman's description. The fire has burned itself out. Sherman exits, satisfied with the destruction with which he has left his mark on the landscape. Barnard dwells on the implications of the destruction, showing the occupation (since citizens were evacuated, the wagons must belong to the Federal army). These bleak scenes of Atlanta prepare us for the restorative power of the subsequent five views from the vicinity of Savannah.

In "City of Atlanta, Ga., No. 2," Sherman continues to possess Atlanta by means of his representatives, the soldiers. Sherman's *Memoirs* also suggest that Atlanta in some sense continued to possess *him*: "Then we turned our horses' heads to the east; Atlanta was soon lost behind the screen of trees and became a thing of the past. Around it clings many

Fig. 22. "Savannah River, near Savannah, Ga.," Barnard, *Photographic Views of Sherman's Campaign,* plate 47. Library of Congress.

a thought of desperate battle, of hope and fear, that now seem like the memory of a dream; and *I have never seen the place since*" (2:179, emphasis added). Sherman superimposes a picturesque landscape view on the image of Atlanta in his memory, thus dissolving it into a "memory of a dream." Already he has subjected his consciousness of the devastation he commanded to an extensive network of mediations, one node of which is the text of the *Memoirs.* His insistence at this particular point that he never returned in person (which is equally true, but not mentioned, with respect to most other locations) suggests that he did return often, in memory.

Sherman views and then blocks the destruction effected by his representatives, the soldiers. They, especially as embodied in Sherman's act of vision, are the viewer's representatives as well, for they work for the United States government, which has acted in the supposed interest of

Fig. 23. "Buen-Ventura, Savannah, Ga.," Barnard, *Photographic Views of Sherman's Campaign.* Library of Congress.

all Americans in prosecuting the war (even, ironically, in the supposed interest of the Southerners who used the railroad before it was destroyed). Both Barnard and Sherman thus escape from the oppressive scene of Atlanta into a pleasant landscape. Barnard views and then displaces the destruction, like Sherman. The album moves immediately from Atlanta in ruins to a picturesque view of the Savannah River that bears no trace of war (fig. 22). Similarly, Sherman continues to develop the scene suggested by the "screen of trees" that blocks his memory of Atlanta: "The day was extremely beautiful, clear sunlight, with bracing air, and an unusual feeling of exhilaration seemed to pervade all minds—a feeling of something to come, vague and undefined, still full of venture and intense interest. Even the common soldiers caught this inspiration" (2:179). It seems unlikely that the soldiers would have shared fully Sherman's enthusiasm for the grueling march ahead. Nevertheless, Sherman represents them

FIG. 24. "Chattanooga Valley from Lookout Mountain, No. 2," Barnard, *Photographic Views of Sherman's Campaign,* plate 14. Library of Congress.

as being of a common mind (his) that has felt the restorative power of "nature" and, thus refreshed, can continue.

In Barnard's photographs the remains of Atlanta bake, along with the viewer, under an open sky. On the Savannah River, the position designated for the viewer is shaded by the tree that partly frames the scene. The next image, of a path shaded by moss-draped trees, is a sort of visual pastoral elegy (fig. 23).[8] A gravemarker (perhaps a small mausoleum) at the end of the path adds compositional interest to the image and reveals that it is a view of a cemetery. It is clear, from the luxuriant yet ordered vegetation, that the marker in the background long antedates the Federal occupation. The melancholy emotion evoked by the image blocks any consideration of war. The caption identifies the scene as "Buen-Ventura," "good fortune." If this is an ironic comment on Sherman's presence in Georgia, the image seems not to admit it. It is hard even

FIG. 25. Thomas Cole, *Oxbow* (*The Connecticut River Near Northampton*) (1836). The Metropolitan Museum of Art, Gift of Mrs. Russell Sage, 1908.

to imagine the presence of Sherman's troops in this scene, because the landscape has apparently never been despoiled—although in fact Sherman devotes some space in his *Memoirs* to "the cemetery of Bonaventura" as one of the few places outside the city that would be of interest to a "stranger" (2:230).

Momentarily Sherman, like Barnard, interpolates a travelogue into his military history; on "the ride along the Wilmington Channel by way of Thunderbolt, there might be seen some groves of the majestic live-oak trees, covered with gray and funereal moss, which were truly sublime in grandeur, but gloomy after a few days' camping under them" (2:230–31). More extensively than Sherman, Barnard seems to regard Savannah as a mine of aesthetic value. "Fountain, Savannah, Ga." (*Views*, plate 51), seeming to transport us to an Italian city, feels especially incongruous with the facts of war until we realize that we are viewing a fine specimen of the spoils that Sherman captured (luckily intact, since Savannah was surrendered without a fight).

That Barnard's photographic aesthetic derived from the contemporary theory of the picturesque is especially apparent in the three views from Lookout Mountain. "Chattanooga Valley from Lookout Mountain, No. 2" (fig. 24) recalls Cole's "The Oxbow" (fig. 25) in composition and style. Barnard's "Lu-La Lake, Lookout Mountain" (*Views*, plate 15) is a less expansive but similarly styled scene of a small waterfall and the pool below it, framed by rock cliffs. There are no specific images of appropriation within these panoramic scenes, but there are some present in a photograph that represents pioneers' tents, "Pass in the Racoon Range (Whiteside No. 2)" (plate 7). Pioneers are those who built or repaired bridges, cleared roads, and so forth, in advance of occupation by the rest of the troops. Whitman's "Pioneers! O Pioneers!" draws an explicit analogy between the military sense of the term and the more familiar sense of those who settled new American territories to the west (*DT*, 25–30). Barnard's caption does not mention that his image represents pioneers, but the preceding image of a newly built wooden bridge— "Pass in the Racoon Range (Whiteside No. 1)"—shows that the tents are of a pioneer camp. As Whitman realized, both senses of the term are ideologically appropriate to such images.

However, even in the views from Lookout Mountain, from which indices of occupation such as pioneers' camps are absent, the politics of ownership are inscribed in the compositional form of the representation. The position and contemplative attitude of the spectator had been preinscribed in the picturesque scene when Barnard inherited its form from the school of Cole. Placing the form within the context of military history modifies the inscription of the spectator. We now find that the perceiving subject, whose position we occupy in viewing the image, is the figure of Sherman or Barnard. What Holmes claimed metaphorically for all landscape photography approaches literal truth here: "We steal a landscape from its lawful owners, and defy the charge of dishonesty" ("Sun-Painting," 13). The picturesque aesthetic found value in the American landscape, we recall, not so much because it was scenic, but because its scenes were peculiarly *American*. Since these Southern scenes are now again part of "America" they can function, like Cole's "The Oxbow," as a repository of the American values of appropriation and control of new lands.

It was in this spirit, of the awareness of the Federal repossession of the seceded states, that *Harper's Weekly* began in 1866 to publish two series of visual representations of the South. One, "Pictures of the South," consisted eventually of well over one hundred landscape and genre sketches, representing typical topographies, employments, and activities. This series began to appear in the spring. *Harper's* had sent its best artists, Theo Davis and Alfred Waud, on tours of the Southern states after the war to send back these scenes; they found, for example: a magnolia grove in Alabama (8 September), freedmen harvesting moss in Louisiana (15 September), or farming Jefferson Davis's plantation in Mississippi (15 September), Acadians washing their clothes on a Louisiana bayou (20 October), white Georgians gathered for a barbecue (10 November). While landscape and genre sketches had always been an important part of the material in *Harper's*, the caption now attached to every view—"Pictures of the South"—indicates a direct attempt to organize this sort of material under a political rubric. By subsuming all of these scenes under the category of "the South," *Harper's* locates them with respect to the manifest seat of power, "the North."

Equally significant was another project that also inscribed a hierarchical opposition of North and South. In the 6 January 1866 issue there appeared the first of a series of maps of the Southern states (fig. 26) accompanied by relevant statistics and the following rationale: "In the present situation of the country the material condition of the Southern States is of primary importance. We give on page 12 A MAP OF THE STATE OF MISSISSIPPI, surmounted by an emblematic representation of that State. ("Mississippi").[9] Elsewhere in this issue, a more general statement of the aims of the project is prefaced by an anecdote about a Virginian who, having no money to farm his land, "should like nothing so much" as to sell half of it to "a company of Vermont farmers." *Harper's* applauds the "common sense" with which the Virginian viewed his situation. "For it is by actual immigration and social and industrial intercourse that the hostility springing from separation and ignorance will be removed" ("Our Maps"). This is a geographical and economic version of the spiritual Unionism proposed by Whitman; as such, it appears to be a similarly impractical proposal (for very few Vermonters would go south to farm). But it is noteworthy that a Virginian should be represented as welcoming the control of Southern soil by Vermonters, who might be said to epitomize Yankee cultural values. Farming the land is not the real issue here; the Virginian's problem is that he has no Southern source of capital and so must turn to the North. Agriculture thus functions as a metonymy for economic and political control.

In order to encourage this political transformation, under the guise of restoring the South to its antebellum fecundity, *Harper's* announced,

157

FIG. 26. "Mississippi," *Harper's Weekly*, 6 January 1866, p. 12.

We propose to publish a series of carefully prepared maps of the
Southern States, beginning with MISSISSIPPI in this number of the
Weekly, accompanied by concise and complete industrial statistics,
that the general character and special advantages of the Southern
part of the country are understood by those who are thinking of
settling there. . . . Knowledge, knowledge, knowledge—that is the
key with which the golden treasure of the Future is to be unlocked;
and we shall do what we can to put it into the hands of every body
who can read. ("Our Maps")[10]

The South is treated as an object of ethnographic study, complete with
the iconography of typical native inhabitants (in the "emblematic representation" that heads each map). Cartography and ethnography are, as
is usual in the course of empire, early steps in the process of colonization
and exploitation of natural resources.

Thus *Harper's* reinscribes the will to empire that produced the United
States and, eventually, the war. The left sides of the emblems for Mississippi and for Georgia (figs. 26 and 27) represent early contact between
European explorers and Native Americans. Both parties are well armed;
although the confrontations appear to be peaceful, the images evoke the
wars waged to subjugate the native peoples of the South. The subjugation
of Southern whites was of course a touchier issue—for they in fact had
participated in the imperialism that informs these emblems. The left-hand
side of the emblems for Alabama (13 January) and Louisiana (3 February)
show images of slavery rather than the images of confrontations between
whites and native Americans that we see in the emblems of Mississippi
and Georgia: mounted white overseers direct the labor of blacks who
are sorting cotton (Alabama) or cutting sugarcane (Louisiana). These
emblems represent the South as it was (although the representations of
Native Americans do not show their antebellum persecution). In fact one
could not infer from any of them that the Civil War had occurred. There
are no representations of destruction nor any of emancipation—even
though *Harper's* published many sketches on these topics during and immediately following the war.[11] On the right-hand side of the emblem
for Mississippi, the ambiguous image may represent the present time (fig.
26). According to the accompanying text, in this image "field laborers
[are] bringing in their baskets of cotton to the huge cotton-press which
rises in the back-ground." Minerva, patroness of commerce, is described
as "bearing the Liberty cap on her spear"; the cap hangs there, as if
it is a trophy of war ("Mississippi"). Yet the need for this verbal explication

FIG. 27. "Georgia," *Harper's Weekly*, 12 May 1866, p. 301.

betrays a contradiction in the iconographic code—that is, in this context the conventional allegory of "Liberty" does not go without saying. Minerva in fact directs her gaze as if to act as overseer, mimicking the poses of the overseers in the antebellum scenes from the emblems of Alabama and Louisiana: the blacks no longer serve the agrarian slavocracy, for their new master is mercantile capitalism. If liberty is one of the products of the war, these emblems show that it is unequally distributed.

None of the emblems suggests that the war brought about any changes in the social structure of the South. Since victor and vanquished were both white (and equally "Americans"), the emblems disguise the discourse of empire by usurping the place of Southern whites. The picture is of a land of abundant resources (including the indigenous labor power of black persons) ripe for expropriation. As Marx argues in *Capital*, colonialist operations display the inner structure of capitalism—the expropriation of the worker by means of the accumulation of capital—in a particularly revealing way. The American Civil War "brought a very rapid centralization of capital" in its aftermath; according to Marx it marked a transition from a colonial to a fully capitalized economy as indicated by the final "annihilation of that private property which rests on the labor of the individual himself" (940). The maps published by *Harper's* display the subjugation of the colored races, while veiling a more sophisticated proposal for the economic and political domination of Southern whites. Racial ideology represented the former structure as "natural," but the American rhetoric of democratic political representation would not permit the *display* of the latter structure. The blacks and Native Americans, of course, would suffer (in different ways) under the weight of both.

By photographing landscapes and cityscapes, Barnard supplies information on the material condition of the Southern states, of the sort called for by *Harper's*. The maps, emblems, and genre sketches disseminated by *Harper's* show us part of the context within which these photographic representations could be transformed into cultural symbols. Very few Vermonters would migrate to Virginia to farm the land, as *Harper's* explicitly proposed; but they would go south to "carpetbag," accompanying the substantial migration of Northern capital southward during Reconstruction. The land in Barnard's photographs is generally depopulated—and this is not only because the conventions of military history dictate the erasure of the experience of the common soldier. The depopulated landscape in nineteenth-century America symbolizes an open invitation to colonization. In the case of the South, the paradigm could no longer maintain the literal force that it still commanded in the set-

FIG. 28. "Ruins in Charleston, S.C.," Barnard, *Photographic Views of Sherman's Campaign,* plate 60. Library of Congress.

tlement of the western territories. But Barnard's photographs offer the invitation symbolically, as Cole's "prehistorical" landscapes had done in the 1820s and 30s.

The few persons represented in Barnard's photographs contemplate scenes of destruction, as for example in "Ruins in Charleston, S.C.," the penultimate image in the *Views* (fig. 28). An important convention attached to the picturesque ruin since the seventeenth century had been the topos of *sic transit gloria mundi* (for example, Gray's "Elegy" and Shelley's "Ozymandias"). In analogous visual representations, the figure of the contemplative spectator in the image had prescribed our position as viewer, and had inspired our meditation on this topic. Even in the absence of a represented figure, the convention exerted a strong influence.[12] Thus Trachtenberg, whose reading of "Ruins in Charleston" seems informed by this convention, suggests that the "two contemplative figures" involve the viewer in the act of "reclaiming the scene for culture by aestheticizing it" (25). In this scene of cultural ruin the dominant ideology of social hierarchy survives, allegorized in the composition of the image. Upon glancing at the photograph, we immediately notice the white man sitting on the summit of a pile of rubble; a bit later the black youth, whose clothing provides less contrast with the ground, comes clearly into view. The respective position of the figures implies that while much of the culture of the South has been destroyed, one ideological structure, supposedly natural and equally valuable to Northern and Southern whites alike, has been preserved.

An innovation in the representation of the contemplative figure functions on a deeper ideological level. Neither white nor black Southerner commands the complete view to which we, as Barnard's Northern spectators, are privileged. The scaffold signifies that Reconstruction is already beginning, but it seems as if the white Southerner and the black youth whose position he "oversees" refuse to acknowledge it; their gazes are directed elsewhere. "Knowledge," *Harper's* assured its readers in 1866, "is the key with which the golden treasure of the Future is to be unlocked" ("Our Maps"). Thus from the perspective of the camera—which occupies a privileged position and surveys the entire scene—the Southerners, like the constricted field of their nostalgic gaze, become symbolic objects of appropriation. They look at their past in ruins; we see the future that will be constructed for them.

It is doubtful that Barnard's "Ruins in Charleston" had any direct economic or cultural impact on the South, just as the maps and sketches in *Harper's* did not cause an immediate influx of New Englanders into Virginia. Any significant political effect achieved by the *Photographic Views of Sherman's Campaign* (by means of their influence on the wealthy and powerful Northerners who purchased them from Barnard's New York gallery) would be nearly impossible to demonstrate. Barnard's album does not even display the overtly propagandizing tone of parts of Gardner's *Sketch Book*. But it does reveal an important contemporary response to the war. The most visible photographs of the Civil War were "Brady's" Antietam series (fig. 8) and his contemplative view of a pond and woods at Gettysburg, which were available for mass consumption as engravings in *Harper's*. Barnard refines the picturesque aesthetic that prescribed both the composition and selection of these images. The *Photographic Views of Sherman's Campaign* thus exemplify the restorative but evasive pastoralism that structured the production and reception of Civil War photography.

In general, the photographic work of the Brady circle proposes a naturalizing ideological attitude toward the violence of the war. As Roland Barthes describes the terms of such an attitude,

> it purifies [historical conditions], it makes them innocent, it gives them a natural and eternal justification, it gives them a clarity which is not that of an explanation but that of a statement of fact. If I *state the fact* of French imperiality without explaining it, I am very near to finding that it is natural and *goes without saying*: I am reassured. (*Mythologies*, 143)

Barthes identifies this attitude as "myth." The myth of the Civil War as a legitimate instance of the violation of human bodies was conveyed, contemporarily, by the aesthetic forms most suited to historical evasion and ideological naturalization; these forms were the realistic pastoral and the picturesque. The realism of the photograph lent its legitimacy to the ideology inscribed therein (for even obviously staged images such as Barnard's "Ruins in Charleston" and Gardner's "What Do I Want, John Henry?" seem to contain a large portion of natural truth). Under the impression that they were merely documenting the facts in aesthetically appropriate ways, Civil War photographers were making a more subtle kind of documentary, by representing the "nature" of the Union.

6. Melville's *Battle-Pieces* as a Trace of War

THE TITLE of Melville's *Battle-Pieces and Aspects of the War* (1866) alludes to a representational problem by inviting us to look for "the war" in the "pieces" and "aspects" as they appear in the volume. The poems engage the tendencies of contemporary representations of the Civil War to aestheticize the effects of violence and to evade questions about the historical contingency of politics. Whitman, Gardner, and Barnard propose the recovery of a natural image of America as a means to restore the Union; in their representations, the wounds of war disappear into a rhetoric of nature and necessity. Melville criticizes the naturalizing tendency of such representations, finding in the pastoral-organic aspect of the war only the promise of further disintegration and destruction. He displaces the conventional inscriptions that harmonize nature, the human body, and ideology with images of chaos and disruption. His view argues against the possibility of legitimating the political outcome of the war in terms of Nature or any other external category.

The political agenda of *Battle-Pieces* sometimes seems to consist in a simple affirmation of Unionism; in "Dupont's Round Fight," for example, the Federal navy is described as "the Fleet that Warred for Right" and the defeat of "the rebel" as a "victory of Law" (*CP*, 15). In other poems, however, Melville criticizes the political and aesthetic assumptions that might ground such an affirmation. Since the beginning of his artistic career, Melville had explored the means by which both political and aesthetic structures of representation prescribe the relations between the subject and the state. In *Battle-Pieces* he continues this exploration to discover that the violence of the Civil War cannot be attached in any meaningful way to a democratic ideology. Rather than providing a stable ideological foundation for the restoration of the American state, the war merely prefigures its own endless repetition. The violence that is predicted is not necessarily physical (although sometimes it is just that, as when Melville hints that racial violence could follow the war). More broadly, Melville is concerned with the mode of political subjectivity prescribed by a militaristic state. As he traces the history of the violent conservation of the Union, he reopens the wounds of war at the level of representation.

I.   *Say what some poets will, Nature is not so much her own ever-sweet in-*
     terpreter, as the mere supplier of that cunning alphabet, whereby selecting
     and combining as he pleases, each man reads his own peculiar lesson
     according to his own peculiar mind and mood. (Pierre, 342)

Several contradictory models for the representation of the war are proposed in *Battle-Pieces*. The production of poetry is figured variously as:
recollecting a "memory," transcribing the airs of an Aeolian harp, writing
a classical drama, and rewriting the journalistic record of the war. Critics
have interpreted Melville's conflicting metacommentaries on poetic representation as claims for the underlying unity of *Battle-Pieces*—suggesting
for example that the essence of the volume is the conception of "historic
tragedy" and that the "wayward winds" are only figures for this essence.[1]
But tragedy is only enacted; it is a masquerade that demands the confidence
of the spectator. Michael Paul Rogin argues that the war restored Melville's
confidence—that he "found political renewal in the Civil War" because
it "reconnected him to public events in America." Thus the war, for
Melville, "sanctified the 'political edifice'" of the Union, as represented
by the dome of the Capitol building which "dominates the landscape
of *Battle-Pieces*" (*SG*, 256, 262, 263). But it did not at all sanctify a particular
mode or apparatus of representation. It was not clear just what the iron
dome represented, or how it did so. We know that Melville saw that
the dome was painted to assume the appearance of stone; a symbol that
was central to his ideology (according to Rogin) was a facade, a structure
whose only function was ornamentation.[2]

The preface to *Battle-Pieces* states that "with few exceptions, the
Pieces in this volume originated in an impulse imparted by the fall of
Richmond." Although the poems were composed at a time when Northern
victory was imminent and the war thus could be regarded as an event
with historically delimited boundaries, Melville writes that

> the aspects which the strife as a memory assumes are as manifold
> as are the moods of involuntary meditation—moods variable, and
> at times widely at variance. Yielding instinctively, one after another,
> to feelings not inspired from any one source exclusively, and un-
> mindful, without purposing to be, of consistency, I seem, in most
> of these verses, to have but placed a harp in a window, and noted
> the contrasted airs which wayward winds have played upon the
> strings. (*CP*, 446)

At the outset we are at a double remove, as the winds of war are translated
from one medium to another. Neither medium seems reliable; the memory

166

of the war is fading even as Melville writes, and the vagaries of the harp seem incongruous with the decisions necessary to produce a coherent historical account of the war.

The preface may have been inspired by Coleridge's association of the sound from the harp with the vicissitudes of the mind:

> Full many a thought uncall'd and undetain'd
> Traverse my indolent and passive brain
> As wild and various as the random gales
> That swirl and flutter on this subject lute. (399)

In Coleridge's usage, the harp is not a metaphor for memory (the thoughts are "undetain'd").[3] Thus if Melville is alluding to Coleridge, his use of the figure suggests that the vagrancy of poetic thought impedes the goal of historical representation. The figure would seem to prohibit him from writing *memoranda* of the war; and yet he is concerned with the "aspects which the strife as memory assumes."

The last sentence of the volume provides an artistic model very different from that of airs playing on an Aeolian harp. Concluding his prose "Supplement," in which he argues for the reconciliation and mutual tolerance of North and South, black and white, Melville writes: "Let us pray that the great historic tragedy of our time may not have been enacted without instructing our whole beloved country through terror and pity; and may fulfillment verify in the end those expectations which kindle the bards of Progress and Humanity" (*CP*, 467). Aristotelian tragedy, honoring the unities to produce catharsis, may be an apt metaphor for a war that restored the Union. (Perhaps the "bards of Progress" will next write a comedy.) Unity may be perceived in "*historic*" tragedy if history is regarded teleologically and "God appears in apt events" ("The Battle for the Mississippi," *CP*, 42). But the alternate model for history supplied by Melville's preface, in which "the strife as memory" can only be compared to the "contrasted airs" of "wayward winds," suggests that this sort of unity is inaccessible, unknowable, and therefore not susceptible of representation.

Tragedy suggests necessity; the prefatory image of the Aeolian harp suggests an equally significant model of chance. A middle term, choice, appears in Melville's use of textual and visual sources. His footnotes to the individual poems indicate that in composing the *Battle-Pieces* he relied heavily on accounts of battles and other events as he found them in *The Rebellion Record*, a thirteen-volume compendium of journalistic reports, speeches, maps, and other documents published by Putnam's (Cohen, 15–

18). By thus displaying his dependence on textual sources, Melville is claiming that the poet of war does not bare his soul to the event (as Whitman, following the Romantics, had pretended to do). In this mode he does not invite the *genius loci* to inscribe itself, but insists that he transcribes only prior transcriptions. The event, object, or experience to be represented is not its "own ever-sweet interpreter" (*Pierre*, 342). But while the poems of *Battle-Pieces* self-consciously admit (to a much greater extent than those of *Drum-Taps*) that their relation to the war is mediated by an apparatus of previously inscribed facts, at the same time they attempt to maintain their status as poetry, a representational apparatus significantly different from reportage. Hence Melville's conflicting assertion that he had "but placed a harp in a window" and "noted the contrasted airs."

Melville uses the image of the Aeolian harp in two texts other than *Battle-Pieces*, associating it in both instances with destruction. These uses suggest the aptness of the harp as a figure for the representation of the war as a historical rupture. In *Moby-Dick*, the sound of the wind in the rigging warns that the *Pequod* will be destroyed if Ahab is allowed to indulge his monomania. Ahab is deaf to "the presaging vibrations of the winds in the cordage." Starbuck, who cries "let the Typhoon sing, and strike his harp here in our rigging," explains to Stubb "what's in the wind": "Yonder, to windward, all is blackness of doom; but to leeward, homeward—I see it lightens up there; but not with the lightning" (164, 504–05). Starbuck does not confuse prophecy with necessity, arguing repeatedly for the *Pequod* to turn back. The harp presages destruction, but the submission of Starbuck and the crew to Ahab's authority permits the catastrophic end of the voyage.

A second instance of the figure occurs in *John Marr and Other Sailors*. "The Aeolian Harp," although composed long after the Civil War, is suggestive in its treatment of memory and pictorial representation. Melville describes the remains of a shipwreck, caused by a gale like that which now resonates on the strings. Unlike the rigging of the *Pequod*, this harp is not prophetic but retrospective:

> List the harp in window wailing
>   Stirred by gales from fitful sea:
> Shrieking up in mad crescendo—
>   Dying down in plaintive key!
>
> Listen: less a strain ideal
>   Than Ariel's rendering of the Real.

> What that Real is, let hint
> A picture stamped in memory's mint.　　　　　　(*CP*, 194)

The switch from sound to picture in the middle of the second stanza, at the point where "memory" is invoked, suggests that the harp interested Melville as a (failed) mode of representation. The currency of memory is said to be permanent here, a tangible record that contrasts with the vagaries of the wind. The "Real" is unknowable (although it is privileged over the even less relevant "Ideal"); it can only be approached through the detour of a different image impressed in the mind. And yet, like the tune of the Aeolian harp, the visual mode of representation also fails to connect with "the Real." A coin bears a picture, and "memory's mint" is said to be as substantial in itself as a coin; but, like the relation of money to labor-power, this picture is only a substitute (a "hint") for the unnamed referent of the "Real." The shipwreck described in the middle section of the poem is not the particular wreck signified by the wailing of the harp, but a reconstruction from memory. Melville cannot give a picture or any other representation of the crew's experience of the wreck:

> O, the sailors—O, the sails!
> O, the lost crews never heard of!
> Well the harp of Ariel wails
> Thoughts that tongue can tell no word of!　　　　　(196)

In these, the final lines of the poem, Melville describes the limits of pictorial representation, which memory cannot transcend.

In *Battle-Pieces*, Melville explores another visual model for representation—the relatively new medium of photography. The photograph is added to the list of metapoetic figures (memory, reportage, tragedy, Aeolian harp) that frame the question of representation. Prior to the war he had addressed the limitations of daguerreotypy, reporting Pierre's reasoning that "instead of, as in old times, immortalizing a genius, a portrait now only *dayalized* a dunce." By preserving only one moment in an individual's history and presenting it as the truth, the daguerreotype hypostatizes a representation to which one would have to conform oneself in the future. Thus Pierre concludes that "when every body has his portrait published, true distinction lies in not having yours published at all. For if you are published along with Tom, Dick, and Harry, and wear a coat of their cut, how then are you distinct from Tom, Dick, and Harry?" (254). Pierre realizes that, at this stage of his career, he would be "dayalized

[as] a dunce" if he had his portrait taken. A daguerreotype may reveal the truth of a moment; but Pierre, the prospective genius, does not want to have to live in that moment for the rest of his life.

In "On the Photograph of a Corps Commander" Melville meditates on the regularizing tendency of photographic representation he had identified in *Pierre*; but he displays a more complex attitude toward this tendency. The historical text to which the poem alludes has prevented any objection that this photograph only "dayalized a dunce." The subject is identified as "the soul that led / In Spotsylvania's charge" (*CP*, 69).[4] Although a heroic history frames the image, Melville remains relatively uninterested in its historicity. The image is not important because it represents a specific person, but because of what it shows about "man" as a type (about all the Toms, Dicks, and Harrys, to use Pierre's expression). The poem opens with a regularizing tautology—that "man is manly." The aesthetic response to this tautologous perception is that the photograph is

> A cheering picture. It is good
>   To look upon a Chief like this,
> In whom the spirit moulds the form.   (70)

Melville responds to the portrait as an epitome of masculinity. Yet since "man" and words derived from it appear ten times in this twenty-four line poem, the claim that "the spirit moulds the form" seems finally to be a hollow, pro forma assertion (70).[5]

Melville's interpretation of photographic signs marking gender reveals what we have always known—that war can define aspects of what is "manly." But if the "warrior-carriage of the head" and other icons of militarism are sufficient signs of masculinity, it is not clear that they are therefore necessary signs (69). Since Melville is not a soldier, he himself ("a fellow-man") would not be "manly" according to such an exclusive definition. The poem does not show any way to attach its characterization of gender to a contemporary ideological position with regard to the Civil War. Whitman found, in his poetics of adhesiveness, a certain configuration of masculinity that was supposed to epitomize his democratic ideology. Neither Melville's poem nor the photograph suggests any basis for judgment about political positions: "man" can be said to be "manly" under a wide range of ideologies. Still, we might criticize Melville for not envisioning an alignment of masculinity with pacifism. If a certain icon of masculinity is one result of the war, as is clear from this poem, such an icon might also have contributed to the causes of the war. But this is a question that, contemporarily, no one seems to have asked.

Melville concludes with an attempt to transform the opening tautology into a bond between men not unlike Whitman's idea of adhesiveness. The image is said to "kindle strains that warm." But unlike Whitman, Melville does not draw, in the final stanza, any political inference from this possibly homoerotic response:

> Nothing can lift the heart of man
>   Like manhood in a fellow man.
> The thought of heaven's great King afar
> But humbles us—too weak to scan;
> But manly greatness men can span,
>   And feel the bonds that draw.   (70)

Where Whitman described a bond between man and man, and drew from this description an ideological paradigm of democratic Unionism, Melville describes a bond between man and an *image* in a political vacuum. He hints that narcissism is the real ground of the wartime camaraderie Whitman valorized. The viewer of the photograph is supposed to identify himself, "a fellow man," with the idealized subject of the photograph; but he remains locked in his own narcissistic gaze.[6] His eyes are averted from the one source of ideological narrative mentioned in the poem— theodicy. The removal of theodicy as an ideologically productive structure ("heaven's great King *afar*"), like the inscrutability of "the Real" in "The Aeolian Harp," reveals the trace that the war leaves, in Melville's aesthetic, as a crisis of representation.

The *Battle-Pieces* explore the consequences of this crisis on two levels. First there are the problems of representational politics that produced the war, and which the war only seems to have resolved; here the poems demonstrate a discontinuity between the prosecution of war and certain values supposed to characterize the American ideology, such as democratic politics, the autonomy of the subject and the like. Second, and especially significant with respect to the work of Whitman and the photographers, is the way in which Melville negotiates the meaning of an unspeakable event—death in war—at the level of representation. Photographic captions attempt to inject meaning into a potentially meaningless image of a corpse; Melville, as we have seen, shows how limited the legitimate production of photographic meaning must be even in the case of a representation of a living person. Whitman had attempted to produce meaning by mobilizing the contemporary rhetorical topoi of embodiment, sacrifice, and exchange, and (like the photographers) by drawing a pastoral frame around the war. Melville is skeptical of recuperative activity. In several poems he ironizes the topoi used by Whitman and envisions the degeneration of the pastoral topos; the crisis of pastoralism becomes a figure for the larger representational problems posed by the war. In *Battle-Pieces*, the attempt to legitimate the war by means of a naturalizing rhetoric produces only disruption.

II.   *Political institutions, which in other lands seem above all things intensely artificial, with America seem to possess the divine virtue of a natural law. (Pierre, 9)*

From Tommo's paranoiac apprehensions to Billy Budd's uncomprehending last words, Melville's texts exhibit a fascination with the apparatuses of political representation and political repression. He is continually "trying out" different metaphors for political subjectivity and the state. His first essay in comparative political science takes him to a land of cannibals; we shall see that in the *Battle-Pieces* he returns there.

When Tommo jumps ship at Nukuheva, he justifies his decision by claiming that political authority on the *Dolly* was not structured as it first appeared to be. "The usage on board of her was tyrannical," he explains, and the "captain was the author of these abuses" (*Typee*, 21). He had perceived political authority to be a matter of contract: "I signed as a matter of course the ship's articles, thereby voluntarily engaging and legally binding myself to serve in a certain capacity for the period of the voyage . . . . But in all contracts, if one party fail to perform his share of the compact, is not the other virtually absolved from his liability?" (20). Believing that he has shipped as a subject of a constitutional monarchy, he discovers that the real form of the state on board the *Dolly* is tyranny. The captain has in effect erased the ship's articles; his "prompt reply to all complaints and remonstrances was—the butt end of a handspike, so convincingly administered, as effectually to silence the aggrieved party" (21).

Having lived for so long under this very palpable structure of political authority, Tommo is puzzled by the absence of anything resembling a state apparatus among the Typees: "To all appearances there were no courts of law or equity. There was no municipal police for the purpose of apprehending vagrants and disorderly characters. In short, there were no legal provisions whatever for the well-being and conservation of society, the enlightened end of civilized legislation" (200). Tommo comes to discover, however, that an invisible state is manifested in several forms.

He discerns a sort of benevolent paternalism, in which "the natives appeared to form one household, whose members are bound together by the ties of strong affection" (204). The hierarchy within the family of the state is displayed in a system of tatoos: "In the decoration of the chiefs it seems to be necessary to exercise the most elaborate penciling; while some of the inferior natives looked as if they had been daubed over indiscriminately with a house-painter's brush" (220). These structures of authority have analogues in antebellum America, although Tommo seems not to recognize it (perhaps because, in relation to his skin color, his political status among the Typees is an inversion of his status as an American citizen). The model of benevolent paternalism was commonly used by Southerners as a legitimating description of the slave system (Rogin, *SG*, 214). Skin color marked the sociopolitical status of the Europeans, Africans, and Native Americans living on American soil (as citizens, current or former slaves, and noncitizens, respectively). Similarly, the practice of tattooing among the Typees writes an individual's sociopolitical being onto the surface of his or her body. By means of these representations one becomes a walking description of one's relationship to the state, an embodied representation of one's political subjectivity. This semiotic structure is authorized by a legal text both among the Typees (although here the text is only implicit) and in the United States. Among the Typees, tattooing is interconnected with the structure of "taboo," the "dictates" of which "guide and control every action of [the Typee's] being" (221). Tommo confesses that he is "wholly at a loss where to look for the authority which regulates this potent institution" (224). He does not recognize the source of political authority because he looks for it beyond itself, in an external regulatory structure. But the structure of authority is inscribed on the body of every citizen; it is its own self-authorizing and self-perpetuating source. This (in)visible relationship between the state and inscribed representation bears significantly on the question of representation as it is posed in *Moby-Dick* and the *Battle-Pieces*.

In *Moby-Dick*, political representation is shown to have no transcendent ground: one cannot find, external to the structure of authority itself, any justification for the primacy of one model of representation over another.[7] The metaphors for the state that Melville explores derive from Hobbes's complex analogy, part of which is quoted in the "Extracts" that preface the book: "By art is created that great Leviathan, called a Commonwealth or State—(in Latin, Civitas) which is but an artificial man" (xx). There is a confusion between organic and mechanistic models, since the state in Hobbes's sentence is, by turns, a monster, a mechanical apparatus, or a human body.[8] Initially, the structure of authority that Ahab creates is represented as a machine: "my one cogged circle fits into all their various wheels, and they revolve" (167). Ishmael internalizes the mechanistic model: "my oath had been welded with theirs . . . and more did I hammer and clinch my oath, because of the dread in my soul" (179). As they approach nearer to Moby-Dick, however, the mechanism begins to transform itself into an organism: "They were one man, not thirty. . . . all varieties were welded into oneness, and were directed to that fatal goal which Ahab their one lord and keel did point to" (557). The transformation into an organism is completed on the third and final day of the chase, when Ahab cries, "Ye are not other men, but my arms and my legs; and so obey me," asserting a kingly role as the head of the body politic (568). Ahab's death and the sinking of the Pequod reveal the destructive potential of the various metaphors comprising Hobbes's model of the state. After the catastrophe, Ishmael calls himself an "orphan," yet again transforming the model of the state, from single body to family. He is taken in by the Rachel, "search[ing] after her missing children" (573). If this ending represents, in contrast to Ahab's illegitimate authority, the benevolent face of a maternalistic model, Melville would go on to show its destructive face in Pierre.

As Michael Ryan points out in a critique of Hobbes's Leviathan, an "absolute political state is necessarily logocentric because it depends on law, which in turn depends on the univocal meaning of words." The state must banish "the open possibility of displacement which metaphor represents" (3, 5). With metaphor, of course, goes poetry, since poetry is generally thought to be the least univocal discourse, the most dependent for its effects on rhetorical slippage. But Hobbes's own model for the state metaphorically (even "poetically") introduces this sort of slippage— which Melville explores in his book about the Leviathan. As in Tommo's puzzlement over the question of the state of the Typees, the confusion over models of political authority in Moby-Dick reveals the relation between the discourse of the state and the formation of the subject; once the state is destroyed, Ishmael escapes, but only to reproduce its discourse in his own text.

"The Battle for the Bay," in Battle-Pieces, shows that for the military man autonomous subjectivity is wholly displaced by the discourse of the state. Unlike the apparatus of political authority on Typee, which had been inscribed visibly on the body, the texts of heroism and duty that maintain authority in America are internalized. The sailors are less self-aware of this internalization than Ishmael had been; the displacement is now invisible to the subject himself:

> Below, the sleeping sailors swing,
> And in their dreams to quarters spring,
> Or cheer the flag, or breast a stormy tide. (73)

The rhetorical outside has taken over the experiential inside of the sailors. The effect of martial discipline is such that they maintain their loyalty to the state, and speak its language of subjugation, even in their dreams. Melville describes a similar phenomenon among the crew of the *Bellipotent*: "True martial discipline long continued superinduces in average man a sort of impulse whose operation at the official word of command much *resembles* in its promptitude the effect of instinct" (*Billy Budd*, 127, emphasis added). The ideological efficacy of this displacement of subjectivity results from its miming of biological instinct, which naturalizes the mechanism of political authority.

When the sailors described in "The Battle for the Bay" are at "quarters" in anticipation of acting out what they had lately dreamed, "The decks were hushed like fanes in prayer; / Behind each man a holy angel stood" (*CP*, 73). We realize that this transformation of consciousness through discipline has a palpable, material source, if we recall Melville's comments on a very similar tableau in *White-Jacket*: "Nor seems it a practice warranted by the Sermon on the Mount, for the officer of a battery, in time of battle, to stand over the men with his drawn sword . . . and run through on the spot the first seaman who showed a semblance of fear" (314). Subject to the repressive power of the state even while, in fighting a war "for the Union," they also act as its material representatives, sailors in "The Battle for the Bay" live according to a semblance of bravery and loyalty that becomes their only reality. They are, like Plato's hypothetical statue of Cratylus, what they imitate.

While many of the *Battle-Pieces* describe the bonds of duty that subjugate the soldier, this metaphor was supplied most readily by the new topic of ironclad ships. The commander of the *Monitor* declaims, "Ay, Turret, rivet me here to duty fast!" ("In the Turret," *CP*, 37). As with the sailors represented in "The Battle for the Bay," the commander's internalization of the rhetoric of the militaristic state he serves is so extensive that he submits his autonomy to the war machine. (Melville reminds us that his name was "Worden" (35); history seems to have supplied a pun here, in the sense that he polices himself.) "A Utilitarian View

175

of the Monitor's Fight" argues that the sailor is similarly subservient to his machine, a laborer

> in War now placed—
> Where War belongs—
> Among the trades and artisans.
> . . . .
> War yet shall be, but warriors
> Are now but operatives; War's made
> Less grand than Peace,
> And a singe runs through lace and feather.   (CP, 40)

This representation does not go as far as White-Jacket's assertions that the sailor in a man-of-war is a slave. But it does hint, in its reorientation of the rhetoric of heroism, at the repressive relationship in war between labor and capital—"a rich man's war and a poor man's fight," in contemporary parlance (McPherson, 607).[9] It locates war within the emergent structure of the American political economy; if it is "Less grand than Peace" it nevertheless may be regarded as a business that is practical, given a plentiful labor supply and a confidence in the ideological market. As Melville had already shown in "The Tartarus of Maids," there is no provision in industrial capitalism for the autonomy of the laborer; they are one with the mechanism that structures their lives.

The metaphor of a ship of state, an artificial Leviathan, no doubt suggested itself to Melville as he composed Battle-Pieces.[10] In "Misgivings" it is aligned with the metaphor, made famous by Lincoln, of the state as a house threatened by structural division:

> With shouts the torrents down the gorges go
> And storms are formed behind the storm we feel:
> The hemlock shakes in the rafter, and the oak in the driving keel.
>   (CP, 4)

But Melville does not belabor the metaphor in Battle-Pieces, and in fact questions its relevance in "The Stone Fleet," which describes how several decrepit wooden ships were filled with stones and sunk in an unsuccessful attempt to block Charleston Harbor. Melville includes some names that have Southern associations, now obsolescent:

> Four were erst patrician keels
> (Names attest what families be),
> The Kensington, and Richmond too

Leonidas, and Lee:
> But now they have their seat
> With the Old Stone Fleet. (16)

These—names and ships—are replaced by a new order, a technologized method of warfare that reveals a repressive system of politics as well: "The rivets clinch the iron-clads, / Men learn a deadlier lore" ("The Temeraire," *CP*, 39). It is not literally true that ironclad warfare was "deadlier" than a traditional naval battle; men were maimed and died in each. The reference instead suggests the increasingly repressive effects of technologized warfare on men such as Worden.

As ironclads were replacing oaken ships, so a new iron dome replaced the old wooden dome of the Capitol building. In "The Conflict of Convictions" Melville does not envision the new state as a machine with moving parts, like an ironclad ship or like the early figures for Ahab's political power on the *Pequod*. The American state Melville envisions is an immobile, unresponsive edifice:

> Power unanointed may come—
> Dominion (unsought by the free)
> > And the Iron Dome,
> Stronger for stress and strain,
> Flings her huge shadow athwart the main;
> But the Founder's dream shall flee. (7)

Unlike a mechanistic model of political authority—which implies that the state-machine can be adjusted and even rebuilt, if necessary, but will eventually break down if it is not maintained—the architectural model of the "Iron Dome" is eternally secure and even stress-hardened by the winds of war. (Melville creates an engineering fiction here; in fact, repeated stress and strain will weaken a metal structure and eventually cause its failure.) Democracy—"the Founder's dream"—is not in this poem the representational foundation of the state, as it is sometimes said to be, but an evanescent light chased away by the dark shadow of the dome. In alternate stanzas an oppositional voice criticizes the project of empire and the prosecution of the war, claiming to see "rust on the iron Dome" (5).

The prose "Supplement" which concludes the volume questions whether the war has truly silenced this oppositional voice. The war, Melville fears, has not settled any important political questions. It has, for example, solved the problem of slavery only by leaving a substantial part of its

ideology intact. The resolution of the representational issues (among them
the question of slavery) by means of war—a structure of violence that
demands the subservience of the subject to the state—has not produced
a legitimate ideological consensus. Melville hints at the popular, white
attitude toward the question of emancipation in "A Meditation." The
subtitle of the poem identifies it as a dramatic monologue spoken by "a
Northerner after Attending the last of Two Funerals from the Same
Homestead—Those of a National and Confederate Officer (Brothers)."
The speaker is also a soldier, who recalls the wartime feelings of both
Northern and Southern whites:

> Warm passion cursed the cause of war:
> Can Africa pay back this blood
>> Spilt on Potomac's shore?
> Yet doubts, as pangs, were vain the strife to stay,
> And hands that fain had clasped again could slay.   (154)

As Rogin argues, these lines give "blacks the responsibility for redeeming
America" (SG, 279). They do not necessarily reveal Melville's own attitude, since the poem is clearly a dramatic monologue. The sentiment
is placed within the context of a retrospective account of a conflict now
over, given by one who fought in it. The question it raises is how to
prevent violence from resurfacing, how in the context of Reconstruction
the political inequality between black and white is to be resolved. If,
as a result of the war, even Northerners hold such attitudes, then the
prospects of a genuine resolution are dim.

The image of slavery occupies the center of two other poems. One,
"Formerly a Slave," describes "an idealized portrait by E. Vedder" on
view "in the spring exhibition of the National Academy, 1865." Since
the portrait is "idealized" it invites a sentimental, optimistic textualization:

> The suffrance of her race is shown
>> And retrospect of life,
> Which now too late deliverance dawns upon;
>> Yet she is not at strife.
>
> Her children's children they shall know
>> The good withheld from her.   (CP, 101)

"The Swamp Angel" provides a marked contrast. The title refers to the
name given by soldiers to "the great Parrot gun, planted in the marshes
of James Island" (453).[11] Their description of the cannon as "a coal-black
Angel / With a thick Afric lip" (70) raises the same question that had

troubled the Northern soldier of "A Meditation." It locates the source of violence in the former slaves, identifying the tendency of Northerners and Southerners alike to make them responsible for the war. Even more drastically than the sailors in the ironclads, the black person's subjectivity is prescribed only by the limited, violent images of the military state. The prospects for the gradual amelioration sentimentally described in "Formerly a Slave" seem questionable.

The supposed resolution of ideological questions provided by the war itself, Melville suggests, merely threatens the repetition of violence and the perpetuation of racism. (Indeed, the nation would suffer from racial violence in the coming years.) In the concluding "Supplement" to *Battle-Pieces*, he cautions that "it is vain to glide, with moulded words, over the difficulties . . . . Wherefore in a clear sky do we still turn our eyes toward the South as the Neapolitan, months after the eruption, turns his toward Vesuvius? Do we dread that the repose may be deceptive? In the recent convulsion has the crater but shifted?" (465). The image of the volcano significantly replaces the image, developed in the poetry, of the "Iron Dome" and resonates with the image of the "coal-black" cannon of "The Swamp Angel." But the source of eruption is the white South; its direction double: Southern blacks and Northern whites. "There has been an upheaval affecting the basis of things," a violence which threatens to resurface (461).

Thus in order to contribute toward reconciliation Melville develops a modest proposal for the restoration of the South. His metaphors for the peacetime state, however, are as ominous as those for the state of war. The emancipation poses the most acute political problem of peacetime. Melville first suggests a program of "philanthrop[y] toward the blacks" (465). This recommendation is well-intentioned if ineffective; but its terms are ironic, for they imply a paternalism that had been Melville's own metaphor for the Southern state: Confederates had been "allied by family" to Robert E. Lee; in seceding from the Union they "cleaved to the natural part" ("Lee in the Capitol," *CP*, 148, 151). Thus a paternalistic model would reinscribe the antebellum state that ruptured in the war, and would reproduce the legitimating metaphor of slavery.

Shifting from philanthropy to a more politically minded program of meliorating legislation (which, however, remains unspecified), Melville also switches metaphors for the state: "Our institutions have a potent digestion, and may in time convert and assimilate to good all elements thrown in, however originally alien" (465). We now find ourselves where Melville began his career-long analysis of political power and authority—

in a cannibal land. In envisioning a model capable of maintaining authority and controlling political chaos, Melville develops the organic metaphor of the state to a point where it implicitly threatens to consume everyone, including himself. Tommo escapes being devoured by the Typees; it remains an open question whether the Americans will be able to escape their own cannibalistic state. Ishmael alone had detached himself from the body politic whose head was Ahab; the rest of that body destroyed itself.

Melville realizes that his own poems are implicated in the "upheaval affecting the basis of things" (461). He admits that he has "been tempted to withdraw or modify some of them, fearful lest in presenting, though but dramatically and by way of poetic record, the passions and epithets of civil war, I might be contributing to the bitterness that every sensible American must wish at an end" (463). Thus he suggests that his poetic representations of the war are not restorative—that in substituting words for wounds, in what appears to be a healing, reconciliatory gesture, he is only perpetuating a representational crisis of the sort that produced the war in its confusion over the relations between representation, the subject, and the state.

To write poetry about war is, in some sense, always to aestheticize it; poetry necessarily evades "the real war" (mentioned but not represented by Whitman) because it is only a representation. If war poetry is never quite about war, in *Battle-Pieces* it is often about the trace that the Civil War has left on the apparatus of poetry. But poetry's concern with its own status as an apparatus of representation is not a merely self-referring, politically irresponsible gesture. Whitman's "Lilacs," for example, is self-reflexively about poetry, but it is also about the cultural and political activity of attempting to make an ideologically productive image of America. Poetry is connected to the state by virtue of its place within the general network of representation and inscription that constructs the political experience of the individual. The *Battle-Pieces* reflect critically on the cultural function of the affirmative poetry of the Civil War, which was to aestheticize and thereby legitimate war, patriotism, and the state.

III. *As a statue, planted on a revolving pedestal, shows now this limb, now that; now front, now back, now side; continually changing, too, its general profile; so does the pivoted, statued soul of man, when turned by the hand of Truth. Lies only never vary; look for no invariableness in Pierre. Nor*

*does any canting showman here stand by to announce his phases as he
revolves. Catch his phases as your insight may. (Pierre, 337)*

There has been some disagreement over the "realism" of the representation of violence and its aftermath in *Battle-Pieces.*[12] By modern standards
there are relatively few signs of pain or injury. Unlike Whitman, Melville
did not nurse the wounded and so did not see firsthand the vast effects
of wartime violence; he was never near the fighting, although he did
visit a camp behind the lines where his cousin was stationed (Miller, 306).
In many poems, however, a dramatization of the lack of firsthand experience of the war permits a critical perspective—one that Whitman
never quite manages, and which is completely beyond the optimistic view
of the photographers, who were confident that their cameras were recording for posterity images of "the real war." In writing *Battle-Pieces*
Melville was conscious that he was critically re-presenting extant verbal
and visual representations of the war. Poems such as "Donelson," "Running the Batteries," and "The House-Top," versify and otherwise ma-
nipulate (without apology) previously published journalistic accounts from
the *Rebellion Record*; in doing so they demonstrate the mystifying political
effects of the prevalent journalistic and poetic tendencies to aestheticize
the war. The recuperative tropes of the rhetoric of war—of the sort
that structure the poetics of *Drum-Taps*—are ironized in these poems.

"Donelson," which appears early in the volume, dramatizes Melville's compositional method by interweaving versified dispatches from
the front with descriptions of and commentaries on the reactions of the
civilian readers of those dispatches. One dispatch reports the following
grisly view of the field outside of Fort Donelson:

> Our heedless boys
> Were nipped like blossoms. Some dozen
> Hapless wounded men were frozen.
> During day being struck down out of sight,
> And help-cries drowned in roaring noise,
> They were left just where the skirmish shifted—
> Left in dense underbrush snow-drifted.
> Some, seeking to crawl in crippled plight,
> So stiffened—perished.
> . . . .
> And this they say, yet not disown

> The dark redoubts round Donelson,
>   And ice-glazed corpses, each a stone—
>   A sacrifice to Donelson.   (*CP*, 26)

Like Gardner's caption for his photograph of corpses ("A Harvest of
Death"), the first lines of the dispatch draw a pastoral frame around
the corpses. When the references to pain and suffering in the subsequent
lines might question the relevance of this frame, the text of the dispatch
responds by invoking the recuperative trope of ritual "sacrifice," which
writes the ideological sign of theodicy over the dead body. Two laconic
lines set off from the rest schematize the general process of recuperation:

> For lists of killed and wounded see
> The morrow's dispatch: to-day 'tis victory.   (33)

No continuity is proposed between the events of the battle ("killed and
wounded") and their ideological signification (the Union "victory"); they
are even reported in different dispatches on different days. The dispatches
regard death as simply a part of the aftermath; the confrontation with
this grim reality is deferred until tomorrow. These two lines dramatize
the way in which ideological discourse displaces the body, once the body
has served its purpose in war.

In his *Memoranda during the War* Whitman lamented the underrepre-
sentation of the individual heroisms and brave deaths of the war. Melville
describes a similar tendency toward interdiction, showing the ideological
purpose it serves. After the news of victory there are celebrations and
prayers of thanksgiving;

> But others were who wakeful laid
>   In midnight beds and early rose,
>   And, feverish in the foggy snows,
> Snatched the damp paper—wife and maid.
>   The death-list like a river flows
>   Down the pale sheet,
> And there the whelming waters meet.   (33)

Whitman thought, "Likely their very names are lost" (*M*, 16). Melville,
more accurately describing the normal practice of publishing the names
of the dead, locates the loss differently. His simile taken from nature
illustrates the erasure, by means of textual representation, of all traces
of the autonomy of the body. It does not frame the corpse, which is
lost to representation; rather, it erases even the textual sign of the body.

Such an erasure enables the transformation of the violated body into a sign of the legitimation of the state.

The displacement of the body by the disembodied sign is more complete in "Dupont's Round Fight"; here there are no names or any other signs of human life. The poem represents the minor battle of Port Royal, South Carolina, in which the Union fleet sailed down the mouth of Broad River to bombard Fort Walker and then "circled back upstream" to bombard Fort Beauregard on the other bank (*CP*, 447). The path of the fleet is proposed as a type of divine harmony of the spheres, a prophecy of Union victory in the war, and a sign of the political legitimacy of the outcome of the war:

> In time and measure perfect moves
>   All art whose aim is sure;
> Evolving rhyme and stars divine
>   Have rules, and they endure.
>
> Nor less the Fleet that warred for Right,
>   And, warring so, prevailed,
> In geometric beauty curved,
>   And in an orbit sailed.
>
> The rebel at Port Royal felt
>   The Unity overawe,
> And rued the spell. A type was here,
>   And victory of Law.   (15)

The structure of the poem is of a piece with the allegory; the hymn meter does not admit of any variation that would disrupt symmetry.[13] The final word of the poem seems to gesture toward the transcendent. But the typography, insisting on itself as typography (note a supplementary sense of "type"), reveals the self-referentiality of the assertion and so displaces the supposed transcendental referent, much in the way that the interdependent apparatuses of tatoo and taboo among the Typees are seen to have no authorizing referent outside of the political subjects themselves. "Law" is what the Union victory at Port Royal (by synecdoche, the outcome of the war) substantiates. One can say no more than this; one could say it equally truly had the Confederacy won the battle and the war (with rhetorical support from the Declaration of Independence). The argument for the legitimation of the ideology of the victor in war, like the path of Dupont's fleet and Melville's tautological inference from the "Photograph of a Corps Commander," is circular and cannot be conclusively grounded by means of an external moral, natural, or transcendental reference. The argument can be made with such purity only in the absolute interdiction of any trace of the human body.

"Dupont's Round Fight" is not an "inside narrative." The only trace of the actual event is the description of the path of the fleet, "In geometric beauty curved, / And in an orbit sailed." This graceful form, which aestheticizes the battle and thus obscures the centrality of violence, was a fact emphasized in the journalistic account from which Melville worked.[14] And yet, Melville was later to write, the "symmetry of form attainable in pure fiction cannot so readily be achieved in a narration essentially having less to do with fable than with fact" (*Billy Budd*, 128). This distinction, according to which "Dupont" would be a representation more fabulous than factual, is a function of the perspective of the observer. The perspective of "Dupont" is only the depersonalized perspective of the state.

"Running the Batteries, As Observed from the Anchorage above Vicksburgh" is also an outside narrative of an engagement between the Union navy and Confederate shore forces. Although the poetic structures are less symmetrical than those of "Dupont" (the meter distractingly uneven at times), the perspective of the observer, as described in the title, is nearly as aloof. "Running the Batteries" dramatizes the ideological function of perspective, describing the tendency of the politically interested observers to aestheticize the battle. The poem begins as a nocturne, in which nature is perceived by the observers on shore to be sympathetic to the Union cause:

> A moonless night—a friendly one;
> > A haze dimmed the shadowy shore
> As the first lampless boat slid on.   (*CP*, 49)

We can assume that some of the observers are war correspondents.[15] As they silently watch for signs that the Union ships have successfully slipped past the Confederate sentries, they witness instead a developing battle. The ships are attacked and return fire:

> How we strain our gaze. On the bluffs they shun
> > A golden growing flame appears—
> Confirms to a silvery steadfast one.
> > "The town is afire!" crows Hugh: "Three cheers!"
> Lot stops his mouth: "Nay, lad, better three tears."   (50)

There is a trace of voyeurism in these eager gazes through the darkness at the "secret" event (49). The adjectives ("golden," "silvery") are wholly conventional, indicating the rhetorical stance of the spectators. Both fleet and town are on fire; yet the spectators, no doubt because they have read the sort of poetry evoked by these adjectives, are prepared to perceive the battle more as an aesthetic object than as an event in which human life is destroyed:

> A baleful brand, a hurrying torch
>   Whereby anew the boats are seen—
> A burning transport all alurch!
>   Breathless we gaze; yet still we glean
> Glimpses of beauty as we eager lean.
>
> The effulgence takes on an amber glow
>   Which bathes the hill-side villas far;
> Affrighted ladies mark the show
>   Painting the pale magnolia—
> The fair, false, Circe light of cruel War.   (51–52)

The poetic voice thus turns against the observers (except for "Lot," with whom the voice may empathize) to point out the seductive appeal of the aesthetic view of war—a temptation to orient one's perceptions toward "glimpses of beauty" rather than admit the horror of the scene. In the last line we see the battle as if it were the statue of Pierre's soul, revolving on a pedestal. By turns we see it under "fair," "false," and "Circe" lights. If these contrasting views do not enlighten most of the spectators, this is because their perspective is conditioned by a false identification with the combatants, which entails a patriotic, but dull final line:

> So burst *we* through their barriers
>   And menaces every one:
> So Porter proves himself a brave man's son.   (52, emphasis added)

The concluding assertion of Porter's bravery has been dictated by the ideological stance of the spectators.[16] But its rhetorical flatness is a product of the critical perspective of the speaker of the poem, who, while occupying a spatial and ideological position similar to that of the other spectators, is rhetorically self-aware in a way that they are not.

"The March into Virginia, Ending in the First Manassas" more directly disrupts the pro forma rhetoric of heroism that characterizes Porter as a "brave man's son." The first several lines describe the attitude of new recruits on the eve of battle:

> In Bacchic glee they file toward Fate
> Moloch's uninitiate;

> Expectancy, and glad surmise
> Of battle's unknown mysteries.
> All they feel is this: 'tis glory
> A rapture sharp, though transitory,
> Yet lasting in belaureled story. (10-11)

At this point the young men share the view of the war correspondents above Vicksburg, having internalized the empty rhetoric of heroism that aestheticizes war in "belaureled story." We get outside of this rhetoric, but only to return to it in the final two lines of the poem. Some of the recruits

> Shall die experienced ere three days be spent—
> Perish, enlightened by the vollied glare;
> Or shame survive, and, like to adamant,
> Thy aftershock, Manassas, share. (11)

Robert Penn Warren points out the multivalence of "enlightened," arguing that the moment of death produces "a blaze of knowledge which, for all its deadliness [is], somehow, a blaze of glory, a glare of glory" (809). Where the war correspondents in the previous poem had imagined an identification in which "we" become members of the crew who run the batteries, here the single word "enlightened" separates the perceiving subject from the subject of the war. The "glare" of battle enlightens the scene, perhaps in an aesthetic sense; but the soldier finds a different (although undescribed) sense of enlightenment in the moment of death. The nature of that enlightenment is clarified in "Shiloh, A Requiem," which describes a scene

> Of dying foemen mingled there—
> Foemen at morn, but friends at eve—
> Fame or country least their care:
> (What like a bullet can undeceive!) (CP, 41)

Those who "survive" the first battle of Manassas and represent that experience to themselves as "shame" (for it ended in the panicked retreat of Union forces witnessed by many civilians who rode out from nearby Washington) are not "enlightened," not "undeceived" about the legitimacy of dying to settle a political conflict.

Aesthetic distance can result in the simple affirmation of war. But, critically handled, it is not without value in the perception of ideological structures. "The House-Top, A Night Piece," has been read as evidence

of a "reversal" of Melville's attitude toward the repressive power of the
state, from rebellion (in *White-Jacket* and earlier texts) to endorsement
(Rogin, *SG*, 266). But in its critical detachment it refuses any such definitive
statement. A dramatic monologue on the New York draft riots of July
1863, spoken from the perspective of a civilian observer, "The House-
Top" displays the issues of the war in at least some of their ideological
complexity. The attitude of the speaker is not monological, and this is
the point of the poem. By describing the disruption as the "Atheist roar
of riot" in line 8 he seems to be setting a distance between himself and
the rioters and their goals. But the opening lines indicate a hidden identification as well:

> No sleep. The sultriness pervades the air
> And binds the brain—a dense oppression, such
> As tawny tigers feel in matted shades,
> Vexing their blood and making apt for ravage.
> Beneath the stars the roofy desert spreads
> Vacant as Libya. (*CP, 57*)

Thus when the rioting draftees "roar," later in the poem, we remember
that the speaker has felt himself to be a "tiger" who also lives in an
atmosphere of "dense oppression" that "binds" him. If he does not sympathize with mob violence, he nevertheless also criticizes the blindness
of New York to the material causes of the uprising and the ideological
contradictions revealed by its violent suppression.

Melville dramatizes an attempt to make sense of the violence that
is perpetrated by both the mob and the Draconian state:

> The town is taken by its rats—ship-rats
> And rats of the wharves. All civil charms
> And priestly spells which late held hearts in awe—
> Fear-bound, subjected to a better sway
> Than sway of self; these like a dream dissolve,
> And man rebounds whole aeons back in nature.
> Hail to the low dull rumble, dull and dead,
> And ponderous drag that jars the wall.
> Wise Draco comes, deep in the midnight roll
> Of black artillery; he comes, though late;
> In code corroborating Calvin's creed
> And cynic tyrannies of honest kings;
> He comes, nor parlies; and the Town, redeemed,

> Gives thanks devout; nor, being thankful, heeds
> The grimy slur on the Republic's faith implied,
> Which holds that Man is naturally good,
> And—more—is Nature's Roman, never to be scourged. (57)

The Irish immigrants responded with violence to the imposition of the draft—especially to the clause that permitted a draftee to buy a substitute body for $300—because, subject to "sway of self," they had no interest in fighting and dying to maintain the Union or to free the slaves. The characterization of the rioters as "rats of the wharves" refers specifically to the stevedore's strike of June 1863, when blacks, under police protection, replaced the striking stevedores, most of whom were Irish. This action ignited existing racial tensions; the mob turned on the blacks, killing eleven of them in the ensuing violence. The riots were put down only when Union troops, newly arrived from Gettysburg, fought with the rioters and killed over eighty of them in several small street battles (McPherson, 609–10). Although the Archbishop of New York publicly supported the draft (Cohen, 240), the "priestly" religion that nominally controlled the rioters proved ineffective. Military force (the "midnight roll / Of black artillery"), identified specifically with the rule of law in the figure of "Draco," was the only effective means to enforce compliance with the draft.[17] The "Town," that is, the Protestant middle classes whose lives were restored to normal by the "artillery" under "Draco's" command, are shown to use religious rhetoric to obscure the mechanisms of repression; "redeemed" by the violence, they offer prayers of thanksgiving.

The poem admits the effectiveness of repressive force in maintaining civil order, but also recognizes the incompatibility of the structure of such a state with the ideology in the name of which that state was supposedly fighting the Civil War. The image of the whip in the last line of the poem brings the issue of slavery into the ideological debate. White-Jacket had argued that flogging—the summary synecdoche in "The House-Top" for all uses of repressive force—violates both "the genius of the American Constitution" and "the Law of Nature" (143, 145). The claim that the rioters had "rebound[ed] whole aeons back in nature" controverts White-Jacket's appeal to natural law. But White-Jacket had claimed that "Calvin's creed" described not man in a state of nature, but man as the product of a repressive culture: "Depravity in the oppressed is no apology for the oppressor; but rather an additional stigma to him, as being, in a large degree, the effect, and not the cause and justification of oppression" (142). The speaker of "The House-Top" is not White-

Jacket, of course, but his words do reveal the contradictions within the prowar Northern ideology. If man is "never to be scourged," slavery must be abolished (although, strictly speaking, slavery was constitutional until the ratification of the Thirteenth Amendment in 1865). But must that abolition be accomplished by the military state—which White-Jacket had identified as another institution of slavery—by means of the deaths of its citizens? The argument against slavery is also the argument against military servitude, but "the Town" refuses to recognize the ideological contradictions entailed by the prosecution of the war. (Although, as McPherson points out, many Democrats argued that conscription was unconstitutional [608–9].) The exercise of violence to maintain order is a "grimy slur on the Republic's faith" and cannot be openly acknowledged to form a part of the ideology of a nation supposedly warring in the name of freedom.[18]

By choosing to write a nocturne such as "The House-Top," Melville has dissociated his poem from the dictates of unthinking Unionism (which prompt him in other poems to develop, for example, easy and unconvincing analogies between Federal forces and the Israelites). He thus seems to be free to speculate on politics in the abstract. Still, although the poem does not represent a battle between Union and Confederate troops, violence is a central part of its subject, and Melville refuses to represent it. His own note to the poem appeals to the inexpressibility topos, much in the way Whitman had done to justify his assertion that "the real war will never get in the books": "'I dare not write of the horrible and inconceivable atrocities committed,' says Froissart, in alluding to the remarkable sedition in France during his time. The like may be hinted of some proceedings of the draft rioters" (*CP*, 452). The violence is doubly buried; a justification of its interdiction appeals to a prior alibi for a prior interdiction. The ideological point is ambiguous, in keeping with the detachment of the poem. Melville's allusion displaces the actual violence of the riots into a very obscure past.[19] The meditative detachment, which seems to have permitted a relatively unfettered exploration of an ideological issue, also prohibits any concrete representation of the violation of bodies. In his refusal to take full account of violence, Melville shows that it cannot be attached to an ideology of autonomy in any meaningful way. There is no room for autonomy in either violent rebellion or its equally violent suppression.

IV. *Stark desolation; ruin, merciless and ceaseless; chills and gloom, —all here lived a hidden life, curtained by that cunning purpleness, which, from the piazza of the manor house, so beautifully invested the mountain.* (*Pierre*, 344)

Pastoralism, as it appeared in "Lilacs" and the *Memoranda* and structured the contemporary reception of Civil War photography, attempted to naturalize the events and especially the outcome of the war, evading the reality of historical forces in its legitimation of the ideology of the victor. Pastoralism in *Battle-Pieces* sometimes takes such a restorative, beneficent turn, such as the assertion in "Shiloh" that "April rain / Solaced the parched ones stretched in pain" (*CP*, 41). (There is a literal truth in these lines: one effect of loss of blood is extreme thirst, which pools of collected rainwater might relieve.) In "Magnanimity Baffled," a reference to dead soldiers is sentimental: "Like plants that flower ere comes the leaf— / Which storms lay low in kindly doom" (105). Often, however, such pastoral tropes are invoked only to be deconstructed. The plight of the men at Andersonville prison camp, for example, is said to be beyond the restorative power of nature:

> But withering famine slowly wore,
> And slowly fell disease did gloat.
> Even Nature's self did aid deny;
> In horror they choked the pensive sigh. (114)

Pastoral tropes are ineffective to recuperate such suffering; even the pathetic fallacy—the trope of last resort in the pastoral response to human pain—is denied.

Although the pastoral representations of *Battle-Pieces* are distanced from the war, they do not hide the fact of their distance. "The March into Virginia" addresses the topos of pastoralism not in an attempt to mobilize its recuperative power to heal the wounds of war, but in order to demonstrate the incongruities between the pastoral mode of representation and the realities of war. The "green" recruits marching toward Manassas perceive a bucolic scene. The representation of the landscape in the pastoral mode conflicts with the historical events that will occur in it:

> No berrying party, pleasure-wooed,
> No picnic party in the May,

> Ever went less loth than they
>> Into that leafy neighborhood. (10)

Some members of that "berrying party" will form a burying party, as the idyll gives way to the devastation of battle. As with the double sense of "enlightened," the pun here suggests the delusionary nature of aestheticized representations of war.

"Ball's Bluff, A Reverie," which also invokes pastoralism in describing troops marching to battle, is structured, as the subtitle indicates, by an even greater aesthetic distance. Here we remain in town with the speaker, watching the troops marching out to battle:

> They moved like Juny morning on the wave,
>> Their hearts were fresh as clover in its prime
>> (It was the breezy summertime),
>>> Life throbbed so strong,
> How should they dream that Death in a rosy clime
> Would come to thin their shining throng?
> Youth feels immortal, like the gods sublime. (14)

In locating death in Arcadia, Melville trivializes his poem. But this evasion is a product of the very distance between the pastoral "reverie" of the dramatized speaker and the experience of the men who fight in the battle that is mentioned (but not represented). Pastoralism, the poem implies, is an attitude toward war that becomes easier to assume as the distance between the perceiver and the war increases and "Death" becomes an abstraction rather than a concrete reality. Any poetic attempt to represent the war now finds itself at an ever increasing distance; it is less than a year after the war and already Melville finds its reality retreating from him.

Unlike Whitman and the photographers, Melville permits himself to speculate on the possibility that the violence and suffering of civil war might again erupt on American soil. Such critical moments reveal organicist, American nationalism to be a failed project—failed, not because it had proven to be ideologically ineffective, but because in its very effectiveness it repressed the representational crises that were the origin of the war. It idealized the war-torn nation instead of asking hard questions about race, freedom, autonomy, and the individual's relation to the state. Melville asks these questions, not directly but in the images of disruption that recur in *Battle-Pieces*. These images do not, in retrospect, appear to be serious predictions of another national civil war (postwar political violence would be directed against blacks or working class whites, which minimized any critical representation in contemporary political discourse). Melville's concern that "we still turn our eyes toward the South, as the Neapolitan, months after the eruption, turns his toward Vesuvius" (CP, 465) appears naive at first; after all, the South was pacified and reconstructed, and order restored. Nevertheless, Melville finds beneath the pastoral surface of postwar America something that threatens to disrupt its harmony—named variously as a volcano, a shark, or Gorgon. The structure of American political representation was altered only by means of violence—that is, the Thirteenth Amendment, formally freeing the slaves, and the subsequent amendments that seemed to guarantee their civil rights, were only ratified after the territory they primarily affected was subsumed once again into the Union by means of war. Melville recognized that as an end, the emancipation was an unqualified good. His figures of disruption indicate uneasiness over the use of violence as a means to this end. He has no confidence that violence will have accomplished more than to reproduce itself, if not in war then in other forms.

We have seen that Whitman used pastoral images to marginalize or interdict representations of death. Gardner went beyond even this, matching a photograph showing Federal troops occupying a town (fig. 7) with a text that claimed, "with returning peace, the husbandman finds that nature has not forgotten its fruitfulness in the years of war and devastation" (4)—thus implying that the Federal forces supervise and aid the restorative processes of nature, preventing further devastation in the form of a Southern attack. In Barnard's photographs of the territory covered by Sherman's campaign, the troops themselves are absent; picturesque nature is restoring itself, in Sherman's wake, providing a landscape ripe for economic and political appropriation. Melville, too, treats Sherman's march in the pastoral mode, in "The March to the Sea." But this poem questions the conventional recuperative power of the pastoral or picturesque view, showing that Sherman's operations were not restorative, but destructive. In the early stanzas, the Federal army is represented by means of natural metaphors; for example:

> The columns streamed like rivers
> > Which in their course agree,
> And they streamed until their flashing
> > Met the flashing of the sea. (84)

Continuing this alignment of Sherman's army with the forces of nature, the poem compares the flanking companies to flocks of pigeons ranging over the landscape, construing the event as an idyll: "Fighting was but frolic" (85). The consummation of the pastoral conceit occurs in the penultimate stanza:

> The grain of endless acres
>   Was threshed (as in the East)
> By the trampling of the Takers,
>   Strong march of man and beast;
> The flails of those earth-shakers
>   Left a famine where they ceased.   (86)

But the expected harvest—a natural event in a pastoral narrative—does not produce the ideological fruit that we might expect. Instead the harvest produces only famine, fear, and destruction,

> For behind they left a wailing,
>   A terror and a ban,
> And blazing cinders sailing,
>   And houseless households wan,
> Wide zones of counties paling,
>   And towns where maniacs ran.   (87)

Compared, especially, with other contemporary representations of Sherman's march—for example, the peaceful, rural interlude of Thomas Nast's "The Soldier's Halt" (fig. 18)—Melville's critique is quite revealing. The troops, who first appeared to be acting in concert with the beneficent processes of nature, are shown to be destroying not only the land but also any hopes that the devastation could be recuperated by means of pastoral representation.

"Frenzy in the Wake," the companion piece to "The March to the Sea," is narrated from the perspective of the Southerners who witnessed the destruction of the march to the sea. These Southerners are also prepared to read events of the war in pastoral terms:

> From frozen Maine they come,
>   Far Minnesota too;
> They come to a sun whose rays disown—
>   May it wither them as the dew!

But they find that Sherman's march cannot be recuperated in terms of the sympathy of nature with their cause:

With burning woods our skies are brass
　　The pillars of dust are seen;
The live-long day their cavalry pass—
　　No crossing the road between.

We were sore deceived—an awful host!
　　They move like a roaring wind,
Have we gamed and lost? but even despair
　　Shall never our hate rescind.　　　　　　　　　　(88)

Federal troops are identified with the power of nature ("the roaring wind"), but this power is not beneficent. Its effect on the landscape is, under the terms of the pastoral, *unnatural*, as it turns the sky to "brass"; thus the supposedly natural power of Sherman's army is revealed metaphorically for the mechanic power it actually possessed. The final metaphor for the war, gambling, can be read alternately as an assertion of random chance or foreordained fate—an assertion of nature as chaos or nature as divinely ordered harmony. More important than this metaphor, though, is the final assertion of enduring hate, the "frenzy" in Sherman's "wake."

　　Melville's deconstruction of the restorative status of pastoralism recurs in different forms and gestures throughout the volume. It appears especially significant in contrast to other, more popular poems that were being written in the North, in response to the end of the war. In 1866 Whittier published *Snow-Bound: A Winter Idyll* to satisfy his editor's request for a "New England pastoral"; it was the most popular volume of verse since Longfellow's *Song of Hiawatha* (1855), far outselling either *Battle-Pieces* or *Drum-Taps* (Leary, 70). The war has left its trace in this text, in the recollection of a former time "when all the land / Was clay in Slavery's shaping hand" (Whittier, 401). For Whittier, far more than for Melville, Whitman, or Lincoln, the Civil War had been fought over slavery. Thus the occasional mentions of the topic in *Snow-Bound* describe a history of the war that freed the slaves. Whittier also prescribes a narrative of the restoration of the land after this war. This prescription is evident in the section devoted to the schoolmaster that used to board with Whittier's family. The teachings of the schoolmaster will "the cruel lie of caste refute"; the values he represents provide a model for the restoration of the land that culminates in a national unification that is set in the pastoral scene:

　　　　of such as he
Shall Freedom's young apostles be,

Who, following in War's bloody trail,
Shall every lingering wrong assail;
All chains from limb and spirit strike,
Uplift the black and white alike;

. . . .

A schoolhouse planted on every hill,
Stretching in radiate nerve-lines thence
The quick wires of intelligence;
Till North and South together brought
Shall own the same electric thought,
In peace a common flag salute,
And, side by side in labor's free
And unresentful rivalry,
Harvest the fields wherein they fought.   (404)

Whittier closes the memory of the war with restorative, naturalizing images; the technology of the telegraph is made organic ("nerve-lines") and even the schoolhouses are not built but "planted" in this vision of America's future. These images are more cooperative and egalitarian than, for example, the proposal *Harper's* made of giving Virginia land to Vermont farmers. Whittier's agrarianism envisions an America restored to its pastoral past, yet purified of the evil of slave labor. And yet this vision contains a trace of war, the resonance of which Whittier seems unaware, in a refiguration of the late violent contest between North and South as an "unresentful rivalry."

   In the earlier poems of Whittier devoted specifically to the war, his pastoralism dictates a complete, predictive narrative of American history. "The Battle Autumn of 1862" shows that throughout the war Whittier had appealed to a hopeful idea of the permanence of nature's restorative power:

And, calm and patient, Nature keeps
    Her ancient promise well,
Though o'er her bloom and greenness sweeps
    The battle's breath of hell.

And still she walks in golden hours
    Through harvest-happy farms,
And still she wears her fruits and flowers
    Like jewels on her arms.   (339)

The poetic conventions within which Whittier is working exclude any representation of violence potentially repulsive to his Quaker sensibility. They also prevent him from confronting the contradictions within his ideology that his endorsement of the war entailed. He had criticized John Brown's use of violence and would later argue that Quakers must refuse to fight but ought to support the Northern war effort by other means (Leary, 65–66). His evasion of violence thus not only attempts to heal the nation and restore the idyllic scene; it effaces the question of his personal relation to the use of violence to achieve the political end he so valued.

Whittier's pastoralism was a heavily Christianized one, so we would expect to find images of swords being beaten into plowshares to commemorate the war's end. We do in "The Peace Autumn," the title of which alludes to the earlier "Battle Autumn of 1862." "Peace Autumn" describes the fulfillment of nature's "ancient promise" invoked in the earlier poem:

> Thank God for rest, where none molest,
>   And none can make afraid;
> For Peace that sits as plenty's guest
>   Beneath the homestead shade!
>
> Bring pike and gun, the sword's red scourge,
>   The negro's broken chains,
> And beat them at the blacksmith's forge
>   To ploughshares for our plains.
>
> Alike henceforth our hills of snow,
>   And vales where cotton flowers;
> All streams that flow, all winds that blow,
>   Are Freedom's motive powers.   (346–47)

There is no trace of the "frenzy" in Sherman's "wake," no sense that the war left unsolved a great many ideological problems. Whittier is so intent on arguing for an undifferentiated, pastoral America that the oddity of the equation of Northern, winter snow with Southern, summer cotton does not concern him: it is enough that an image of unification is produced. Thus Whittier validates Lincoln's image of "our" infinitely reproducible "national homestead" which is said to guarantee an end to the war's unnatural violation of American politics and economics (5:529).

Melville's "The Apparition, A Retrospect," is devoted wholly to a critique of pastoralism. It is especially suggestive when read against

Whittier's "Peace Autumn." Melville imagines an animated, beneficent landscape (blending "picturesque" and "body politic" metaphors). But this scene is disrupted by a volcanic catastrophe:

> Convulsions came; and, where the field
>   Long slept in pastoral green,
> A goblin-mountain was upheaved
> (Sure the scared sense was all deceived),
>   Marl-glen and slag-ravine.
>
> The unreserve of Ill was there,
>   The clinkers in her last retreat;
> But, ere the eye could take it in,
> Or mind could comprehension win,
>   It sunk!—and at our feet.
>
> So, then, Solidity's a crust—
>   The core of fire below;
> All may go well for many a year,
> But who can think without a fear
>   Of horrors that happen so?   (*CP*, 102)

Melville does not deny the appearance of the image that Whittier describes. He simply supplies a counter-schema that is at least equally persuasive and allows us to choose what value we will find in the American landscape—or allows us to deny, in the face of contradictions, that the landscape is the source of any political value. In some respects "The Apparition" is a companion piece to the thematically opposite "Dupont's Round Fight" (discussed in section III). The meter (respectively smooth or rough, to match the theme) and stanzaic structure are similar, except that an extra tetrameter disrupts the symmetry and rhyme scheme, as the volcano forces its way to the surface: the "field" goes unrhymed. If this is an allegory, two political implications are clear. First, the war, like the eruption, is incomprehensible and any attempt to recuperate the meaning of the war, especially by means of naturalizing tropes, is subject to the disruption figured here. Second, despite peaceful appearances, a war or some other violence—an "unreserve of Ill," a "core of fire below"—lurks in America's future. Melville found the sort of political vision exemplified by Whittier's pastoralism too simple, at the least. It failed to confront the political realities of relations between a conquered and a conquering state that were further complicated by an ideology of race which threatened the return, in another form, of the violence of slavery.

It was not enough merely to imagine "North and South . . . Harvest[ing] the fields wherein they fought" or the "negro's broken chains" being forged into plowshares (404, 347).

Melville also suggests that the experience of war had a profound effect on the combatants' adaptability to peacetime structures of existence. "Commemorative of a Naval Victory" develops an image of sailors whose wartime experiences appear, at first, to have produced in them an inner peace (an effect, as "The Battle for the Bay" suggests, of the displacement of subjectivity by the text of duty):

> Sailors there are of gentlest breed,
>   Yet strong, like every goodly thing;
> The discipline of arms refines,
>   And the wave gives tempering.
>   The damasked blade its beam can fling:
> It lends the last grave grace.   (*CP*, 114)

Yet this temper may not always reach the core, and sailors may not be entirely forged of fine hammered steel. The grim pun on "grave" does not adequately prepare us for the image of disruption that emerges in the last lines of the poem; like the "pastoral green" that conceals a volcano, in peacetime:

> Elate [the sailor] never can be
> He feels that spirit which glad had hailed his worth,
>   Sleep in oblivion.—The shark
> Glides white through the phosphorous sea.   (115)

The shift of topics announced by this remarkable image is disorienting; the calm tone set by the opening image is destroyed. We are taken beneath the peaceful surface of the preceding images to glimpse a lower layer of chaos. This is a warning that American men, who believed that a war was the only effective resolution to political conflict and acted on that belief, may have become unfit to govern or be governed by peaceable structures of political representation.

In "America," a prophetic allegory of the republic, the war appears to have been a momentary, incomprehensible rupture, like the volcano of "The Apparition." A female allegorical figure of the sort drawn by Thomas Nast (e.g., fig. 1), identified with the American flag, gazes over an idealized landscape prior to the Civil War:

> Where the wings of a sunny Dome expand
> I saw a Banner in gladsome air—

Starry, like Berenice's hair—
Afloat in broadened bravery there;

. . . .

The Land reposed in peace below;
    The children in their glee
Were folded to the exulting heart
    Of young Maternity.   (*CP*, 105)

Nast's allegory is fused with the scene of contemporary landscape and genre painting, producing a sense that patriotism and pastoralism are a single phenomenon in antebellum America. The second stanza describes the effect of war on this scene:

I saw the ambiguous lightning play.
Valor with Valor strove, and died:
Fierce was Despair, and cruel was Pride;
And the lorn Mother speechless stood,
Pale at the fury of her brood.   (106)

In the third stanza, America, distressed by this disruption of the harmony of the early republic, falls into a sleep resembling death:

But in that sleeps [*sic*] contortion showed
The terror of the vision there—
    A silent vision unavowed,
Revealing earth's foundation bare,
    And Gorgon in her hidden place.
It was a thing of fear to see
    So foul a dream upon so fair a face,
And the dreamer lying in that starry shroud.   (106)

The description is more detailed than in the previous two stanzas, because while the pastoral scene of antebellum America can go without saying, the unusual vision of horror needs to be clarified. As in "The Apparition," the disruptive figures are then dispersed. America awakens from this nightmare in the fourth stanza with a "clear calm look,"

Power dedicate, and hope grown wise,
    And youth matured for age's seat
Law on her brow and empire in her eyes.   (107)

It is not clear whether such an awakening has yet taken place as Melville writes. The idea of a renewed dedication to empire after the war shows political acumen, but Melville is narrating both prophecy and

199

history. He uses the past tense in the fourth stanza—"from the trance she sudden broke"—as is consistent with the rest of the poem. The second stanza seems to represent the fighting of the Civil War, yet is less horrific than the third. "Yet later," the third stanza is given over to a nightmare which may refer to the war that is now ended; or, given another chronology, it may refer to the political problems Melville foresees for Reconstruction. The disruptive figures of "earth's foundation bare, / And Gorgon in her hidden place," like the "ambiguous lightning" of the previous stanza, are overtly metaphors for the war itself and for the disruption of the American system of political representation manifested by secession. But they may also represent the political future, in which a "silent vision" impinges on the experience of attempting to forget the violence of the war. The disruption is represented in such a way that it is always threatening to return.

The peaceful views at the beginning and end of "America" are shown from the perspective of the allegorical figure who looks down on the American landscape. This figure is the embodiment of American political subjectivity, the means by which we represent the mythos of America to ourselves—that is, we are supposed to see with the eyes of the one body politic and share its consciousness and values. Yet the scenes of the nightmare and the pastoral seem to be interchangeable environments for this body: "empire," the concluding peacetime note of the poem, was an important motivation for the nightmare of the Civil War that exposed the "Gorgon." The prophetic chronology is underdetermined such that both visions apply to Melville's present of 1866. Both also continue to provide us with representations of the American state. We are living beneath the apparently peaceful dominion of the postwar empire ("Power dedicate, and hope grown wise"). And we are living through an "unavowed" nightmare—which is the same militaristic empire, viewed from a critical perspective—still waiting to wake up.

200

Epilogue: "For the Union Dead"

ROBERT Lowell, as Whitman, Melville, Brady, Gardner, and Barnard had done a century before, locates the significance of the American Civil War in the landscape. But he doubts that any restorative, integrative power lies there. He finds instead, in the conventions that structure images of the landscape, what Melville had found: traces of instability that demand a critique of representation. "For the Union Dead" opens on a blighted, antipastoral scene in the present:

> The old South Boston Aquarium stands
> in a Sahara of snow now. Its broken windows are boarded.
> The bronze weathervane cod has lost half its scales.
> The airy tanks are dry.

The disintegration of pastoralism imaged in the opening stanza suggests that the nominal power of the pastoral mode to produce a beautiful reconciliation of nature and civilization (in this case, the American state) is no longer effective. A key moment in this disintegration, perhaps its origin, is the Civil War. The war has left its traces in gradually eroding memorials that occupy the landscape without producing any sense of the integration of their presence there: "frayed flags / quilt the graveyards of the Grand Army of the Republic."

The image of the aquarium is the ideological center, locating the poem in the pastoral topos which had often been invoked to negotiate the meaning of the Civil War. An aquarium is a formal landscape under water, self-enclosed and composed as an aesthetic object.[1] The "cowed, compliant fish" are analogous to the eighteenth-century peasants who, because of their compliance, can be idealized by landscape painters such as Gainsborough. (The adjective "cowed" also compares the fish to the cattle that appear often in the pastoral.) The poet at first attempts to identify himself with the anthropomorphized organisms that inhabit the underwater "kingdom," by imagining that his "nose crawled like a snail on the glass." Yet beyond projecting himself into the scene, he wants to intervene in it: "my hand tingled / to burst the bubbles." But the formal qualities that, literally, structure the aesthetic apparatus prevent him from doing so. There is glass between him and the scene, and so:

> My hand draws back. I often sigh still
> for the dark downward and vegetating kingdom
> of the fish and reptile.

The "sigh" encodes the conventional nostalgic attitude prescribed by the pastoral, reinforcing the distance the poet perceives between himself and the beautiful life of the aquarium.

The entire vignette of the aquarium is an exercise in nostalgia, initiated by the desolation of the present scene in which the aquarium building, now boarded up, "stands / in a Sahara of snow." The landscape in which the poet now finds himself is unnatural, animated by "yellow dinosaur steamshovels" enclosed in the "cage" of a "barbed and galvanized fence." The poet, "pressed against" this fence, regards the steam shovels with much the same attitude that had structured his perception of the fish. But there is a crucial difference: the formalization of pastoralism has, in the dinosaur image, expanded its boundaries to encompass the actual landscape in which the poet lives. Convention has taken over nature. But this is not Arcadia, for the pastoral topos does not provide an effective apparatus for the integration of civilization and nature.

No longer an image contained within its own structure—and aesthetically and ideologically effective in the very assurance that had been supplied by its own containment—pastoral now seems to have taken over all of life. This bursting of boundaries produces only a confusion of representational modes, revealed most powerfully in the concluding lines of the poem:

> The Aquarium is gone. Everywhere,
> giant finned cars nose forward like fish;
> a savage servility
> slides by on grease.

The image recalls a similar one from *Battle-Pieces*, with which Melville had disrupted a representation of the calming, tempering virtue of military service to the state (one of the supposed ideological lessons of the war): "The shark / Glides white through the phosphorous sea" (*CP*, 115). But there is not even the sublime force of Melville's image of potential rupture—no suggestion that rebellion offers any alternative to the present state. The romantic sublime is, for Lowell, as mystified as the pastoral. He finds that the apt metaphor for the apparatuses of representation that structure modern American existence is neither animistic (fish) nor mechanistic (cars), but a begrimed confusion of models.

The penultimate line resonates with *servare*, ironizing the epigraph "Relinquunt Omnia Servare Rem Publicam" ("they gave up everything to preserve the state"). *Servility* twists *servare* into *servire*, a near homonym signifying "to be a slave."[2] The war nominally ended slavery, but the figures in Lowell's disintegrated postwar landscape, like the Americans typified in the picturesque or the corpses in Brady's and Gardner's versions of pastoral, remain servile. If the Union dead saved the state, that preservation has resulted not in civilization but in savagery. By developing this antipastoral image, Lowell has gotten inside of pastoralism (as he could not get inside the beauty of the aquarium) to reveal its ideological infrastructure. Representation produces an abstraction of subjectivity— in the "statues of the abstract Union Soldier," in the present absence of the disembodied, "drained faces of Negro school-children" represented on the television screen, and in the cars that have displaced human figures in the modern landscape. This abstraction is the trace left by the war in the structure of all representation. Far from restoring representation as the ground of the American state, the war has left only a representational crisis. The war is shown to be thoroughly mediated in this poem, which is not about the Civil War itself so much as it is about its (dis)appearance in representation. The poetic image of Shaw "lead[ing] his black soldiers to death" derives not directly from the events in which Shaw participated, but rather from the textualization of those events in historical discourse and, finally, in the bronze relief. (Similarly, "a commercial photograph / shows Hiroshima boiling.") This is a poem thoroughly aware of the mediated nature of experience.

Of course, the revelation of the poem is not simply that the Civil War is one hundred years and thousands of texts and images distanced from the present. The image of "The stone statues of the abstract Union Soldier" that, subject to erosion, "grow slimmer and younger each year" suggests a deeper failure of representation.[3] The identification of the monuments as "abstract" signifies the initial referential gap between the actual, individual soldiers and their typification in heroic abstractions. The structures of representation that fill the gaps between the actual soldier and his ideologically abstracted image *are* those structures that the Union dead fought to preserve. This "preservation" has produced only disintegration, just as the artistic attempts at preservation are shown to be unsuccessful, subject to the disintegrative forces of wind and rain which continually reduce any resemblance between the statued image of the soldier and the appearance of the actual soldiers the statues were intended to represent. Initially distanced from the reality of the war by means of their abstract aesthetic form, and further distanced by the erosion of even that form, these statues have come to represent only the perpetual failure of representation.

"Relinquunt omnia servare rem publicam"—and yet what is preserved is only the representational crisis that erupted in the war. (Inflecting the title with a Latin syntax borrowed from the epigraph, it is possible to read the poem as commemorative of the "Dead Union.") Lowell ironizes the claim that memorials to the dead memorialize the war as a restorative event in any sense:

> Two months after marching through Boston,
> half the regiment was dead;
> at the dedication,
> William James could almost hear the bronze Negroes breathe.

The sentimentalism attributed to James is a symptom of a misplaced faith in representation, the tendency to read representation as presence. James's attitude is analogous to Gardner's reading of his pastoral, memorial photograph of the Union dead on the field at Gettysburg: "The faces of all were pale, as though cut in marble, and as the wind swept across the battle-field it waved the hair, and gave the bodies such an appearance of life that a spectator could hardly help thinking that they were about to rise to continue the fight" (37). Reading the corpses as marble monuments, Gardner appeals to the animating power of Nature to restore the dead to life. By ironizing James's similar claim, Lowell demonstrates the discontinuity of memorialization and preservation.

The bronze of Shaw "sticks like a fishbone/in the city's throat," in an image that continues the disintegration of the memory of the aquarium. The bronze also memorializes dis-integration: relations between white commander and black subjects are structured by military hierarchy, a most repressive apparatus mediating between the subject and the state. The bronze—in which all the men appear to be the same color—becomes a fit image for the failure of representation in modern America. The state-sponsored discourse of civil rights (the policy of color blindness) disguises the hierarchical economic structures that prohibit the realization of egalitarian, autonomous political subjectivity.

Nominally a commemoration of one of the most ideologically significant moments in the war, in which blacks were given equal status with whites (the opportunity to serve their country and, symbolically, to fight for their own emancipation), the monument to Shaw and his troops reopens the political wounds of the war. The status of black Americans in 1964 is similarly dis-integrated:

> When I crouch to my television set,
> the drained faces of Negro school-children rise like balloons.

Disembodied, enclosed, framed, and placed on display by this new representational apparatus, the faces of the black children are like the "bubbles / drifting from the cowed, compliant fish" in the aquarium that the poet remembers from his own childhood. The poet seems to be outside the form, a perceiver. The children, like the fish, are inside, captive of the representational apparatus—visual yet also political—that structures the American state. Yet the poet and the children together are also inside the sinister, antipastoral scene in which animated mechanical structures have replaced natural organisms. It is not only the televised image that is "drained," but the subjectivity of those represented in the image. As Lowell realizes in 1964, a time when the realities of racism and segregation (dis-integration) were beginning to occupy the center of political discourse, this sort of representation does as much to construct the ideology of race relations as any less apparently mediated perception (such as direct political dialogue between blacks and whites). Races, indeed all political subjects, exist only in the ways in which they are represented to themselves and each other. Representation has been in crisis for more than a century. Lowell locates the political as well as the aesthetic meaning of this crisis in traces of the Civil War.

Notes

Introduction

1. Quotations from Emerson's writings are documented in the text using the following abbreviations: *JMN*: *Journals and Miscellaneous Notebooks of Ralph Waldo Emerson*; *W*: *The Complete Works of Ralph Waldo Emerson* (1904).

2. James McPherson suggests that the Kansas-Nebraska controversy was "the most important single event pushing the nation toward civil war" (121). Other commonly cited causes of the Civil War (larger issues of economic sectionalism and disputes over slavery and over "states' rights" versus "Federalist" interpretations of the Constitution) are also accurately described as crises of representation. The vote on the Wilmot Proviso (1846), which would have excluded slavery from territories recently acquired from Mexico, was the first that cut across party lines to align North against South (McPherson, 52–54). This was an early sign that normal representational politics would break down. Northern politicians would argue that the "slave powers" of the South were conspiring to govern the entire country; Southerners insisted on the contrary that Northern politicians were conspiring to privilege the economic interests of the Northern states. Southerners often pointed to conflicts in the interpretation of the Constitution as the fundamental justification of secession. Some historians argue, however, that Southerners did not consistently hold the position of states' rights and that Northerners did not consistently hold the position of the supremacy of the Federal government—each side shifting its views "when it was convenient to do so." Each side accused the other of failing to understand the true nature of democratic government; thus the war resulted from "a complete breakdown of the democratic process" (Stampp, 7, 63, 42, 140).

3. In "Politics" (1844), Emerson had argued that the only true government would consist in absolute self-representation; this was to be accomplished by an increase of self-reliance, including "the growth of the Individual; the appearance of the principle to supersede the proxy; the appearance of the wise man; of whom the existing government is, it must be owned, but a shabby imitation. . . . The tendencies of the times favor the idea of self-government, and leave for the individual, for all code, to the rewards and penalties of his own constitution" (*W*, 3:215–16, 219). During the Civil War, however, Emerson renounces his earlier "radical egoism" and even suggests that "self-reliance" now means the obedience of the soldier to state-imposed structures of discipline (Fredrickson, 177, 178). His own antebellum language is in crisis here, in its new reliance on the state; a key term in his rhetoric of representation has taken on an apparently opposite meaning. As he affirms in 1862, "Government . . . has, of necessity, in any crisis of the state, the absolute powers of a dictator" (*W*, 11:302). George M. Fredrickson finds a permanent transformation of Emerson's attitude toward the individual's relation to the state. Leonard Neufeldt, however, argues that after the war, his "old pessimism about politics seems to have returned in full force" (512).

4. On a hypothetical scale of one hundred degrees, Scarry suggests, the degree of consent in conventional war "may fluctuate between, for example, eighty-eight and one hundred" (153). One is tempted to ask what it would be like to hold a belief with 88 percent of one's body and reject it with the other 12 percent (and also to ask if the nonconsenting fraction would be spared death or injury).

5. The most extreme form of aesthetic response to state icons, Walter Benjamin argues, is characteristic of fascism (241–42); however, the general aesthetics of patriotism long antedate the rise of twentieth-century fascist governments.

6. The Maine recruit reports that, on the march to Gettysburg, his regiment was greeted by "young ladies [who] came out of a house as we passed, and sang 'The Red, White, and Blue' and 'The Star Spangled Banner.' They were dressed all in white, carrying little flags, and appeared intensely loyal to the North" (Haley, 97). Nast's illustrations will be discussed in Chapter 1.

7. But Dickinson's poetry, for example, was greatly affected by the war, despite Wilson's assertion to the contrary. Although Dickinson dissociated herself from the public sphere to an extreme degree, Shira Wolosky argues that "inner violence confronted outer violence" in her poetry and that the war "dramatically confirmed the anguish and confusion that constituted her world" and left its trace in her art (38, 41).

8. *Collected Poems of Herman Melville*, abbreviated in the text as *CP*; all quotations from *Battle-Pieces* are taken from this edition.

9. Quotations from Whitman's writings are documented in the text using the following abbreviations:

AP	*An American Primer*
C	*The Correspondence*
DL	*The Death of Abraham Lincoln*, in *Memoranda during the War [and] Death of Abraham Lincoln* (1875)
DT	*Drum-Taps* (1865), in *Drum-Taps and Sequel to Drum-Taps*
LG 1855	*Leaves of Grass: The First (1855) Edition*
LGV	*Leaves of Grass: A Textual Variorum of the Printed Poems*
M	*Memoranda during the War*, in *Memoranda during the War [and] Death of Abraham Lincoln* (1875)
PW	*Prose Works 1892*
SDT	*Sequel to Drum-Taps* (1865–66), in *Drum-Taps and Sequel to Drum-Taps*

10. The typical American, writes Crèvecoeur, begins as a landless immigrant, labors on another's farm to acquire knowledge and a small amount of capital, and then buys some land, after which "He is now an American . . . . He is naturalised, his name is enrolled with those of the other citizens of the province" (55). In the South, pastoralism was often used to naturalize the institution of slavery; but the attempt was often unsuccessful, for the American pastoral narrative, as schematized by Crèvecoeur, emphasized free labor. Simms, for example, found himself forced to choose between pastoralism as a literary ideal and as an ideological paradigm for the legitimation of the slave system; he preserved the literary ideal "at the expense of his defense of the institution of slavery" (Simpson, 64).

1.   Whitman's *Drum-Taps* and the Rhetoric of War

1. The early critics were often more concerned with the form, which was strange, than with content, which was accessible (if somewhat vulgar). Charles A. Dana, in the very first review, found the verses to be "shaped on no pre-existent model," "disfigured," hiding "the essential spirit of poetry beneath an uncouth and grotesque embodiment." Charles Eliot Norton used more precise terms: "The poems . . . are neither in rhyme nor blank verse, but in a sort of excited prose broken into lines without any attempt at measure or regularity, and, as many readers will perhaps think, without any idea of sense or reason" (quoted in Hindus, 23, 24).

2. The importance of typification in Whitman's poetics is apparent in the semiotics of the catalogue. Stanley R. Coffman argues that Whitman found a justification for his use of the catalogue technique in Emerson's ideas about the power of "bare lists of words" to create in the mind "a heightened sense not only of reality but of the variety and abundance of its manifestations" (225).

3. In light of the reading proposed in this essay, Wilson's claim that in *Drum-Taps* Whitman "does not write editorials on current events but describes his actual feelings" will need to be reassessed. It is true that Whitman occasionally "makes a sketch from the life," as in "Cavalry Crossing a Ford," but for the most part he does a good deal more (or, from Wilson's perspective, a good deal less) than describing events or feelings (483, 482). Aaron is more sensitive to the political force of *Drum-Taps*, finding the poems to be "more calculating and concessive than the early *Leaves*"; but he insists that the volume should be read as "a personal if not necessarily a powerful expression of the War's impact on [Whitman]" (68, 69).

4. Roger Scruton points out that the "body politic" is the central metaphor of "organicist" political theory (42). The representation of the state as an organism, especially a human body, was prevalent in eighteenth- and nineteenth-century political theory, especially among German philosophers (Coker). Such ideas were imported into Anglophone theory by Coleridge, Carlyle, Bancroft, and Emerson. On Whitman's debt to German thought, see Stovall (193–95, 205–07). F. O. Matthiessen, among others, argues that Whitman's poetics is heavily influenced by Coleridge's "organic principle" (593–94). Whitman's claim in the 1855 preface that "the United States themselves are essentially the greatest poem" seems to be an attempt to combine poetic and political organicism in a single representational system.

5. Harold Aspiz argues that in the antebellum *Leaves* Whitman made his own body into "an exalted poetic theme" and thereby, in the face of a cultural reticence which kept the body under wraps, "created a model" of an idealized body "that his fellow Americans could emulate" (x, 239). Jon Rosenblatt argues that "tropes of embodiment" function, in the context of Whitman's uneasiness about his sexual orientation, to present the poet to the reader in the form of a second, tangible body; this doubling of the poet's body offers Whitman "the possibility of purifying his own mortal body, which has failed to provide him with the guiltless sexual contact with others that he desires" (104).

6. "Copperhead" (literally a member of the pit viper family of reptiles) was a term of reproach for Northern Peace Democrats, who were thought to sympathize with the Confederacy. William Lloyd Garrison extends the metaphor in describing their threat to the body politic of the Union: "I think that this bellowing, bullying, treasonable party at the North has, after all, but very little left, either in point of numbers or power; the fangs of the viper are drawn, but the venomous feeling remains" (66).

7. Regarding Whitman's preference for certain Spanish words, Matthiessen suggests that Whitman found *libertad* inscribed on the Mexican dollar coin and *camerado* in Scott's romances (529). The gender of *libertad* is feminine. Whitman's reasons for this choice, as opposed to the French *liberté* (also grammatically feminine) or the English *liberty* (conventionally feminine in allegory) may have been metrical. The masculine inflection of *camerado* reinforces Whitman's sense of male homo-eroticism in the poems of "adhesiveness."

8. The *Variorum* edition reprints the table of contents page that bears the inscription (*LGV*, 2:557).

9. Nast's engraving of the figure of Liberty praying at the altar of Union, commemorating Thanksgiving Day, appeared in the 5 December 1863 issue of *Harper's*.

10. Hobbes, who argues for the artificiality of any governmental structure, nevertheless maintains that "an earthly Soveraign [*sic*] may be called the Image of God" (669). The theological roots of organicist political theory are in the medieval notion of the sovereign as mediating body, representative both of the people and of God. The theory was formalized in the Elizabethan age. It was readily available in American culture, since it had been criticized by revolutionaries such as Thomas Paine (Rogin, "King's Two Bodies," 81–82).

11. In his "Second Inaugural Address" Lincoln suggests that "American Slavery is one of those offenses which . . . [God] now wills to remove, and . . . He now gives to both North and South, this terrible war, as the woe due to those by whom the offence came" (8:333). The extent to which Lincoln actually believed this is not clear. The topic was popular in pulpit oratory, especially in the early years of the war (Moorhead, 23–81).

12. An engraving and text in *Harper's* entitled "Uncle Tom and His Grandchild" exemplifies the perception: the old man is identified as "a pure negro" while the girl, "almost white, and very beautiful," is said to have "far more of 'Southern Chivalry' in her veins than of negro blood" (3 November 1866, 690). Stowe's *Uncle Tom's Cabin* was a popular source of such information. In his *Narrative of the Life of an American Slave*, Frederick Douglass records how the identity of his white father is withheld from him.

13. Michael Adams argues that the early "military failures" of the North— e.g., McClellan's unwillingness to engage the Army of the Potomac in battle with opposing armies that he always outnumbered—resulted from the "popular conception" of the "Southerner as a superior martial figure," an aristocrat who even in peacetime lived by a code of honor and violence. These conceptions resulted in "what may be loosely termed the inferiority complex of some Northerners in the Civil War" (vii, viii).

14. Yet for both Lincoln and Whitman the war was not about slavery, but about the nature of the Union. Lincoln's emancipation proclamation was entirely a political expedient, which he felt would cease to apply after peace had been negotiated. At the outset of the war, he hoped to preserve the Union without the need for an executive or legislative order of abolition, because he viewed such governmental interference as unconstitutional (McPherson, 502–4).

15. What Grossman seems to mean here is that Whitman finds a transcendent meaning in Lincoln's death that does not depend on the logic of exchange; it is a case of representation without substitution.

16. The following discussion depends on Marx's analysis of commodity fetishism (*Capital*, 163–77).

17. James A. Rawley summarizes the congressional debate during the war over the Legal Tender Act, which authorized the printing of $150 million in U.S. notes— the first instance of a national fiat currency (49–51).

18. There is little point here in attempting to settle the question of Whitman's sexual experiences. Joseph Cady concludes that several of the poems in *Drum-Taps*, "when viewed 'from the inside' of gay experience at the time, emerge as purposeful homosexual visions"; thus they "truthfully expressed [Whitman's] developing positive sense of homosexual identity" (50, 58). On the other hand, Gay Wilson Allen finds that "clear evidence of his homosexual life is lacking" and argues for "sublimation" (57, 58). These critics agree, however, that there is some connection between Whitman's homoeroticism and his idea of democracy.

19. The other terms commonly used in this conceptualization are "resemblance" and "reflection" (61). Thus the representative is regarded as static rather than active.

2.   "The Real War Will Never Get in the Books"

1. Some passages were transcribed verbatim from these notebooks; others were revised (Basler, 19). Whitman had hoped to publish some of this material during the war, in a book to be entitled *Memoranda of a Year (1863)*. He proposed this idea to a Boston publisher who showed some interest but decided that the venture would be too great a financial risk (Allen, 141). When finally published in 1875, the *Memoranda* incorporated some articles that had previously appeared in the *New York Times* in 1863–65 (*PW*, 1:vii). Only about a hundred copies were printed (Basler, 11); but the complete text, with some revisions, was later included in *Specimen Days* (1881) and saw widespread distribution in this form.

2. This phrase does not appear in the 1875 text of the *Memoranda*, although there are many similar phrases; it was added as a summary comment when they were reprinted in *Specimen Days*.

3. Allen describes Whitman's use of organic rhythm and parallel structure to give form to his verse (230–42). Whitman sometimes suggested that while traditional rhyme and meter had been essential mnemonic devices in an oral tradition, they were "arbitrary" impositions in written poetry (Matthiessen, 580). In the 1855 preface, he claims that traditional rhyme "drops seeds of a sweeter and more luxuriant rhyme"

and is thus a sign of the more subtle, essential organic principle of poetry that derives "from beautiful blood and a beautiful brain" (*LG 1855*, 10).

4. In *Specimen Days* the words "We . . . things?" are deleted, but the emphasis of the passage on the problems of historical representation—the impossibility of giving full details and so on—is not appreciably altered (*PW*, 1:45). The passage, evidently revised from Whitman's journals during the war—as many of these passages were—was originally dated May 12, 1863. In 1863 the first volumes of histories of the war by Joel Tyler Headley, John Cabot Abbott, and Horace Greely were becoming "best sellers" (Pressly, 38).

5. In *Specimen Days*, the passage is set off with a subtitle: "Unknown Remains of the Bravest Soldier" (*PW*, 1:48).

6. John Singleton Mosby raised and commanded a guerrilla company of cavalry that operated in northern Virginia, at times within ten miles of Washington; the proximity of these attacks to the seat of the Federal government was a continual source of embarrassment (McPherson, 737-38).

7. Yet Ernst Robert Curtius's exhaustive rhetorical analysis of medieval European literature shows that the inexpressibility topos was traditionally used only in quite special circumstances—eulogies or other poems of praise to rulers and saints, or hymns to God. He does not address the "inexpressibility" of repulsive subjects (159-62).

8. Roland A. Dukerson documents Whitman's familiarity with Shelley's "Defense of Poetry" and other prose works, arguing for Shelley's influence on some passages of Whitman's poetry and on the 1855 preface (148).

9. An alternate title appears in the manuscript as "The Primer of Words." Horace Traubel's foreword to the 1904 edition reports that most of the notes, originally intended for a lecture series, were written on endpapers and filler sheets of unbound copies of the 1855 edition of *Leaves of Grass*—the theory is, so to speak, written in the margins of the poems. With the business of the war, Whitman abandoned the project, always intending to bring it out, but never succeeding.

10. No critic has, to my knowledge, attended to the violence of the passage, despite the fact that Whitman wrote the *American Primer* at a time when the country was preoccupied with the possibility of a coming war. The passage is generally regarded as a central statement of Whitman's poetics (Allen, 245; Kaplan, 229; Rosenblatt, 101). Howard Waskow (19) cites a related passage: "A perfect user of words uses things—they exude in power and beauty from him" (*AP*, 14). C. Carroll Hollis's speech-act analysis of *Leaves* does not cite this or any related passage from *AP*, although it is relevant to his argument. Challenging J. L. Austin's distinction between poetic discourse and performative language, Hollis notes the overwhelming abundance of pure performatives in the early editions of *Leaves*, and sees Whitman as calling attention to the fact that he is doing things with words, especially dramatizing his desire to secure uptake—that is, to make communicative contact with his reader. (It must be noted that Austin's distinction is, more precisely, between "serious" and "nonserious" uses of language; all language has, according to Austin, a "performative" aspect.)

11. The inner voice of the subject, which produces its identity, grounds the

possibility of representation in general, while simultaneously producing a latent consciousness of death: the proposition "I am" entails the proposition "I am mortal." Nevertheless, discourse about representation always marginalizes death (describes it as "latent") if it appeals—as Whitman's text so often does—to the speech *act* (the living utterance) as a guarantee of meaning (Derrida, *Speech*, 96–97, 54). For a brief, clearly articulated argument that the possibility of representation depends logically on the possibility of the death (the absence) of the speaking or writing subject, see Derrida, "Signature."

12. Leo Marx argues that the pastoral "ideal," as disseminated by Renaissance texts, determined the perception of the New World as a pastoral garden; in this sense *The Tempest* is "a prologue to American literature." The center of the American pastoral tradition is Jefferson's *Notes on the State of Virginia* (*Machine*, 34–72, 116–44). Whitman was familiar with Shakespeare, of course, and with the complete works of Jefferson (Stovall, 42). He probably also knew Emerson's views on the subject as expressed in essays such as "The Young American," which, according to Marx, expressed "the popular conception" of "the philosophy of romantic American pastoralism" and bore "a striking resemblance" to Jefferson's ideas (*Machine*, 230, 238). Whitman's ideas on pastoralism may also have been influenced by Bryant, Longfellow, Milton, Shelley, and many others. Especially suggestive is his interest in the reveries of McPherson's *Ossian* and in American "primitivists" such as Martin Tupper and Samuel Warren (Stovall, 115–16, 188–90). But the list of Whitman's sources is so vast, as Stovall demonstrates, that to single out any few would be inadequate. I will go on to propose that a relevant contemporary theorist of the pastoral in politics was Abraham Lincoln.

13. By the time of the Renaissance, the words were no longer thought to be spoken by Death, and were transformed instead into the shepherd's elegy, signifying that "I, too, lived in Arcadia" (and thus led a happy life, and so on) (Panofsky).

14. Matthiessen remarks on the similarity between the image this poem develops, in its final version, and the open-air paintings of W. S. Mount (599).

15. Floyd Stovall documents Whitman's general familiarity with Milton's *Poetical Works* (e.g., for a review written in 1848); he does not single out "L'Allegro" and "Il Penseroso," but does argue for Whitman's interest in the pastoral masque *Comus* (125–29).

16. James L. Machor argues that "beneath the surface opposition, the poem actually links the two scenes [rural and urban] as mirror images" such that it becomes an "expression of the urban pastoral ideal" (333). Uninterested in the wartime context of the poem, Machor minimizes important differences between the two halves, especially the representation of two kinds of poetics—one spontaneous, eternal, and focused on nature, the other politically prescribed, temporally specific, and focused on the war effort—each in its appropriate sphere.

17. E.g.: "Entering a Long Farm-Lane," "To the Spring and Brook," "Cedar-Apples," "Summer Sights and Indolencies," "The Lesson of a Tree," "The Sky—Days and Nights—Happiness" (*PW*, 1:xiii–xiv).

18. The text of this lecture, from which all quotations will be taken, is transcribed in the same volume in which the *Memoranda* are reprinted. Whitman delivered the

lecture, always with great success, many times from 1880 to 1890 (Basler, 35-46).

19. The advertisements for the lecture did not mention the poem to which Whitman alludes, trading instead on references to the widely popular "O Captain! My Captain!" (Basler, 36-37). In the mention of the "lilacs" Whitman may have been indulging in his characteristic self-promotion, reminding potential readers of what he thought to be a much better poem about Lincoln.

20. In discussing its relation to the genre, Richard P. Adams describes "some remarkably specific resemblances in thought and imagery" between "Lilacs" and Shelley's pastoral elegy on Keats, "Adonais"; he argues that Whitman learned the conventions of the genre from this poem and Milton's "Lycidas" (480). Mutlu Konuk Blasing takes more account of the poem's self-reflexivity, describing a "progression" of "various poetic 'stages' [that] are set up only to be abandoned in a quest for a poetic speech adequate to the poem's occasion" (31).

21. Stanza 11 is literally the center of the text of 1865, which contains twenty-one numbered sections or stanzas. Some stanzas were combined to form the sixteen of the 1891 edition. Stanzas 10, 11, and 12, however, retain their original numbering through all editions and remain untouched by revision except for accidentals (*LGV*, 2:529-39).

22. The visual composition of Whitman's image—an agricultural landscape with a city in the background—evokes the origins of the pastoral tradition of landscape painting in Renaissance Venice, especially the work of Giorgione and Campagnola; for a survey of this tradition, see Rosand.

23. Manifest Destiny had decreed "the expansion of American institutions across the whole of North America whether the residents—Indians, Spaniards, Mexicans, Canadians—wanted them or not"; the United States acquired all Mexican territories north of 31 degrees as a result of the Mexican war (McPherson, 47-48). Edmund Wilson remarks that during the Civil War "the Canadians became so alarmed at the increasing aggressiveness of the Washington government that they for the first time began to take steps to consolidate their diverse provinces in a single federal system" (xv).

24. Buchanan, for example, had begun three of his four annual addresses with a similar formula: "Since the adjournment of the last Congress our constituents have enjoyed an unusual degree of health. The earth has yielded her fruits abundantly and has bountifully rewarded the husbandman" (10:129; see also 10:339, 11:7). Buchanan violates the convention, displacing the pastoral with politics, in 1858. Earlier that year he had recommended the admission of Kansas as a slave state (McPherson, 167). In his 1858 "Annual Message" he forgoes the usual opening reference to bountiful harvests and moves immediately to the Kansas issue, praising the Supreme Court decision allowing the importation of slaves into the territories and proclaiming thanks to "Almighty Providence" that sectional strife had thus been allayed (10:235).

3. Photography and the Scene of History

1. My use of the term *naturalization* derives in part from the early work of Barthes, especially *Mythologies*. The sign systems of bourgeois culture, Barthes argues,

efface our consciousness of historical processes to make their results seem natural, thus inevitable and just.

2. Neither addresses the question of photographic representation. White, unlike Jameson, does not attempt to describe the nature of the historical referent, claiming only to analyze the ideologies of the "structural components" (4) of various histories. His very approach is possible, however, only on the assumption that there is little point in attempting "to decide whether a given historian's work is a better, or more correct, account of a specific set of events or segments of the historical process" (3).

3. The appearance of the images (engravings made from daguerreotypes) could not have been markedly different from that of the engravings with which the public was already familiar; this similarity to existing images may account for the apathetic popular reception of the volume.

4. Even though Brady claimed to have been on the field at First Bull Run, no authenticated photograph survives to substantiate his claim. The one surviving photograph supposedly from Bull Run, "Confederate dead on Matthews Hill" (which remained unknown until 1954), was probably staged, because there exists a similar photograph in which all the "bodies" are in identical positions, but upright and very much alive, and dressed in Federal uniforms (Frassanito, *Antietam*, 29–32).

5. A two-plate view of the Gettysburg battlefield was reproduced as a wood engraving in *Harper's Weekly* (22 August 1862, 532). Since all positives were contact prints, the size of the negative plate determined the size of the finished image; these ranged from 2.5 x 4 inches for *carte-de-visite* portraits to 10 x 14 inches and sometimes larger for landscapes. In 1875 William Henry Jackson packed a 20-x-24-inch plate camera into the Rockies and brought back views that "astounded the photographic world" (Newhall, *History*, 100). Enlargement was not a feasible practice until the turn of the century.

6. The camera obscura had existed since the sixteenth century. It consisted of a box fitted with a lens, a mirror oriented at 135 degrees to the focal axis of the lens, and a ground-glass plate parallel to the axis of the lens. The image projected onto the plate could be traced with pencil and paper.

7. Talbot at first called his photographs "calotypes" but later attempted to name the process after himself, mimicking Daguerre. In 1843 he set up a photofinishing laboratory called "The Talbotype Establishment"; the new name gained some currency in England (Newhall, *History*, 43).

8. By the time Holmes is writing, the "picturesque" and the "sublime" were not distinct or mutually exclusive categories of aesthetic experience. This realignment of modes is, as I will suggest below, due largely to the work of Cole and other painters of the Hudson River school. The first English theorist of the picturesque, William Gilpin (circa 1790), enlarged Burke's category of "the beautiful" to include the irregular form and complex harmony he found in the paintings of Gainsborough (Bermingham, 63–64). However, Gilpin's contemporary Uvedale Price suggested that the picturesque was a distinct third category. Martin Price defines the "picturesque moment" of the late eighteenth century as "that phase of speculation . . . where the aesthetic categories are self-sufficient," arguing that Words-

worth's *Prelude* marks the end of this moment and the passing of the picturesque into the sublime (which, unlike the picturesque, invites moral or metaphysical speculation) (262, 287–89). But in the United States the term *picturesque* was commonly used as late as the 1870s as both an adjective and a noun in reference to both contemporary paintings and the landscape itself. At this time, the term could connote moral or metaphysical value.

9. The volume was dedicated to Durand, "President of the National Academy of the Fine Arts." It was evidently quite a popular book. Another publisher reprinted it under a different title later in 1852; Putnam reissued it in 1868 in an expanded form under the title *A Landscape Book*. In 1872 Bryant edited *Picturesque America*, a similar, two-volume collection (Deakin, vi–vii).

10. Even though photographic conventions derived largely from the conventions of painting (especially as they were popularly disseminated in engraved reproductions), photography was from the beginning a commercial, democratizing, and possibly vulgar industry. As Emerson remarked, "'Tis certain that the Daguerreotype is your true Republican style of painting. The artist stands back and lets you paint yourself" (*JMN*, 8:142). In response to the public perception of the photographer as a mere tradesman, noted photographers such as Southworth, Hawes, Root, and Snelling cultivated an image of the photographer as a sophisticated artist (Rudisill, 175–91).

11. In the terms of C. S. Peirce's semiotic theory an *index* is related to its referent by means of a physical connection, an *icon* by means of resemblance (which need not be visual, as in Peirce's claim that algebraic equations are sometimes icons of physical laws), and a *symbol* by means of cultural convention other than resemblance (2:156–73). Thus a photograph is both an index, in its material origin, and an icon, linked to its referent by means of a structure of detailed visual resemblance. Yet a photograph can easily become a Peircean symbol as well, standing for something (perhaps a sentence or an abstract concept) by means of cultural conventions. Barthes elaborates a semiotic theory that is similar to Peirce's in important respects: he identifies as "myth" that which in Peircean terms would be a system of "symbols." Barthes argues that the apparent guarantee of resemblance in the photographic semiotic establishes a "first-order" significance, on the basis of which a mythology, a "second-order," ideological significance, appears in the image. Thus for example a photograph of a black soldier saluting the French flag published on the cover of *Paris-Match* signifies "that France is a great Empire, that all her sons, without any colour discrimination, faithfully serve under her flag" and so on (116). The "second order" of photographic signification is the realm of the Peircean "symbol." Cabot denies that this level of significance is possible in photographic representation.

12. See, for example, George Barnard's lecture on "Taste," discussed in Chapter 5.

13. This review—the second of three that the *Times* devoted to Brady's New York gallery—was written before any photographer had publicly displayed images of the war dead. The first negatives of battlefield dead were made at the scene of the battle of Antietam during September 1862 by Alexander Gardner, who was at that time employed by Brady. The other two reviews will be quoted in the following chapter.

14. Marx identifies the "middle landscape" of cultivated land as a system that mediated between the terror of the wilderness and the claustrophobia of the city—it functioned in the American consciousness as "the landscape of reconciliation, a mild, agricultural, semi-primitive terrain" that signified the plenty, opportunity, and security available to all (87). It seems odd that he does not mention the Civil War.

15. Of course an absence of represented human labor is not the only possible sign that a landscape painter has evaded the conditions of history. John Barrell's analysis of the representation of the rural poor in English landscape painting from 1730 to 1840 suggests that the georgic mode (the representation of rural labor) was even more effective than the formal, Arcadian pastoral in creating depoliticized, nonthreatening images of the laboring classes, because the georgic pretended greater realism. The poor work "blithely" (in Gainsborough), "cheerfully" (in Moreland), and "automatically" (in Constable), the representation of labor being determined by social forces, but indirectly, in the form of aesthetic constraints that permitted only "half an image" of rural life to be presented (21, 16). Direct representation of social relations is mediated by the harmony of the composition, which denies class conflict and presents an ahistorical image of "an English countryside innocent of division" (5).

16. John Mowitt has pointed out to me that Antonio Gramsci's ideas on the "organic intellectual" controvert the claim that "organicist" political theories are necessarily conservative. In a recent reconsideration of the thesis of *The Machine in the Garden*, Marx examines the recent emergence in America of pastoralism as "a nascent left-wing ideology" ("Pastoralism," 36). He finds that environmentalists, envisioning "the possibility of a cultural revolution grounded in opposition to the technocratic idea of material progress," have been attracted to the "recovery of 'the natural'" characteristic of pastoralism, but argues that in order to accomplish anything concrete, left-pastoralists would have to form alliances with "the hitherto disadvantaged carriers of emergent values—those for whom 'the recovery of the natural' as yet has, in itself, little or no appeal" (65–66).

17. See, for example, daguerreotypes made at logging and mining camps from two "wilderness" areas—California and Minnesota—reproduced in Rudisill (295–311).

18. McPherson locates the origin of secession in the debates over the political control of the territory acquired in the Mexican War, which was contemporarily recognized to be an imperialist enterprise (47–77).

19. The idea of a photographic standard is not so odd as it may seem at first. Scientific disciplines such as crystallography and microbiology have come to depend on photographic representations of data which are regularized for comparison through a standard system of powers of magnification.

20. Fredric Jameson's work in *The Political Unconscious* provides some direction for an argument that aesthetic form itself has political significance.

4.   Some Versions of Pastoral: Brady and Gardner

1. This chapter concentrates exclusively on the work of Northern photographers. A few Southerners made photographs related to the war, but this work remained unknown in the North until the publication of F. T. Miller's ten-volume *Photographic History of the Civil War* in 1911. The Confederate army evidently did not invest in battlefield photography as the Federal army did. Nor did any Southerner publish a photographic album of the war, as Barnard and Gardner did. However, the works of two Southern photographers have recently received some attention. A. D. Lytle, operating in Baton Rouge during the Federal occupation, made portraits of Federal officers, landscapes showing army camps in and near Baton Rouge, and many photographs of Federal ironclad ships and their crews. Lytle appears to have been a Union sympathizer, but it was rumored after his death that he was a "camera spy" for the Confederacy. Today his pictures seem to carry little information of value as military intelligence (East, 197–232). J. D. Edwards, whose gallery was in New Orleans, produced several photographs of Confederate troops, materiel, forts and the like during 1861–62. These photographs stress the South's preparedness for war (Davis, 1:344–63). In this they resemble the Northern photographs that document "how concretely the Civil War served as a proto-industrial experience" (Trachtenberg, 26–27).

2. Portraits, of course, were taken at fairly close distances. But of the thousands of Civil War photographs in the National Archives and the Library of Congress (including portraits), fewer than fifteen are true close-ups with a focal distance of three feet or less (Snyder). The only major exceptions to the straight-on camera angle are some of Andrew Russell's photographs, made for the Army Corps of Engineers, of bridges taken from the bottom of a bed or gorge. In these images the camera is angled approximately thirty degrees upward. As Trachtenberg argues, such images glorify the technological achievements of the war. "High Bridge, Crossing the Appomattox" (Gardner, *Sketch Book*, plate 98) presented an opportunity for an upward camera angle (the river bed is smooth and dry), but Gardner chose instead to shoot straight on.

3. Gardner first published his *Catalogue* in 1863. Brady did not publish a catalogue until 1869; several of the photographs it lists were made by Gardner (Cobb, 132).

4. Compare also photographs of wounded men in the Vietnam war, which clearly show the wounds while making it difficult in many cases to determine whether the man lives or dies—for example, the work of Larry Burrows and Catherine Leroy (Lewinski, 211, 212, 217).

5. The Milhollen and Mugridge index to the Brady archive in the Library of Congress lists sixteen photographs of Confederate dead and three of Federal dead. Of these latter three, one is mislabeled (see the discussion below of Gardner's "Harvest of Death"), one represents skeletal remains being collected for reinterment (impossible to identify as Confederate or Union), and one shows an embalming surgeon posed behind a body partially covered by a sheet (which may have been a posed scene). Gardner's *Sketch Book* maintains a similar proportion of Confederate to Federal dead.

6. My generalizations about the representation of the wounded are based on photographs reproduced in Davis (4:231–74) and on the microfilm reproductions indexed by Milhollen and Mugridge. One view depicting men sitting and lying on the ground near a field hospital at Savage Station, Virginia, would have provided the opportunity for the documentation of the wounded. Yet this group portrait is taken at a distance that obscures any view of the wounds from which the men might be suffering; in the foreground, for example, is a group of soldiers playing cards (Milhollen and Mugridge, 6, LC-B8171-491). Generally, if the wounded are shown it is only after they have recovered (e.g., Davis, 4:262–63). Medical techniques such as anaesthesia were documented by posing healthy soldiers as wounded men (4:241). One remarkable and exceptional photograph, probably taken by a surgeon who worked in an army hospital, shows a pile of eight or nine amputated legs (4:244). The differences between this image, first published in 1983, and the conventions of the images produced by official army photographers and commercial photographers cannot be emphasized too strongly.

7. For example, Gardner's photograph of a Union burial detail at Antietam documents this military presence, showing a row of four corpses arranged beneath a tree in the left middle ground and a group of soldiers with picks and shovels in the right middle ground (Frassanito, *Antietam*, 145).

8. Louis Althusser's distinction between "repressive" and "ideological" state apparatuses is helpful here. The repressive state apparatus is the state itself—that is, the law and the physical power to enforce it by means of the military, the police, and the penal system (135). Ideological apparatuses, which function to legitimate the existing class system and power structure, include religion, the educational system, the family, the political process, the media, and "culture" (literature, art, and the like) (136–37). These apparatuses ought not in general be regarded as consciously "conspiratorial," but rather as sign systems within which a representation of the relationship of the individual to his or her "reality" is constructed. Under a capitalist system of production, such apparatuses legitimate the absence of egalitarian social and economic relations by constructing representations (such as "the free market") that propose that such relations are in fact present.

9. On the general operations of this redescriptive rhetoric, see Scarry (63–81).

10. Numbers used to document quotations from Gardner's *Sketch Book* refer to the number of the plate that the text accompanies.

11. "Gun-cotton" was the common term for cellulose nitrate, an important ingredient in recently developed smokeless gunpowder. In wet-plate photography, a viscous "collodion" made from gun-cotton (or "nitrocellulose") and potassium iodide dissolved in alcohol was used to coat a glass plate, which, when dry, was dipped in a solution of silver nitrate. The resulting reaction formed an evenly distributed layer of light-sensitive silver iodide on the negative plate (Newhall, *History*, 59).

12. John Kasson, however, argues for a more heavily technologized aesthetic and ideology, citing the nineteenth-century ideal of the factory community (e.g., Lowell, Massachusetts) and visions of technological utopia; like Marx, Kasson does not discuss the Civil War in any detail. The aesthetic and ideology that inform

the Civil War photography with which I am concerned more closely resemble Marx's descriptions than Kasson's; but the naturalizing impulse was redirected toward the politics of the war.

13. I erroneously attribute the Antietam series to "Brady" in order to reflect the contemporary perception. Frassanito's analysis of the photographs from Antietam demonstrates that this series was made not by Brady, who was never near Antietam, but by Gardner and his assistant, James Gibson, both of whom were employed by Brady at the time. In May 1863 Gardner left Brady's company, taking Gibson with him, and set up a rival gallery in Washington (Cobb, 127). From the view of Burnside Bridge reproduced in the *Sketch Book*, it is evident that Gardner retained at least some of the negatives from the Antietam series.

14. In the Dover reprint of the *Sketch Book* the negatives of the Manassas photographs are attributed to George Barnard and James Gibson, the positives to Gardner. I treat "Gardner" as the "author" of the *Sketch Book*, assuming that he selected the images to be included.

15. I borrow the phrase from Frassanito, who points out that more Americans died on 17 September, 1862, than on any other day in history. While the site of Antietam Bridge was of little military importance, "there can be little doubt, judging by the quantity of negatives expended on it, that the bridge was considered by Alexander Gardner to be a good subject" (*Antietam*, 17, 87).

16. *Harper's Pictorial History of the Great Rebellion* (1866–68) claims that Reynolds was shot in the head but does not give an exact location. This volume includes three engravings of photographs from Gettysburg, including the "Brady's" two-plate view, "Wheat-Field in Which General Reynolds Was Shot," and two views of stone houses. The authors state that Brady permitted "access to, and free use of his immense collection of scenes and portraits" (Gurnsey and Alden, 402–3, 507–8, 401).

17. Another image excluded from the *Sketch Book* shows a blanket under the corpse, on which it was probably carried. The musket is not of the kind used by sharpshooters (Frassanito, *Gettysburg*, 192). Since this musket appears identical to the musket in the *Sketch Book* photographs, it seems likely that Gardner composed "A Sharpshooter's Last Sleep" as well.

18. Antigone says, in response to Creon's edict that the body of her brother remain unburied, "Nor did I deem that your decrees were of such force that a mortal could override the unwritten and unfailing statutes of heaven. For [they are] not of today or yesterday, but of all time " (Sophocles, 127).

19. I found it interesting that, unlike most of the Civil War photographs housed in the Prints and Photographs Division of the Library of Congress, this one has apparently never been copied. If a print has been copied, a copy negative is kept on file for future print requests; no copy negative was on file for this image.

5. Barnard and the American Picturesque

1. Of the four maps included in the original edition, the Dover reprint (1977) reproduces only one; the other three "requir[ed] color-coding which was not feasible in the present edition" (Newhall, Preface, iii). The original edition is extremely

rare; the National Union Catalogue lists seven extant copies. The copy in the Library of Congress Prints and Photographs Division includes no maps.

2. The full text of this pamphlet is included in the Dover reprint (Barnard, *Views*, ix–xviii).

3. Encamped near Raleigh, Sherman realized that "Johnston's army could not be caught; the country was too open; . . . the men could escape us, disperse, and assemble again at some place agreed on, and thus the war might be prolonged indefinitely" (2:344).

4. Presumably the relevant "theory of color" was the study of the photographic representation of colors by means of gray tones. Rich and varied gray tones were notoriously difficult to produce.

5. This is evidently the only published notice. Since the price of one hundred dollars placed the volume beyond the reach of the middle class, the relative lack of publicity is not surprising. The choice of *Harper's* to notice the book is note-worthy—especially since Barnard (unlike Brady or Gardner) had no commercial connection with the magazine or the publishing house of Harper & Brothers—and probably derives from the general interest of the editors in illustrations of the war.

6. Joseph Glatthaar's recent "social history" of Sherman's army is no real exception to the conventional perspective of the military historian. Although he takes "the viewpoint of the soldiers," he deals with regularities, emphasizing "the veteran character that utterly dominated Sherman's army" and arguing that Sherman "captur[ed] the hearts and minds, or 'souls' of his men" (xi–xiii, 17).

7. For the reader's convenience, plate numbers refer to the widely available Dover reprint of the *Views*. Discrepancies between the Dover edition and the copy in the Library of Congress, from which my illustrations are reproduced, will be noted where relevant.

8. As with all photographs reproduced here from Barnard's *Views*, "Buen-Ventura" is taken from a copy of the album owned by the Library of Congress. The Dover edition, reprinted from a copy of the *Views* owned by the New-York Historical Society, includes a slightly different image, also captioned "Buen-Ven-tura" (plate 48). To avoid confusion, I have not given a plate number to the photograph reproduced in the present essay. Plate 48 of the Dover edition shows more emphatically that a cemetery is being represented: two grave markers, sur-rounded by a fence, dominate the left half of the image. This composition invites the viewer to enter the scene, but only part way; the iron railing directs the eye toward the path, but the heavy foliage discourages further exploration. One is content to rest on the ground and contemplate the scene, maintaining the aesthetic de-tachment evoked by the experience of the picturesque.

9. Maps and statistics of Alabama (13 January), Louisiana (3 February), and Georgia (12 May) followed, but the projected series was then abandoned without explanation.

10. The "industrial statistics" consisted primarily of topographical descriptions and records of agricultural production.

11. Allegorical engravings by Thomas Nast celebrated the Emancipation Proc-lamation (24 January 1863) and Independence Day (16 July 1864). In the latter image

Liberty has broken the chains and manacles of slavery. On the front cover of the issue containing the map of Mississippi (6 January 1866) is a sketch entitled "The Last Chàttel," in which an old black man contemplates his home in ruins. A whip lying on the ground is a reminder of the past that has been destroyed along with the house, but there seems to be little hope represented for his future.

12. For example, Thomas Cole wrote that he found deserted ruins in Sicily to suggest a contrast between the finitude of human civilization and the eternity of nature (Baigell, 70).

6. Melville's *Battle-Pieces* as a Trace of War

1. Robert Penn Warren points out that in the preface,

> Melville says, "I seem . . . to have but placed"—not "I have . . . but placed"; and his statement is, finally, an affirmation of the inner unity of the book. The "vagrant winds" [*sic*] that touch the harp all blow from Melville's soul, and the "contrasted airs" that play upon the strings constitute a dialectic. The book is not a log of the war, but a log of Melville's attempt to make sense of his feelings about the war—and about life.

If the poems represent political positions in conflict, these for Warren are only metaphors for conflicts universally felt by all sensitive human beings. Differences are subsumed in a "dialectic," manifested especially in "the ironical split between concern with the human being and concern with the idea, between the individual and ideology"; these divisions "were reduced and energy [was thereby] released for creative effort" (806, 805). Michael Paul Rogin, although perhaps more cognizant than Warren that "the individual" is itself an ideological construct, identifies a similar division and consequent reduction: "Living or dying in stoic servitude, the protagonists of *Battle-Pieces* served something larger than themselves. The poems replaced individual, heroic display with the institutional power of the state" (*Subversive Genealogy*, 264; hereafter abbreviated as SG). Joyce Sparer Adler takes her cue from Melville's reference to the war as a "tragedy," identifying a "three-part causal sequence that is characteristic of tragedy: origin and building up of the fate; agony; enlightenment." She is alone among the critics in emphasizing "Melville's passion against war"; in order to reconcile the poems with this passion, she argues for Melville's belief that "the Civil War had a special historical necessity" (133, 3, 134). Daniel Aaron finds in the temporal sequence of poems the key to the unifying design of the volume, but is less intent on producing a monological reading than other critics. He finds "a sustained debate between belief and disbelief, which abounds in paradoxes, ironies, and conflicts, and which keeps denying what it affirms" (79, 88).

2. During the war the decaying wooden dome was replaced, at Lincoln's direction, by a new dome of cast iron, the construction of which Melville witnessed when he visited Washington in 1861 (Rogin, SG, 272).

3. Shelley's use of the figure is similar in "Ode to the West Wind"; here memory is irrelevant as the poet bares his soul to the animating spirit. Melville's familiarity with these poems is open to speculation. Jay Leyda shows that Melville owned the collected works of both Coleridge and Shelley, but does not record checks, un-

derscoring, or other marks of reading in any relevant text. By the middle of the nineteenth century, however, the metaphor was in the air.

4. Hennig Cohen suggests that the officer may have been Winfield Scott Hancock, but may also have been one of several other officers present at Spotsylvania, some of whom performed less than heroically (248). Thus we cannot specify the degree of irony present in the poem.

5. Cohen points out the Emersonian overtones of this line (248). Given the disgust with Emerson's philosophy registered in chapters 36 and 37 of *The Confidence Man* (see also Leyda, 2:648; *Pierre*, 276–77), the image of hollowness—a form filled with wind—seems appropriate.

6. One portrait of Winfield Scott Hancock shows a beard and mustache that are not unlike the way Melville wore his own facial hair (Guernsey and Alden, 338).

7. Critics have identified in *Moby-Dick* several different allegories of antebellum American politics. For example, Willie Weathers reads Ahab as the abolitionist William Lloyd Garrison, the whale as the state, and the real hero as Thomas Jefferson, represented by Bulkington. Charles Foster finds in Ishmael a "representative American" manipulated by Daniel Webster in the figure of Ahab (5). For Alan Hiemert, Webster is the whale, hunted by the proslavery senator John Calhoun, who brings about the destruction of the Union symbolized in the sinking of the *Pequod*. This disagreement over what specific persons and events are being allegorized indicates that *Moby-Dick* cannot be contained by any specific allegorical structure. Nevertheless the text does engage the general problems of "the interracial society, the structure of authority, and the industrial apparatus of nineteenth-century America" (Rogin, *SG*, 108).

8. Hobbes extends and further complicates the system of metaphors: "*Soveraignty* is an Artificall *Soul*, as giving life and motion to the whole body . . . *Equity* and *Lawes*, an artificiall *Reason* and *Will*; *Concord*, *Health*; *Sedition*, *Sicknesse*; and *Civill war*, *Death* (*Leviathan*, 81).

9. As Howard Zinn argues, the war "was not a clash of peoples (most northern whites were not economically favored, not politically powerful; most southern whites were poor farmers, not decision makers) but of elites" (184).

10. Whitman extends the metaphor in "O Captain! My Captain!" which sentimentally mourns the death of Lincoln, the "captain" of the ship of state (*SDT*, 13).

11. This was a "rifle" with an 8-inch bore used to bombard Charleston in 1863; after firing its thirty-sixth round, the gun exploded (Guernsey and Alden, 743).

12. Adler finds a "realistic portrayal of war" which "has, of course, an antiwar effect" to be "one of the main characteristics" of the poems (143). But Rogin argues that the poems show "little of the actual bloody carnage" of the war (*SG*, 260). Edwin Haviland Miller, too, finds a "loss of immediacy" resulting from Melville's perspective "as a distant spectator, observing men and events through a telescope" (309). An early reviewer found the poems to be "phantasms" of Melville's "perturbed" consciousness, "shedding, not words and blood, but words alone." But this reviewer was evidently unprepared to make sense of a work that "possesses the negative virtue of originality in such degree that it not only reminds you of no

poetry you have ever read, but of no life you have known" ("Reviews and Literary Notices," 252).

13. Cohen finds that in this poem "Melville adheres to a degree of regularity in form remarkable for him" (215). Gail Coffler claims that Melville's "theory of art and his artistic method [in *Battle-Pieces*] are finely illustrated in the theme and form" of this poem (108). But in 1862, as he was beginning to experiment with poetry, Melville had checked and underscored the following passage in his copy of the *Poetical Works* of Henry Kirke White: "Harmonious modulations, and *unvarying exactness of measure*, totally precluding sublimity and fire, have reduced our fashionable poetry to mere sing-song" (Leyda, 2:649, emphasis added). Thus there seems to be a degree of irony in the form of the poem—especially in view of Melville's usual insistence on the ambiguity of appearances—and so, implicitly, a potential irony in its "moral" as well.

14. Melville had seen a map of the fleet's path in the *Rebellion Record* (Cohen, 216–17). Of course the actual movements of the ships could not have been so precisely geometrical, as Melville the sailor would have known.

15. Cohen argues that Melville followed his journalistic sources in the *Rebellion Record* so closely that the poem is "little more than versified narration" (236).

16. Melville's note clarifies the allusion to the war of 1812: "Admiral Porter is a son of the late Commodore Porter, commander of the frigate Essex on that Pacific cruise which ended in the desperate fight off Valparaiso with the English frigates Cherub and Phoebe, in the year 1814" (*CP*, 451).

17. Draco's notorious laws had specified death as the punishment for nearly every offense. Thus the figure of Draco may be another allusion to *White-Jacket*: "'*Shall suffer death!*' This was the burden of nearly every Article [of the *Articles of War*] read by the Captain's clerk" (293). It has been suggested that "Draco" is the archbishop of New York, John Hughes, an early advocate of conscription (Cohen, 240; Rogin, *SG*, 266). But this is doubtful. Hughes addressed the Irish community from the balcony of his New York apartment, urging cooperation, only after Federal soldiers had put down the riot; the words "nor parlies" suggest that military force, not Hughes's speech, was the effective mechanism of control. A more likely candidate for "Draco" is General Brown, commander of the troops, who was honored by the mayor for his service in the riots (Cook, 165, 173).

18. As Melville had written before the war: "Is it lawful for you to scourge a man that is a Roman? asked the intrepid Apostle, well knowing, as a Roman citizen, that it was not. And now, eighteen hundred years after, is it lawful for you, my countrymen, to scourge a man that is an American?" (*White-Jacket*, 142). He is referring specifically to flogging in the navy, but the implications are clear for other uses of violence by the state.

19. The event (not) described by Froissart was a peasant rebellion in 1358, which was violently suppressed (Cohen, 240). This event is so obscure that few of Melville's readers could have understood the allusion. A more immediate association, perhaps, would have been the French Revolution of 1848, the ideological status of which was ambiguous. Those in rebellion won—as they did not in the draft riots—and

yet this victory was suspect. At first proclaimed by President Polk to be a triumph of republican principles, the revolution of 1848 degenerated into a brutal class war which ended, eventually, in the accession of Napoleon III as emperor (Rogin, *SG*, 102).

Epilogue: "For the Union Dead"

1. In the context of pastoralism the aquarium image may also evoke the Renaissance genre of piscatorial eclogue (for example, Walton's *The Compleat Angler*), which shares the quietism of the pastoral genre.

2. The MacMillan *Anthology of American Literature* and the *Norton Anthology of American Literature* both translate servare with "to serve," evidently reading the false cognate, servire. (They do not mention, however, that *servire* carries strong connotations of slavery.) William Nelles calls attention to this error, noting that the correct translation should be "to preserve" or "to save." He argues that Lowell the classicist knew what he was writing, and that the irony of Union soldiers giving up everything to be a *slave* to the state would be too strong (639–40). But Lowell the poet also knew what he was writing. He must have been sensitive to the resonance of the word *servility*; thus Nelles seems to underestimate the potential for irony in the reverberations of *servility*.

3. This image, like the title of the poem, reflects on Allen Tate's "Ode to the Confederate Dead" (1937). Tate begins with an image of gravestones in a Confederate cemetery subject to the erosion of the elements. By the end of the poem, it is clear that this decay is a metaphor for the solipsistic dis-integration of the self in the modern age—a plight for which no solution is offered. Despite these similarities, Tate remains uninterested in the specifically political implications of the failure of representation; but such questions (for example, race relations) are central for Lowell.

Bibliography

Aaron, Daniel. *The Unwritten War: American Writers and the Civil War*. New York: Knopf, 1973; Madison: University of Wisconsin Press, 1987.

Adams, Michael C. C. *Our Masters the Rebels: A Speculation on Union Military Failure in the East, 1861–1865*. Cambridge: Harvard University Press, 1978.

Adams, Richard P. "Whitman's 'Lilacs' and the Tradition of the Pastoral Elegy." *Publications of the Modern Language Association* 72(1957): 479–87.

Adler, Joyce Sparer. *War in Melville's Imagination*. New York: New York University Press, 1981.

Allen, Gay Wilson. *The New Walt Whitman Handbook*. New York: New York University Press, 1975.

Alpers, Paul. *The Singer of the Eclogues: A Study of Virgilian Pastoral*. Berkeley and Los Angeles: University of California Press, 1979.

Althusser, Louis. "On Ideological State Apparatuses." In *Lenin and Philosophy and Other Essays*, trans. Ben Brewster. London: New Left Books, 1971.

Andrews, J. Cutler. *The North Reports the Civil War*. Pittsburgh: University of Pittsburgh Press, 1955.

Aristotle. *Poetics*. Translated by Gerald F. Else. Ann Arbor: University of Michigan Press, 1967.

Aspiz, Harold. *Walt Whitman and the Body Beautiful*. Urbana: University of Illinois Press, 1980.

Austin, J. L. *How to Do Things with Words*. 2d ed. Ed. J. O. Urmson and Marina Sbisà. Cambridge: Harvard University Press, 1975.

Baigell, Matthew. *Thomas Cole*. New York: Watson-Guptil, 1981.

Barnard, George N. *Photographic Views of Sherman's Campaign*. 1866. Reprint. New York: Dover, 1977.

———. *Photographic Views of Sherman's Campaign from Negatives Taken in the Field by George N. Barnard*. New York: Press of Wynkoop & Hallenbeck, 1866.

———. "Taste." *Photographic and Fine Art Journal* 8(1855): 158–59.

Barrell, John. *The Dark Side of the Landscape: The Rural Poor in English Painting, 1730–1840*. Cambridge: Cambridge University Press, 1980.

Barthes, Roland. *Mythologies*. Translated by Annette Lavers. New York: Hill & Wang, 1972.

Basler, Roy P. Introduction. In Walt Whitman, *Memoranda during the War and Death of Abraham Lincoln*. Bloomington: Indiana University Press, 1962.

Benjamin, Walter. "The Work of Art in the Age of Mechanical Reproduction." In *Illuminations*, trans. Hannah Arendt. New York: Schocken Books, 1969.

Bermingham, Ann. *Landscape and Ideology: The English Rustic Tradition, 1740–1860*. Berkeley and Los Angeles: University of California Press, 1986.

Bierce, Ambrose. "Chickamauga." 1891. Reprinted in *"In the Midst of Life" and Other Tales*. New York: Signet, 1961.

Blasing, Mutlu Konuk. "Whitman's 'Lilacs' and the Grammars of Time." *PMLA* 97(1982): 31–39.

"Brady's Photographs of the War." *New York Times*, 26 September 1862: 5.

Bryant, William Cullen. *The Poetical Works of William Cullen Bryant.* 1883. 2 vols. Reprint. New York: Russell & Russell, 1967.

Buchanan, James. *The Works of James Buchanan.* Edited by John Bassett Moore. 12 vols. Philadelphia: J. B. Lippincott, 1908–11.

Burgess, Nathan G. "Taking Portraits after Death." *Photographic and Fine Art Journal* 8(1855): 80.

——. "The Value of Daguerreotype Likenesses." *Photographic and Fine Art Journal* 8(1855): 19.

Cabot, J. Eliot "On the Relation of Art to Nature." *Atlantic Monthly* 13(1864): 183–99, 313–29.

Cady, Joseph. "*Drum-Taps* and Nineteenth-Century Male Homosexual Literature." In *Walt Whitman: Here and Now*, ed. Joann P. Krieg. Westport, Conn.: Greenwood, 1985.

Callcott, George H. *History in the United States, 1800–1860: Its Practice and Purpose.* Baltimore: Johns Hopkins University Press, 1970.

Clausewitz, Carl von. *On War.* 3 vols. Translated by J. J. Graham. London: Routledge & Kegan Paul, 1968.

Cobb, Josephine. "Alexander Gardner." *Image* 7(1958): 124–36.

Coffler, Gail. "Form as Resolution: Classical Elements in Melville's *Battle-Pieces.*" In *American Poetry: Between Tradition and Modernism, 1865–1914*, ed. Roland Hagenbuchle. Regensberg: Pustet, 1984.

Coffman, Stanley R., Jr. "'Crossing Brooklyn Ferry': A Note on the Catalogue Technique in Whitman." *Modern Philology* 51(1954): 225–32.

Cohen, Hennig, ed. *The Battle-Pieces of Herman Melville.* New York: Thomas Yoseloff, 1963.

Coker, F. W. "Organismic Theories of the State: Nineteenth-Century Interpretations of the State as Organism or as Person." *Columbia University Studies in History, Economics, and Public Law* 38, no. 2(1910): 1–220.

Coleridge, Samuel Taylor. "The Eolian Harp." In *English Romantic Writers*, ed. David Perkins. New York: Harcourt Brace Jovanovich, 1967.

Cook, Adrian. *The Armies of the Streets: The New York City Draft Riots of 1863.* Lexington: University of Kentucky Press, 1974.

Crane, Stephen. *The Red Badge of Courage.* 1895. Reprint. New York: Penguin, 1983.

Crawley, Thomas Edward. *The Structure of Leaves of Grass.* Austin: University of Texas Press, 1970.

Crèvecoeur, J. Hector St. John de. *Letters from an American Farmer.* 1782. Reprint. New York: E. P. Dutton, 1957.

Curtius, Ernst Robert. *European Literature and the Latin Middle Ages.* Translated by Willard R. Trask. New York: Pantheon, 1953.

Daguerre, Louis. "Daguerreotype." In *Classic Essays on Photography*, ed. Alan Trachtenberg, 11–13. New Haven: Leete's Island Books, 1980.

"Daguerreotypes on Tombstones." *Hutching's Illustrated California Magazine* 1(1857): 519.

Davis, William C., ed. *The Image of War, 1861–1865*. 5 vols. Garden City: Doubleday, 1981.

Derrida, Jacques. "Signature Event Context." In *Margins of Philosophy*, trans. Alan Bass, 309–30. Chicago: University of Chicago Press, 1982.

———. *Speech and Phenomena, and Other Essays on Husserl's Theory of Signs*. Translated by David B. Allison. Evanston: Northwestern University Press, 1973.

Diffley, Kathleen. "The Roots of Tara: Making War Civil." *American Quarterly* 36(1984): 359–72.

Dukerson, Roland A. "Markings by Whitman in His Copy of Shelley's *Works*." *Walt Whitman Review* 14(1968): 147–51.

East, Charles. "A Yankee in Dixie: Baton Rouge Photographer A. D. Lytle." In *Touched by Fire: A Photographic Portrait of the Civil War*, ed. William C. Davis. 2 vols. Boston: Little, Brown, 1985–87.

Emerson, Ralph Waldo. *The Complete Works of Ralph Waldo Emerson*. 12 vols. Boston: Houghton Mifflin, 1904.

———. *Journals and Miscellaneous Notebooks of Ralph Waldo Emerson*. 16 vols. Cambridge: Harvard University Press, Belknap Press, 1960–82.

Empson, William. *Some Versions of Pastoral*. Norfolk, Conn.: New Directions, 1960.

Ettin, Andrew V. *Literature and the Pastoral*. New Haven: Yale University Press, 1984.

Fisher, Philip. "Democratic Social Space: Whitman, Melville, and the Promise of American Transparency." *Representations* 24 (1988): 60–101.

Foster, Charles H. "Something in Emblems: A Reinterpretation of *Moby-Dick*." *New England Quarterly* 34(1961): 3–35.

Frassanito, William. *Antietam: The Photographic Legacy of America's Bloodiest Day*. New York: Scribner's, 1978.

———. *Gettysburg: A Journey in Time*. New York: Scribner's, 1975.

Fredrickson, George M. *The Inner Civil War: Northern Intellectuals and the Crisis of the Union*. New York: Harper & Row, 1965.

Gardner, Alexander. *Catalogue of Photographic Incidents of the War, from the Gallery of Alexander Gardner, Photographer to the Army of the Potomac*. Washington D.C.: H. Polkinhorn, 1863.

———. *Gardner's Photographic Sketch Book of the Civil War*. Washington, D.C.: Philp & Solomons, 1866.

———. *Gardner's Photographic Sketch Book of the Civil War*. Washington, D.C.: Philp & Solomons, 1866. Reprint. New York: Dover, 1959.

Garrison, William Lloyd. "Garrison Endorses the War (1862)." In *William Lloyd Garrison*, ed. George M. Fredrickson. Englewood Cliffs, N.J.: Prentice-Hall, 1968.

Girard, René. *The Scapegoat*. Translated by Yvonne Freccero. Baltimore: Johns Hopkins University Press, 1986.

———. *Violence and the Sacred*. Translated by Patrick Gregory. Baltimore: Johns Hopkins University Press, 1977.

Glatthaar, Joseph T. *The March to the Sea and Beyond: Sherman's Troops in the Savannah and Carolinas Campaigns*. New York: New York University Press, 1986.

Gridley, Roy E. "Some Versions of the Primitive and the Pastoral on the Great Plains of America." In *Survivals of the Pastoral*, ed. Richard F. Hardin. Lawrence: University of Kansas Publications, 1979.

Grossman, Allen. "The Poetics of Union in Whitman and Lincoln: An Inquiry toward the Relationship of Art and Policy." In *The American Renaissance Reconsidered*, ed. Walter Benn Michaels and Donald Pease. Baltimore: Johns Hopkins University Press, 1985.

Gurnsey, Alfred H., and Henry M. Alden. *Harper's Pictorial History of the Civil War*. 2 vols. 1866–68. Reprint. New York: Fairfax Press, n.d.

Haley, John W. *The Rebel Yell and the Yankee Hurrah: The Civil War Journal of a Maine Volunteer*. Edited by Ruth Silliker. Camden, Maine: Down East Books, 1985.

Hiemert, Alan. "*Moby-Dick* and American Political Symbolism." *American Quarterly* 15(1963): 498–534.

Hindus, Milton, ed. *Walt Whitman: The Critical Heritage*. London: Routledge & Kegan Paul, 1971.

Hobbes, Thomas. *Leviathan*. 1651. Reprint. New York: Penguin, 1982.

Hollis, C. Carroll. *Language and Style in* Leaves of Grass. Baton Rouge: Louisiana State University Press, 1983.

Holmes, Oliver Wendell, Sr. "Doings of the Sunbeam." *Atlantic Monthly* 13(1863): 1–15.

———. "My Hunt after 'The Captain.'" *Atlantic Monthly* 10(1862): 738–64.

———. "The Stereoscope and the Stereograph." *Atlantic Monthly* 3(1859): 738–48.

———. "Sun-Painting and Sun-Sculpture; with a Stereoscopic Trip across the Atlantic." *Atlantic Monthly* 8(1861): 13–29.

Horace. "Art of Poetry." In *Critical Theory Since Plato*, ed. Hazard Adams. New York: Harcourt Brace Jovanovich, 1971.

Horan, James D. *Mathew Brady: Historian with a Camera*. New York: Bonanza Books, n.d.

Howe, Julia Ward. "Battle Hymn of the Republic." *Atlantic Monthly* 9(1862): 145.

Hunter, Jefferson. *Image and Word: The Interaction of Twentieth-Century Photographs and Texts*. Cambridge: Harvard University Press, 1987.

Jameson, Fredric. *The Political Unconscious: Narrative as a Socially Symbolic Act*. Ithaca: Cornell University Press, 1981.

Kaplan, Justin. *Walt Whitman: A Life*. New York: Simon & Schuster, 1980.

Kasson, John F. *Civilizing the Machine: Technology and Republican Values in America, 1776–1900*. New York: Viking, 1976.

Kronick, Joseph. "On the Border of History: Whitman and the American Sublime." In *The American Sublime*, ed. Mary Arensberg. Albany: State University of New York Press, 1986.

Leary, Lewis. *John Greenleaf Whittier*. New York: Twayne, 1961.

Lewinski, Jorge. *The Camera at War: War Photography from 1848 to the Present Day*. Secaucus, N.J.: Chartwell, 1986.

Leyda, Jay. *The Melville Log: A Documentary Life of Herman Melville*. 2 vols. New York: Gordian, 1969.

Lincoln, Abraham. *The Collected Works of Abraham Lincoln*. Edited by Roy P. Basler. 8 vols. New Brunswick: Rutgers University Press, 1953.

Lowell, Robert. "For the Union Dead." In *For the Union Dead*, 70–72. New York: Farrar Strauss, 1964.

Machor, James L. "Pastoralism and the American Urban Ideal: Hawthorne, Whitman, and the Literary Pattern." *American Literature* 54(1982): 329–53.

McPherson, James M. *Battle Cry of Freedom: The Civil War Era*. Oxford History of the United States, vol. 6. New York: Oxford University Press, 1988.

Marx, Karl. *Capital: A Critique of Political Economy, Volume One*. 1867. Translated by Ben Fowkes. New York: Vintage, 1977.

Marx, Leo. "The American Revolution and the American Landscape." In *The Pilot and the Passenger: Essays on Literature, Technology, and Culture in the United States*. New York: Oxford University Press, 1988.

———. *The Machine in the Garden: Technology and the Pastoral Ideal in America*. New York: Oxford University Press, 1964.

———. "Pastoralism in America." In *Ideology and Classic American Literature*, ed. Sacvan Bercovitch and Myra Jehlen. Cambridge: Cambridge University Press, 1986.

Matthiessen, F. O. *American Renaissance: Art and Expression in the Age of Emerson and Whitman*. New York: Oxford University Press, 1941; 1980.

Melville, Herman. *Billy Budd, Sailor (An Inside Narrative)*. Edited by Harrison Hayford and Merton M. Sealts. Chicago: University of Chicago Press, 1962.

———. *Collected Poems of Herman Melville*. Edited by Howard P. Vincent. Chicago: Packard–Hendricks House, 1947.

———. *Moby-Dick; Or, The Whale*. Edited by Harrison Hayford et al. Evanston and Chicago: Northwestern University Press and Newberry Library, 1988.

———. *Pierre; Or, The Ambiguities*. Edited by Harrison Hayford et al. Evanston and Chicago: Northwestern University Press and Newberry Library, 1971.

———. *Typee: A Peep at Polynesian Life*. Edited by Harrison Hayford et al. Evanston and Chicago: Northwestern University Press and Newberry Library, 1968.

———. *White Jacket; Or, The World in a Man-of-War*. Edited by Harrison Hayford et al. Evanston and Chicago: Northwestern University Press and Newberry Library, 1970.

Milhollen, Hirst D., and Donald H. Mugridge, compilers. *Civil War Photographs, 1861–1865: A Catalog of Copy Negatives Made from Originals Selected from the Mathew B. Brady Collection*. Washington, D.C.: Library of Congress, 1977.

Miller, Edwin Haviland. *Melville*. New York: Persea Books, 1975.

"Mississippi." *Harper's Weekly* 10(1866): 13.

Moorhead, James H. *American Apocalypse: Yankee Protestants and the Civil War, 1860–1869*. New Haven: Yale University Press, 1978.

Nelles, William. "Saving the State in Lowell's 'For the Union Dead.'" *American Literature* 55(1983): 639–42.

Neufeldt, Leonard. "Emerson and the Civil War." *Journal of English and Germanic Philology* 71(1972): 502–13.

Newhall, Beaumont. *The History of Photography*. Revised ed. New York: Museum of Modern Art, 1982.

———. Introduction. In *Gardner's Photographic Sketch Book of the Civil War*, by Alexander Gardner. New York: Dover, 1959.

———. Preface. In *Photographic Views of Sherman's Campaign*, by George Barnard. New York: Dover, 1977.

"Our Maps of the South." *Harper's Weekly* 10(1866): 3.

Panofsky, Erwin. "*Et in Arcadia Ego*: Poussin and the Elegiac Tradition." In *Meaning in the Visual Arts*. Garden City: Doubleday Anchor Books, 1955.

Patterson, Annabel. *Pastoral and Ideology: Virgil to Valéry*. Berkeley and Los Angeles: University of California Press, 1987.

Paulson, Ronald. *Literary Landscapes: Turner and Constable*. New Haven: Yale University Press, 1982.

Peirce, Charles Sanders. *Collected Papers of Charles Sanders Peirce*. 8 vols. Edited by Charles Hartshorne and Paul Weiss. Cambridge: Harvard University Press, Belknap Press, 1958.

Perkins, Howard Cecil, ed. *Northern Editorials on Secession*. 2 vols. New York: Appleton, 1943.

"Photographic Phases." *New York Times*, 21 July 1862: 5.

(Review of) *Photographic Views of Sherman's Campaign*, by George N. Barnard. *Harper's Weekly* 10(1866): 771.

"Pictures of the Dead at Antietam." *New York Times*, 20 October 1862: 5.

Pitkin, Hanna. *The Concept of Representation*. Berkeley and Los Angeles: University of California Press, 1967.

Plato. *Cratylus*. In *The Dialogues of Plato*, trans. B. Jowett. 2 vols. New York: Random House, 1937.

Poggioli, Renato. *The Oaten Flute: Essays on Pastoral Poetry and the Pastoral Ideal*. Cambridge: Harvard University Press, 1975.

Powell, Earl A., III. "Thomas Cole and the American Landscape Tradition: Associationism." *Arts Magazine* 52, no. 8(1978): 113–17.

———. "Thomas Cole and the American Landscape Tradition: The Picturesque." *Arts Magazine* 52, no. 7(1978): 110–17.

Pressly, Thomas J. *Americans Interpret Their Civil War*. New York: Collier, 1962.

Price, Martin. "The Picturesque Moment." In *From Sensibility to Romanticism: Essays Presented to Frederick A. Pottle*, ed. Frederick W. Hilles and Harold Bloom. New York: Oxford University Press, 1965.

Prown, Jules David. *American Painting: From Its Beginnings to the Armory Show*. New York: Rizzoli, 1980.

Putnam, G. P. *The Home Book of the Picturesque: Or, American Scenery, Art, and Literature*. 1852. Reprint. Gainesville, Fla.: Scholars' Facsimiles, 1967.

Rawley, James A. *The Politics of Union: Northern Politics during the Civil War*. Hinsdale, Ill.: Dryden Books, 1974.

"Reviews and Literary Notices." *Atlantic Monthly* 19(1867): 252–54.

Rogin, Michael Paul. "The King's Two Bodies: Lincoln, Wilson, Nixon, and Presidential Self-Sacrifice." In *Ronald Reagan, the Movie; and Other Episodes in Political Demonology*. Berkeley and Los Angeles: University of California Press, 1987.

———. *Subversive Genealogy: The Politics and Art of Herman Melville*. New York: Knopf, 1983.

Rosand, David. "Giorgione, Venice, and the Pastoral Vision." In *Places of Delight: The Pastoral Landscape*, ed. Robert Cafritz, et al. Washington, D.C.: Phillips Collection, 1988.

Rosenblatt, Jon. "Whitman's Body, Whitman's Language." In *Walt Whitman: Here and Now*, ed. Joann P. Krieg. Westport, Conn.: Greenwood, 1985.

Rudisill, Richard. *Mirror Image: The Influence of the Daguerreotype on American Society*. Albuquerque: University of New Mexico Press, 1971.

Ryan, Michael. *Marxism and Deconstruction: A Critical Articulation*. Baltimore: Johns Hopkins University Press, 1982.

Scarry, Elaine. *The Body in Pain: The Making and Unmaking of the World*. New York: Oxford University Press, 1985.

Scruton, Roger. *A Dictionary of Political Thought*. New York: Hill & Wang, 1984.

Shelley, Percy Bysshe. "A Defense of Poetry." In *Critical Theory since Plato*, ed. Hazard Adams. New York: Harcourt Brace Jovanovich, 1971.

Sherman, William T. *Memoirs of General William T. Sherman, by Himself*. 1875. 2 vols. Reprint. Bloomington: Indiana University Press, 1957.

Simpson, Lewis P. *The Dispossessed Garden: Pastoral and History in Southern Literature*. Athens: University of Georgia Press, 1975.

Smith, Adam. *An Inquiry into the Nature and Causes of the Wealth of Nations*. 1776. Reprint. Edited by Edwin Cannan. 2 vols. London: Methuen, 1950.

Smith, Henry Nash. *Virgin Land: The American West as Symbol and Myth*. Cambridge: Harvard University Press, 1950; New York: Vintage Books, 1957.

Snyder, Joel. "Photographs and Photographers of the Civil War." In *The Documentary Photograph as a Work of Art*. Chicago: David and Alfred Smart Gallery, 1976.

Sobieszek, Robert A., and Odette M. Appel. *The Daguerreotypes of Southworth and Hawes*. New York: Dover, 1980.

Sontag, Susan. *On Photography*. New York: Delta, 1977.

Sophocles. *Antigone*. In *The Complete Plays of Sophocles*, ed. Moses Hadas. New York: Bantam, 1967.

Stampp, Kenneth M., ed. *The Causes of the Civil War*. Revised ed. New York: Touchstone Books, 1974.

Stovall, Floyd. *The Foreground of Leaves of Grass*. Charlottesville: University Press of Virginia, 1974.

Talbot, William Henry Fox. "A Brief Historical Sketch of the Invention of the Art." In *Classic Essays on Photography*, ed. Alan Trachtenberg. New Haven: Leete's Island Books, 1980.

Thompson, W. Fletcher, Jr. *The Image of War: The Pictorial Reporting of the American Civil War*. New York: Thomas Yoseloff, 1960.

Thoreau, Henry David. *The Writings of Henry David Thoreau*. 1906. 20 vols. Reprint. New York: AMS Press, 1968.

233

Trachtenberg, Alan. "Albums of War: On Reading Civil War Photographs." *Representations* 9(1985): 1–32.

Valéry, Paul. "The Centenary of Photography." In *Classic Essays on Photography*, ed. Alan Trachtenberg. New Haven: Leete's Island Books, 1980.

Warner, Maria. *Monuments and Maidens: The Allegory of the Female Form*. New York: Atheneum, 1985.

Warren, Robert Penn. "Melville's Poems." *Southern Review* 3(1967): 799–855.

Waskow, Howard J. *Whitman: Explorations in Form*. Chicago: University of Chicago Press, 1966.

Weathers, Willie T. "*Moby-Dick* and the Nineteenth-Century Scene." *Texas Studies in Language and Literature* 1(1960): 477–501.

White, Hayden. *Metahistory: The Historical Imagination in Nineteenth-Century Europe*. Baltimore: Johns Hopkins University Press, 1975.

Whitman, Walt. *An American Primer*. Edited by Horace Traubel. 1904. Reprint. San Francisco: City Lights Books, 1970.

———. *The Correspondence*. Edited by Edwin Haviland Miller. 6 vols. New York: New York University Press, 1961–77.

———. *Drum-Taps (1865) and Sequel to Drum-Taps (1865–66)*. Reprint. Edited by F. DeWolfe Miller. Gainesville, Fla.: Scholars' Facsimiles, 1959.

———. *Leaves of Grass: The First (1855) Edition*. Edited by Malcolm Cowley. New York: Viking, 1961.

———. *Leaves of Grass: A Textual Variorum of the Printed Poems*. Edited by Sculley Bradley et al. 3 vols. New York: New York University Press, 1980.

———. *Memoranda during the War [and] Death of Abraham Lincoln*. 1875. Reprint. Edited by Roy P. Basler. Bloomington: Indiana University Press, 1962.

———. *Prose Works 1892*. 2 vols. Edited by Floyd Stovall. New York: New York University Press, 1963.

Whittier, John Greenleaf. *The Poetical Works of Whittier*. 1894. Reprint. Boston: Houghton Mifflin, 1975.

Wilson, Edmund. *Patriotic Gore: Studies in the Literature of the American Civil War*. New York: Oxford University Press, 1962.

Wolf, Bryan. *Romantic Re-Vision: Culture and Consciousness in Nineteenth-Century American Painting and Literature*. Chicago: University of Chicago Press, 1982.

Wolosky, Shira. *Emily Dickinson: A Voice of War*. New Haven: Yale University Press, 1984.

Zinn, Howard. *A People's History of the United States*. New York: Harper & Row, 1980.

Index

Aaron, Daniel, 4, 6; on Melville, 5, 222n.1; on Whitman, 5, 209n.3
Adams, Michael, 210n.13
Adams, Richard, 214n.20
Adamson, Robert, 137
Adhesiveness, rhetoric of: in Melville, 171; in Whitman, 12, 16, 34–38, 41–45, 62, 64–65, 67, 170–71
Adler, Joyce, 222n.1, 223n.12
Allen, Gay Wilson, 211nn.3, 18, 212n.10
Alpers, Paul, 7
Althusser, Louis, 219n.8
Andrews, J. Cutler, 80, 110, 145, 147
Anthony, E. & H. T. (firm), 81, 108, 140
Antietam, photographs from battlefield of, 122–23, 163, 216n.13, 219n.7, 220n.15; falsely attributed to Brady, 220n.13; Holmes on, 119–20; reproduced in *Harper's*, 114–16, 123; reviewed in *New York Times*, 116–19
Appel, Odette, and Robert Sobieszek, 81, 82, 83
Aristotle, 52
Aspiz, Harold, 16, 44, 209n.5
Atlanta, Ga., Civil War photographs of, 150–51
Atlantic Monthly, 83, 84, 93, 119, 137
Austin, J. L., 212n.10

Baigell, Matthew, 97–98
Bancroft, George, 39, 209n.4
Barnard, George, 10, 109, 110, 138, 140–43, 165, 192, 201, 220n.14; *Photographic Views of Sherman's Campaign*, reviewed in *Harper's*, 142–43, 145, 221n.5; and Sherman, 142; "Taste" (lecture), 140–42. *Photographic works:* "Buen-Ventura, Savannah," 153, 154–55, 221n.8; "Chattanooga Valley rom Lookout Mountain No. 2," 154, 156; "City of Atlanta No. 1," 150; "City of Atlanta No. 2," 151; "Fountain, Savannah," 155; "LuLa Lake,

Lookout Mountain" 156; "Pass in the Racoon Range (Whiteside No. 1)," 156, "Pass in the Racoon Range (Whiteside No. 2)," 156; *Photographic Views of Sherman's Campaign*, 138–40, 142–45, 148–56, 162–63, 221n.8; "Ruins in Charleston," 162–63, 164; "Savannah River near Savannah," 152; "View from Kenesaw Mountain," 147, 148–49; "Woodsawyer's Nooning, The," 82–83, 103, 140
Barrell, John, 217n.15
Barthes, Roland, 164, 214n.1, 216n.11
Basler, Roy, 211n.1, 214n.19
Battle-Pieces and Aspects of the War (Melville), 5, 7, 165–72, 174–94, 196–200, 202, 222n.1
Benjamin, Walter, 33, 117, 208n.5
Bermingham, Ann, 88–89, 215n.8
Bethune, George, 91–92
Bierce, Ambrose, 4
Blasing, Mutlu Konuk, 214n.20
Body, representational status of, in war, 6, 14, 85, 106, 110; in Barnard, 144; in Gardner, 107–8, 109, 127–32; in Lowell, 203–4; in Melville, 171, 174–76, 182–83, 189; Scarry on, 1–3, 105; in Whitman, 15–16, 42–43, 50, 54, 62. *See also* Adhesiveness, rhetoric of; Body politic, rhetoric of; Embodiment, rhetoric of; Exchange, rhetoric of; Sacrifice, rhetoric of
Body politic, rhetoric of, 39, 209n.4; in Garrison, 210n.6; in Holmes, 119–20; in Lincoln, 73, 74; in Melville, 174, 179–80, 197, 200; in Nast, 18–20; in Whitman, 12–13, 15, 16–24, 71. *See also* Embodiment, rhetoric of
Brady, Mathew, 10, 110, 137, 201, 203, 216n.13; Civil War photographs falsely attributed to, 109, 126, 220n.13; Civil War photographs exhibitions reviewed in *New York Times*, 95, 112–14,

Brady, Matthew, *(cont.)*
116–19, 216n.13; *Gallery of Illustrious Americans,* 79–80, 81, 82; and photographs from Manassas, 80, 121–22, 215n.4; "Wheat-Field in which General Reynolds was Shot," 126, 220n.16
Brownell, Henry Howard, 25
Bryant, William Cullen, 59, 89, 90, 91, 213n.12, 216n.9; on Civil War, 8; "Thanatopsis," 9
Buchanan, James, 214n.24
Bull Run, photographs from battlefield of. *See* Manassas, photographs from battlefield of
Burgess, Nathan, 80, 81
Burke, Edmund, 215n.8
Burrows, Larry, 218n.4

Cabot, J. Eliot, 93–95, 137, 216n.11
Cady, Joseph, 211n.18
Callcott, George, 39
Cameron, Julia Margaret, 82
Campagnola, Domenico, 214n.22
Capa, Robert, 109
Charleston, S.C., Civil War photographs of, 139, 162–63
Church, Frederick Edwin, 89, 92
Clausewitz, Carl von, 14
Cobb, Josephine, 218n.3, 220n.13
Coffler, Gail, 224n.13
Coffman, Stanley, 209n.2
Cohen, Hennig, 167, 188, 223nn.4, 5, 224nn.13, 14, 15, 17
Coker, F. W., 39, 209n.4
Cole, Thomas, 87–89, 92, 103, 162, 222n.12; *Course of Empire, The,* 96, 97–99; *Oxbow, The,* 155, 156; on photography, 103–4
Coleridge, Samuel Taylor, 167, 209n.4, 222n.3
Constable, John, 88, 143, 217n.5
Cook, Adrian, 3, 224n.17
Cooper, James Fenimore, 89, 90
Cooper, Susan, 90–91
Crane, Stephen, 4
Crawley, Thomas, 22
Crèvecoeur, J. Hector St. John de, 8, 208n.10
Crimean War, photographs from, 84–85, 137
Curtius, Ernst Robert, 212n.7

Daguerre, Louis, 91, 215n.7; on daguerreotype, 86
Daguerreotype: Emerson on, 80, 87, 216n.10; genres of, 80–83; Melville on, 169–70; relation to Civil War photography, 84; replaced by photograph, 83; Thoreau on, 86–87
Dana, Charles, 209n.1
Davis, Theo, 145, 157
Davis, William, 126, 218n.1, 219n.6
Derrida, Jacques, 212n.11
Dickinson, Emily, 208n.7
Diffley, Kathleen, 72
Douglass, Frederick, 210n.12
Drayton, Michael, 96
Drum-Taps and *Sequel to Drum-Taps* (Whitman), 5, 6, 11–13, 15–37, 42–48, 58–61, 68–71, 74–77, 168, 181, 209n.3
Dukerson, Roland, 212n.8
Durand, Asher B., 89, 92, 216n.9

East, Charles, 218n.1
Edwards, J. D., 218n.1
Embodiment, rhetoric of: in Barnard, 143, 148; Scarry on, 143; in Whitman, 39–41, 53–54, 209n.5. *See also* Body politic, rhetoric of
Emerson, Ralph Waldo, 78, 209n.4, 213n.12; on daguerreotype, 80, 87, 216n.10; and Melville, 223n.5; on political representation, 1, 207n.3; and Whitman, 13, 39
Empson, William, 7, 58, 101–2
Ettin, Andrew, 7
Exchange, rhetoric of, 28, 38; in Lincoln, 27–28; in Whitman, 12, 16, 29–33, 37, 48

Fenton, Roger, 84–85, 136, 137
Fisher, Philip, 73
Foster, Charles, 223n.7
Frank Leslie's Illustrated Newspaper, 84, 145
Frassanito, William, 116, 122, 126; on Gardner, 85, 127, 128, 130, 132, 220nn.15, 17
Fredrickson, George, 6, 23, 207n.3

Gainsborough, Thomas, 201, 215n.8, 217n.15

Gardner, Alexander, 10, 136, 137, 165, 182, 192, 201, 203, 216n.13, 218n.3, 219n.7, 220n.15; and Fenton, 85. *Photographic works:* "Burial Party, Cold Harbor," 134, 135–36; "Fortifications on the Heights of Centreville," 123, 125–26; *Gardner's Photographic Sketch Book of the Civil War,* 108, 109, 110–11, 120–35, 138, 163, 204, 218n.5; 220nn.13, 14; "High Bridge, Crossing the Appomattox," 218n.2; "Home of a Rebel Sharpshooter," 130–32; "Ruins of Stone Bridge, Bull Run," 121, 122, "Sharpshooter's Last Sleep, A," 129, 130, 220n.17; "Stone Church, Centreville," 110–11, 112; "War, effect of a shell on Confederate soldier," 107–8, 109, 130; "What Do I Want, John Henry?," 133–35, 136, 164. *See also* O'Sullivan, Timothy: photographic works
Garrison, William Lloyd, 210n.6
Gettysburg, photographs from battlefield of, 107–8, 126–32, 215n.5, 220n.16
Gibson, James, 109, 110, 220nn.13, 14
Gignoux, Regis, 90
Gilpin, William, 215n.8
Giorgione, 214n.22
Girard, René, 25–26, 35, 36, 38
Glatthaar, Joseph, 23, 221n.6
Goya, Francisco, 117, 137
Gramsci, Antonio, 217n.16
Grant, Ulysses, 144
Gray, Thomas, 102, 162
Gridley, Roy, 8
Grossman, Allen: on Lincoln, 28; on Whitman, 11, 29, 47, 68, 69

Haley, John, 3–4, 208n.6
Hancock, Winfield Scott, 223nn.4, 6
Harper's Pictorial History of the Great Rebellion, 220n.16
Harper's Weekly, 84, 145, 146, 157–61, 163, 195, 210n.12; Barnard's *Photographic Views* reviewed in, 142–43, 145, 221n.5; Civil War photographs reproduced in, 114–15, 116, 126, 135–36, 215n.5; Nast's illustrations in, 18, 19, 117, 210n.9, 221n.11; "Pictures of the South," 156–57

Hiemert, Alan, 223n.7
Hill, David Octavius, 82, 136–37
Hobbes, Thomas, 173, 174, 210n.10, 223n.8
Hollis, C. Carroll, 212n.10
Holmes, Oliver Wendell, Sr., 116; on Antietam photographs, 119–20; on landscape photography, 87, 103, 156; on photographic encyclopedia, 104; on photography (general), 83, 84, 93–94, 100–101; on war photography, 104
Home Book of the Picturesque, The, 89–92
Homoeroticism. *See* Adhesiveness, rhetoric of
Hood, John Bell, 138
Horace, 28, 52, 53
Horan, James, 80, 81, 121–22
Howe, Julia Ward, 4, 25, 27
Humphrey's Journal, 121
Hunter, Jefferson, 79

Illustrated London News, 85
Inexpressibility, rhetoric of, 212n.7; Horace on, 52; in Melville, 189; Shelley on, 52; in Whitman, 12, 42–43, 47, 50, 54
Inness, George, 70
Irving, Washington, 89, 90

Jackson, Thomas "Stonewall," 121
Jameson, Fredric, 79, 106, 217n.20
Jefferson, Thomas, 73, 213n.12
Johnson, Eastman, 82, 99–100, 133
Johnston, Joseph, 122, 138, 139, 148, 221n.3

Kaplan, Justin, 64, 212n.10
Kasson, John, 219n.12
Keats, John, 214n.20
Kensett, J. F., 90
Kronick, Joseph, 16

Lee, Robert E., 121, 139, 179
Leroy, Catherine, 218n.4
Lewinski, Jorge, 85
Leyda, Jay, 223n.5, 224n.13
Lincoln, Abraham, 106, 131, 138, 176, 194, 196, 211n.14; Address to Wisconsin

Lincoln, Abraham (*cont.*)
  Agricultural Society, 73–74; Annual
  Message to Congress (1862), 72, First
  Inaugural Address, 71; Gettysburg
  Address, 74; on "national home-
  stead" of Union, 9, 72; on recoloni-
  zation of slaves, 23, 73; Second Inaug-
  ural Address, 27–28, 210n.11; and
  "When Lilacs Last in the Dooryard
  Bloom'd," 68, 70–71, 74, 75, 77
Longfellow, Henry Wadsworth, 59,
  213n.12
Lorraine, Claude, 93, 94
Lowell, Robert, 201–5, 225n.2
Lytle, A. D., 218n.1

McClellan, George, 109, 210n.13
McDowell, Irvin, 122
Machor, James, 213n.16
McPherson, James, 3, 23, 176, 188, 189,
  207n.2, 211n.14, 214n.23, 217n.18
Manassas, photographs from battlefield
  of, 110–11, 121–22, 220n.14; Brady and,
  80, 121–22, 215n.4
March to the sea: Barnard's treatment
  of, 144–45; *Harper's* treatment of,
  145–47; Melville's treatment of,
  192–94; Sherman on, 145–46
Marx, Karl, 38, 161
Marx, Leo, 89; on American pastoral,
  8, 68, 73, 96–97, 113, 213n.12, 217nn.14,
  16, 219n.12
Matthiessen, F. O., 33, 70–71, 209n.4,
  210n.7, 211n.3, 213n.14
Melville, Herman, 10, 201; on daguerreotype, 169–70; and Emerson, 223n.5;
  and Whitman, 170–71. *Works:* "Aeolian Harp, The," 168–69; "America,"
  198–200; "Apparition, The," 196–97,
  198; "Ball's Bluff," 191; "Battle for
  the Bay, The," 174–75, 198; "Battle
  for the Mississippi, The," 167; *Battle-
  Pieces,* 5, 7, 165–72, 174–94, 196–200,
  202, 222n.1; *Billy Budd,* 175, 184;
  "Commemorative of a Naval Victory," 198; *Confidence-Man, The,*
  223n.5; "Conflict of Convictions,
  The," 177; "Donelson," 181–82;
  "Dupont's Round Fight," 165, 183,
  197; "Formerly a Slave," 178;

"Frenzy in the Wake, The," 193–94;
  "House-Top, The," 181, 186–89; "In
  the Turret," 175; *John Marr and Other
  Sailors,* 168; "Lee in the Capitol," 179;
  "Magnanimity Baffled," 190; "March
  into Virginia, The," 185–86, 190–91;
  "March to the Sea, The," 192–93;
  "Martyr, The," 71; "Meditation, A,"
  178; "Misgivings," 176; *Moby-Dick,*
  173–74, 223n.7; "On the Photograph
  of a Corps Commander," 170–71, 183;
  Pierre, 168, 169–70, 174, 223n.5; "Run-
  ning the Batteries," 181, 184–85;
  "Shiloh," 186, 190; "Stone Fleet,
  The," 176–77; Supplement to *Battle-
  Pieces,* 167, 177, 179–80; "Swamp
  Angel, The," 178–79; "Tartarus of
  Maids, The," 176; "Temeraire, The,"
  177; *Typee,* 172–73; "Utilitarian View
  of the Monitor's Fight, A," 175–76;
  White-Jacket, 175, 187, 188, 224nn.17, 18
Memoranda during the War (Whitman),
  13, 45, 46–52, 54, 56–57, 63, 65–67, 182,
  211n.1
Milhollen, Hirst, and Donald
  Mugridge, 110, 218n.5, 219n.6
Miller, Edwin Haviland, 223n.12
Miller, Francis Trevalyan, 218n.1
Milton, John, 59, 64, 128, 213nn.12, 15
Moorhead, James, 25, 210n.11
Mosby, John Singleton, 51, 212n.6
Mount, William Sidney, 70, 82, 213n.14
Mowitt, John, 217n.16
Mugridge, Donald. *See* Milhollen, Hirst

Nast, Thomas, 4, 18, 117, 198, 199,
  210n.9, 221n.11; "Our Arms Victorious," 19–20; "Soldier's Halt, The,"
  146–47, 193; and Whitman, 19
Nelles, William, 225n.2
Neufeldt, Leonard, 207n.3
Newhall, Beaumont, 81, 84, 215n.5,
  219n.11; on Barnard, 138, 140; on
  Gardner, 127
New York Times, Civil War photographs reviewed in, 95, 112–13, 116,
  117–19, 216n.13
Norton, Charles Eliot, 209n.1

O'Sullivan, Timothy, 109, 110. *Photo-graphic works:* "Field where General Reynolds Fell," 125, 126, 128–29; "Harvest of Death, A," 124, 126–30
Owen, Wilfred, 28

Panofsky, Erwin, 213n.13
Pastoral, 213n.13; 214n.22; as American ideology, 8–9, 56, 68, 73, 96–100, 113, 139, 208n.10, 213n.12, 217nn.14, 16; in Barnard, 139, 149, 154, 163; in Brady, 95, 126; in Bryant, 8–9; in Cole, 97–99; in Gardner, 110–12, 122–32, 135–36, 192; in Holmes, 100–102; in Johnson, 99–100; in Lincoln, 9, 71–75, 196; in Lowell, 201–3; in Melville, 172, 182, 190–94, 196–200; theories of, 7–8, 101–2, 217n.15; in Whitman, 16, 26, 45, 47, 50, 57–71, 74–77, 139, 213n.16; in Whittier, 132–33, 194–96
Patterson, Annabel, 7, 8
Paulson, Ronald, 88, 91, 143
Peirce, Charles Sanders, 216n.11
Perkins, Howard Cecil, 28, 31, 34
Photographic and Fine Art Journal, 140
Photographic Views of Sherman's Campaign (Barnard), 138–40, 142–45, 148–56, 162–63, 221n.8
Picturesque, the: and American nation-alism, 88, 92, 95, 105–6, 137, 139–40, 156; in Barnard, 139–41, 143, 144, 148–49, 153–54, 156, 162–63; 192; in Cole, 88, 89, 156; in Gardner, 122, 125; *Home Book of the Picturesque,* 89–92; in Melville, 197; in Sherman, 152; theor-ies of, 88–89, 93–95; 215n.8
Pitkin, Hanna, 38, 39
Plato, 38, 175
Poe, E. M., 142, 150
Poggioli, Renato, 7, 101
Pope, John, 122
Powell, Earl, 88, 91
Price, Martin, 215n.8
Putnam, G. P., 89

Rawley, James, 211n.17
Reynolds, John, 126, 220n.16
Robinson, Henry Peach, 82, 117
Rogin, Michael, 173; on Melville, 166, 178, 187, 222n.1, 223n.12, 224n.17; on

rhetoric of body politic, 38–39, 71, 210n.10
Rosand, David, 214n.22
Rosenblatt, Jon, 39, 40, 209n.5, 212n.10
Rudisill, Richard, 80, 88, 140, 216n.10
Ryan, Michael, 174

Sacrifice, rhetoric of, 38; in Holmes, 119–20; in Lincoln, 74; in Melville, 182; Scarry on, 3; in Whitman, 15, 24–27, 35–37
Savannah, Ga., Civil War photographs from vicinity of, 152, 153, 154–55
Scarry, Elaine, 1–3, 42, 50, 105, 143, 208n.4
Shakespeare, William, 96
Shaw, Lemuel, 82, 83
Shaw, Robert Gould, 203
Shelley, Percy Bysshe, 52, 64, 162, 213n.12, 214n.20, 222n.3
Sherman, William Tecumseh, 110, 138, 139, 148, 192, 193, 221n.3; letter to Barnard, 142; *Memoirs,* 144, 145, 148–49, 150–53, 155
Simms, William Gilmore, 208n.10
Simpson, Lewis, 208n.10
Smith, Adam, 15
Smith, Henry Nash, 8
Snyder, Joel, 218n. 2
Sobieszek, Robert, and Odette Appel, 81, 82, 83
Sontag, Susan, 117
Sophocles, 220n.18
Southworth and Hawes (firm), 83
Stampp, Kenneth, 207n.2
Stovall, Floyd, 209n.4, 213nn.12, 15
Stowe, Harriet Beecher, 210n.12

Talbot, William Henry Fox, 85–86, 215n.7
Tate, Allen, 225n.3
Thompson, W. Fletcher, 145
Thoreau, Henry David, 94; on daguer-reotype, 86–87
Trachtenberg, Alan, 6, 78, 109, 218nn.1, 2; on Barnard, 143, 144, 149, 162–63; on Gardner, 111, 133, 135; on Holmes, 119
Trumbull, John, 89, 92
Turner, Joseph Mallord William, 93

Twain, Mark, 3
Typification, rhetoric of, in Whitman, 11–12, 16, 47, 48, 50–52, 55–56, 58, 64–65

Valéry, Paul, 78–79, 120, 122
Vedder, E., 178
Virgil, 7, 8

Walton, Izaak, 225n.1
Warner, Maria, 18, 22–23
Warren, Robert Penn, 186, 222n.1
Waskow, Howard, 212n.10
Waud, Alfred, 157
Weathers, Willie, 223n.7
White, Hayden, 79, 102, 215n.2
White, Henry Kirke, 224n.13
Whitman, Walt, 6, 10, 106, 113, 119, 120, 165, 192, 201, 211n.14; on Drum-Taps, 15, 47; and Emerson, 13, 39; and Melville, 170–71; and Nast, 19. Works: American Primer, An, 41, 53–55, 212n.10; "As I Ebb'd with the Ocean of Life," 13, 39–41, 43, 75; "Calamus" poems, 34–36, 63–64, 67; "O Captain! My Captain!," 214n.19, 223n.10; "Chanting the Square Deific," 22–24, 26; "Come up from the fields, father," 26–27, 76; Death of Abraham Lincoln, 67–68, 71; Democratic Vistas, 54–55; "Dresser, The," 43–44; Drum-Taps and Sequel to Drum-Taps, 5, 6, 11–13, 15–37, 42–48, 58–61, 68–71, 74–77, 168, 181, 209n.3; "Farm Picture, A," 58–59; "First, O Songs for a prelude," 17; "Give me the splendid silent sun," 59–61, 65, 69; "In the New Garden," 62; Leaves of Grass (1855), 11, 13, 17, 37, 53, 57; Leaves of Grass (1860), 34–36, 39, 62, 63; Leaves of Grass (1867), 19, 62; Leaves of Grass (1871),

32, 59; Leaves of Grass, (1876), 12–13, 34, 56; "Lo! Victress on the Peaks!," 24; "March in the ranks hard-prest, A," 42–43; Memoranda during the War, 13, 45, 46–52, 54, 56–57, 63, 65–67, 182, 211n.1; "Origins of Attempted Secession," 21–22; "Out of the Cradle Endlessly Rocking," 60, 63; "Over the carnage rose prophetic a voice," 22, 35–37; "Pensive on her dead gazing I heard the mother of all," 22, 29; "Pioneers! O Pioneers!," 156; "Quicksand years," 43–44; "Reconciliation," 27, 45; "Rise O Days from your fathomless deeps," 18, 20; "Scented Herbage of My Breast," 63, 64; "Sight in camp in the daybreak, A," 45; "So Long!," 39; "Song of Myself," 44, 57–58; "Song of the Banner at Day-Break," 30–33; Specimen Days, 48, 66–67, 211nn.1, 2, 212nn.4, 5; "States!," 34–36; "Of the Terrible Doubt of Appearances, 63–64; "Vigil strange I kept on the field one night," 43; "When Lilacs Last in the Dooryard Bloom'd," 47, 67, 68–71, 74–77, 139, 149, 180; "Years of the unperform'd," 20–21, 143
Whittier, John Greenleaf, 59, 197. Works: "Battle Autumn of 1862, The," 195; "Hive at Gettysburg, The," 132–33; "Peace Autumn, The," 196, 197; Snow-Bound, 194–95
Wilson, Edmund, 4–5, 214n.23; on Whitman, 5, 209n.3
Wolosky, Shira, 24, 208n.7
Wolf, Bryan, 88, 103
Wordsworth, William, 215n.8

Zinn, Howard, 3, 223n.9